Postcolonial Perspectives on
Global Citizenship Education

Routledge Research in Education

For a full list of titles in this series please visit www.routledge.com

Postcolonial Perspectives on Global Citizenship Education

Edited by Vanessa de Oliveira Andreotti
and Lynn Mario T. M. de Souza

Routledge
Taylor & Francis Group

NEW YORK   LONDON

First published 2012
by Routledge
711 Third Avenue, New York, NY 10017

Simultaneously published in the UK
by Routledge
2 Park Square, Milton Park, Abingdon, Oxon OX14 4RN

*Routledge is an imprint of the Taylor & Francis Group, an informa
business*

© 2012 Taylor & Francis

The right of Vanessa de Oliveira Andreotti and Lynn Mario T. M.
de Souza to be identified as the authors of the editorial material, and of
the authors for their individual chapters, has been asserted in accordance
with sections 77 and 78 of the Copyright, Designs and Patents Act 1988

Typeset in Sabon by IBT Global.
Printed and bound in the United States of America on acid-free paper by
IBT Global.

Library of Congress Cataloging-in-Publication Data
Postcolonial perspectives on global citizenship education / edited by
  Vanessa de Oliveira Andreotti and Lynn Mario T. M. De Souza.
    p. cm. — (Routledge research in education ; 68)
  Includes bibliographical references and index.
  1. World citizenship—Study and teaching.   2. International education.
3. Postcolonialism.   I. Andreotti, Vanessa.   II. Souza, Lynn Mario
T. Menezes de.
  JZ1320.4.P66 2012
  370.11'5—dc23
  2011021861

ISBN13: 978-0-415-88496-9 (hbk)
ISBN13: 978-0-203-15615-5 (ebk)

Contents

PART III
Creating Postcolonial Spaces: Global Citizenship
Education 'Otherwise'

Figures and Tables

Acknowledgments

The editors would like to acknowledge all of those who have made this project possible: the authors, reviewers, colleagues and friends who have offered support and encouragement in the completion of the book, especially those working under extreme environmental circumstances following events in 2011. We would also like to recognize the support and inspiration of our families—particularly the children—without whom there would probably be no motivation to write a book like this.

Introduction
(Towards) Global Citizenship Education 'Otherwise'

Vanessa de Oliveira Andreotti and
Lynn Mario T. M. de Souza

The concept of 'global citizenship' has become prominent in Europe and the Americas in government, civil society and educational discourses (Dower 2003; Richardson and Blades 2006; Peters, Britton and Blee 2008; O'Sullivan and Pashby 2008; Abdi and Shultz 2009, 2011). Different agendas and theoretical frameworks inform these discourses which construct different meanings to the words *global, citizenship* and *education* that imply different curricula and intervention packages for education. Educators in these varied contexts are encouraged to 'bring the world into their classrooms' or 'send students into the world' in the form of new content or experiences, which may include school partnerships, fundraising activities, study or volunteer abroad schemes and/or the promotion and deliberation of global issues and perspectives in the curriculum. Some of these initiatives to produce global subjectivities tend to prescribe the adoption of strategies that very often foreclose the complex historical, cultural and political nature of the issues, identities and perspectives embedded in global/local processes and events and in the production of knowledge about the self, the other and the world. In spite of the complexity of contemporary globalization, many of these initiatives seem to echo the simplistic us/them, here/there binarisms that have been denounced and addressed by postcolonial critiques (Andreotti 2006; Andreotti and Souza 2008; Souza and Andreotti 2009; Andreotti 2010; Andreotti, Jefferess, Pashby, Rowe, Tarc and Taylor 2010; Andreotti 2011). Thus, despite claims of globality and inclusion, the lack of analyses of power relations and knowledge construction in this area often results in educational practices that unintentionally reproduce ethnocentric, ahistorical, depoliticized, paternalistic, salvationist and triumphalist approaches that tend to deficit theorize, pathologize or trivialize difference.

Postcolonial studies offer a set of productive questions that can be used to examine and interrogate the frames of reference that shape such approaches and to imagine education 'otherwise.' In terms of critique, postcolonial studies can be particularly useful in the analysis of global ethnocentric hegemonies that reproduce and maintain global inequalities in the distribution of wealth, power and labor in the world. These global ethnocentric hegemonies are enacted in education through initiatives that uncritically embrace the normative teleological project of Western/Enlightenment humanism, which is deeply invested in the production of rational unanimity and unequivocal knowledge

in regard to conceptualizations of humanity/human nature, progress and justice. Such investments structure an epistemic blindness to one's own ontological choices and epistemic categories and thus to radical difference itself.
Postcolonial perspectives can help to question and rearticulate the origins and
implications of these tendencies in order to open up spaces for something
new. However, postcolonial theory itself is not immune from the complexity
and heterogeneity of the contexts in which it arises, and when imagining education otherwise, different strands of postcolonial theory propose different
frameworks for what 'education otherwise' should look like or do. Therefore
it is important to recognize the influences of each strand and acknowledge
both their origins and limitations.

A postcolonial strand informed by historical materialism, for example,
presupposing dialectics as an epistemic framework may propose strategies of
action that often focus on international cross-sectoral mobilization with a view
to shift power relations and decision-making processes to include the voices
and aspirations of those who have been historically oppressed or marginalized.
In contrast, a postcolonial strand informed by poststructuralism may propose
postdialectic or nondualistic educational strategies that focus on the complexities of the construction of self and other, oppressors and oppressed, saviors and
beneficiaries, dispensers (of rights, justice, equality, education, civilization) and
recipients, with a view to enable the possibility of an ethical stance towards
the Other of Western humanism and of uncoercive relationships of solidarity
that do not require homogeneity or a prescribed idea of the future. While the
first strand sees otherness and difference as external to and distant from a
homogeneous, coherent self, the second strand sees otherness and difference as
constitutive of an inescapably heterogeneous and complex self. Thus, whereas
the first strand will tend to focus on the construction of a consensual alternative future, the latter emphasizes the need for a shift in historical patterns of
production of meaning in order to open new possibilities for the relational ongoing co-construction of the present and the future. While one strand can be
accused of overlooking the complexities of power, representation and culture,
the other may be accused of celebrating difference and not offering clear and
immediate options for those facing abject material realities. Both strands are
represented in this edited collection.

In this book, we conceptualize the prefix 'post-' in postcolonialism as a
constant interrogation, a possibility that is 'not yet' but that may announce the
prospect of something new. We define postcolonial theories as tools-for-think-
ing rather than theories-of-truth. In this sense, we acknowledge their situatedness and partiality. By interrogating and examining colonial processes and
institutional suffering, we hope that the postcolonial analyses presented in this
book, which come from different epistemic orientations, may offer insights
and inspirations for addressing neocolonial and imperialistic frameworks that
are still prevalent in global citizenship education—precisely the area that is
pregnant with possibilities for critically informed ethical global solidarities.
The central idea in this edited collection of scholarly work is to support the
development of critical, transnational and political readings that emphasize the

connections between knowledge, power, positionality, cultural assumptions and identity amongst educators and researchers engaged with global citizenship and international development. From a transdisciplinary and postcolonial perspective, the authors offer critiques of notions of development, progress, humanism, culture, representation, identity and education. They also examine the implications of these critiques in terms of pedagogical approaches, social relations and possible future interventions. We hope their work will help move debates in this area beyond current polarizations with a view to enable yet-to-come possibilities (see Table I.1).

Table I.1 Yet-to-Come Postcolonial Possibilities

beyond . . .		and beyond . . .	. . . towards yet-to-come postcolonial educational possibilities of . . .
unexamined ethnocentrisms		absolute relativisms where 'anything goes'	situated and dynamic pluriversalities
ahistoricisms		uncritical historicisms	critical and responsible genealogies
depoliticization of educational agendas		political hijacking of educational agendas	deeper analysis of production and effects of unequal relations of power
essentialisms that reify difference and deny heterogeneity		anti-essentialisms that trivialize power relations and historical contexts	better understanding of the complexity and contingency of the production of subjectivities
deficit theorization and pathologization of difference		romaticization of difference	humility: the awareness of self-insufficiency as the basis for the need for the Other
hedonistic self-interested paternalism based on fantasies of supremacy and entitlement	vs.	detached self-interested indifference based on denial of complicity in harm	mutuality, reciprocity, generosity and co-implication in relationships and exchanges
salvationist agendas based on triumphalism		political alienation based on paralysis in the face of complexity	ethical solidarities that do not require homogenization of identities, memberships or political projects
coercive 'think as I do' education		glorification of 'individual choice' in education	accountable and situated self-reflexive reasoning, listening, feeling, relating, teaching and learning
drive towards making things simple, consensual, certain and unequivocal		drive towards domesticating complexity into 'inclusive' (and still unequivocal) frameworks	knowledge seen as situated, equivocal and provisional and educational pathways that equip learners to respond to context and relate to difference without feeling overwhelmed by complexity, uncertainty, multiplicity and ambiguity

This book is divided into three parts. Part I offers a collection of chapters related to conceptual analyses of global citizenship education and the gifts and limitations of using postcolonial theory as a tool of analysis or a framework for pedagogy. Drawing on the works of Mohanty and Willinsky, Karen Pashby interrogates 'good intentions' in contemporary global citizenship education initiatives. She identifies key challenges in rewriting the agenda for global citizenship from a postcolonial lens focusing on decolonization and relearning through a critical understanding of the history of global relations. David Jefferess examines the concept of benevolence in theorizations of global citizenship in the works of Dower and Appiah. He illustrates the implications of his analysis with reference to policies and programs at the University of British Columbia that frame global citizens as privileged subjects positioned to 'make a difference' for (rather than with) Others. Colin Wright highlights the contributions of postcolonial theory in identifying the violences of Eurocentric forms of universalism. He also draws attention to the limitations of postcolonial theory in tapping the emancipatory potential of different forms of universalism. Drawing on the works of Badiou, Rancière and Žižek, Wright proposes the idea of 'divisive universalisms' as a way of addressing contemporary forms of marginalization in globalized societies. Lynn Mario de Souza draws on Brazilian transdisciplinary work on local indigenous philosophies and little-known conceptions of relations with difference such as 'indigenous perspectivism' and 'equivocal translation' in a search for alternative theoretical frameworks which may be relevant to and inform future educational policy in global citizenship education (GCE).

Part II consists of a collection of critiques of GCE initiatives, including policies, campaigns and study-abroad and volunteering schemes. Talya Zemach-Bersin examines narratives of exceptionalism and nationalism in the U.S. imaginary of study-abroad schemes and the construction of global citizenship not as an alternative to Empire but as a form of empire that perpetuates fantasies of supremacy, entitlement and global expansion. She emphasizes the importance of reclaiming global citizenship agendas through engagements with the historical and cultural roots of global citizenship education. Paul Tarc focuses his critique on historical conjunctures in the production of global citizenship discourses and on the construction of the 'active global citizen' in educational narratives. He uses the international baccalaureate and Oxfam's publication *Education for Global Citizenship: A Guide for Schools* to exemplify the implications of the drive to 'make a difference' under (neo)liberal imaginaries. Nancy Cook looks into colonial constructions of global citizenship that permeate the practice of development volunteering abroad. She provides an analysis of the lives of a group of white Western women development volunteers working in Gilgit, northern Pakistan, to show how notions of self and other can be interpreted as reflecting and reproducing colonial power relations. Cook offers an alternative conceptualization of global citizenship that may enable the emergence of more socially just and less oppressive practices of global solidarities. Nick Stevenson presents a critique focusing on the 'Make Poverty History' campaign emphasizing problematic implications of global justice initiatives that operate under neoliberal systemic structures of consumption, atomism, inequality and waste. He reinterprets the works of Frantz Fanon and Paulo Freire to suggest a politics of hope based on dialogue and reimagined identities grounded on relations of nondomination. Ali Abdi and Lynette Shultz examine the roots of constructions of citizenship grounded on liberal democracy and neoliberal notions of development. They analyze the implications of the universalization of these constructs in the context of Africa and call for the establishment of decolonized spaces of citizenship where a genuine Africanist renaissance can be rebuilt. Shultz also offers a poem related to the difficulties of encountering the Other through international travel that reifies privilege and unequal lines of mobility.

Part III underlines initiatives that aim to create postcolonial pedagogical spaces that support the emergence of global citizenship education 'otherwise.' Lisa Taylor proposes a 'pedagogy of implication' where students are challenged to interrogate their complicities in harm and investments in Eurocentric teleologies in an attempt to learn to learn from, rather than about, Others. She presents an example from a teacher-education course in Canada to show how this can work in practice. Khoo problematizes the 'postcolonial moment' in higher education in Ireland in the context of 'knowledge economies' that place emphasis on transnational mobility and bureaucratic excellence. She calls for a rerouting of human rights and global citizenship education with a view to enable pedagogical openness to otherness and difficulty. Vanessa Andreotti, Cash Ahenakew and Garrick Cooper examine the epistemic blindness, arrogance and violence of projects that seek to construct unequivocal and universal knowledge. They draw on insights from aboriginal and postcolonial scholarship focusing on alternative conceptualizations of language, knowing, being and metaphysics to propose a postcolonial project of global citizenship, which may enable an ethical relationship with the 'Other' of Western humanism.

Although related, the varied theoretical stances of the different contributions brought together in this book seek collectively to themselves perform what is the proposed object of each individual reflection: (1) an unceasing search for understanding and relating to difference in the context of the complex juxtapositions, flows and positionalities of contemporary globalization, (2) the provision of theoretical frameworks for rethinking and rearticulating existing proposals of GCE.

REFERENCES

Andreotti, V. (2006) 'Soft vs. Critical Global Citizenship Education', *Policy and Practice: A Development Education Review*, 3: 40–51.

————. (2010) 'Postcolonial and Post-Critical Global Citizenship Education', in G. Elliott, C. Fourali and S. Issler, *Education & Social Change*, London, Continuum, 223–245.

————. (2011) *Actionable Postcolonial Theory*, New York: Palgrave.

Andreotti, V., Jeferess, D., Pashby, K., Rowe, C., Tarc, P. and Taylor, L. (2010) 'Difference and Conflict in Global Citizenship in Higher Education in Canada', *International Journal of Development Education and Global Learning*, 2(3): 5–24.

Andreotti, V. and Souza, L. (2008) 'Translating Theory into Practice and Walking Minefileds: Lessons from the Project 'Through Other Eyes', *International Journal of Development Education and Global Learning*, 1(1): 23–36.

Abdi, A. and Shultz, L. (eds.) (2009) *Educating for Human Rights and Global Citizenship*, Albany, NY: State University of New York Press.

————. (eds.) (2011) *Global Citizenship Education in Post-Secondary Institutions: Theories, Practices, Policies*, New York: Peter Lang.

Dower, N. (2003) *An Introduction to Global Citizenship*, Edinburgh: Edinburgh University Press.

O'Sullivan, M. and Pashby, K. (eds.) (2008) *Citizenship Education in the Era of Globalization: Canadian Perspectives*, Rotterdam: Sense Publishers B.V.

Peters, M., Briton, A. and Blee, H. (eds.) (2008) *Global Citizenship Education*, Rotterdam: Sense Publishers B.V.

Richardson, G. H. and Blades, D. (eds.) (2006) *Troubling the Canon of Citizenship Education*, New York: Peter Lang.

Souza, L. and Andreotti, V. (2009) 'Culturalism, Difference and Pedagogy: Lessons from Indigenous Education in Brazil', in J. Lavia and M. Moore (eds.), *Cross-Cultural Perspectives on Policy and Practice: Decolonizing Community Contexts*, London: Routledge.

Part I

Conceptual Analyses

Global Citizenship Education
and the Gifts and Limitations of
Postcolonial Theory

1 Questions for Global Citizenship Education in the Context of the 'New Imperialism'
For Whom, by Whom?

Karen Pashby

As is evident from international conferences and recent anthologies and journals,[1] the concept of global citizenship education (GCE) is emerging as a response to a sense of a need to encourage global interconnectedness and global responsibility through citizenship education. While there are divergent views, some common themes define GCE as an educational agenda. My understanding, based on a close reading of the related scholarly literature, is that GCE moves beyond an exclusively national perspective of world affairs and seeks to avoid a social-studies approach that tends to tokenize and exoticize foreign places and peoples. As an ideal, the concept of educating for global citizenship encourages students to adopt a critical understanding of globalization, to reflect on how they and their nations are implicated in local and global problems and to engage in intercultural perspectives (Pashby 2008, 2011). For the purpose of this chapter, I see these tenets as potentially contributing to a project of decolonization in that they work to promote social justice on a global level and work with a critical understanding of the history of global relations. It is significant to point out, however, that the bulk of the writings that theorize and propose GCE on which I draw are from England, the U.S., Canada, Australia and New Zealand, and this is important to contextualizing the way 'the global' and 'citizenship education' are imagined within this emerging field. Indeed, much critical work needs to be done to investigate how an agenda for GCE, while it could be identified as a postcolonial move, is still very much implicated in the colonial legacy of education. This chapter works through some key ideas central to a decolonizing project and examines what important critical questions they raise for GCE as an emergent theory and pedagogical approach in the current context of globalization.

I will outline some overarching rationales and premises of GCE. Then, in order to determine questions to be posed to an agenda for GCE from a framework of decolonization, I begin to frame a working understanding of imperialism and colonialism as they function in contemporary times. This leads to an overview of the legacy of colonialism in education and the articulation of new demands being placed on schooling given a critical understanding of the history of global relations. I draw heavily on the work of Tikly (2004), Smith (1999), Said (1994), Mohanty (1990) and Willinsky (1998) in identifying some of the challenges to a project of decolonizing and 'relearning' by examining political tensions inherent to such a pedagogy. The final section considers key questions arising from the discussion to which an agenda for GCE will have to respond.

GLOBAL CITIZENSHIP EDUCATION: PREMISES AND RATIONALES

My own work theorizing and researching in the area of global citizenship education reflects and is shaped by my past and current experience as an educator. I have taught secondary History and English in northern Quebec and in suburban Brazil as well as in downtown multicultural Toronto. Currently I do occasional secondary-school teaching in Toronto and do instructional work in the inner-city cohort of the initial teacher education (BEd) program at Ontario Institute for Studies in Education at the University of Toronto (OISE/UT). The questions that I pose in this essay relate back to my own work theorizing and practicing global citizenship education (Pashby 2006, 2008, 2009, in press) and are in that sense self-reflective as well as directed at the wider community of scholars and educators working in this area. The scholarly literature on GCE is broad and encompasses a range (Barr 2005) from more liberalist and humanistic frameworks (e.g., Nussbaum 2002; Noddings 2004a) to more critical and social-transformation-oriented frameworks (e.g., Andreotti 2006; Shultz 2007; Richardson 2008; Pike 2008; Andreotti et al. 2010). In this section, I will map out some overarching concepts to loosely define what I mean by GCE in this chapter. This is by no means an exhaustive conceptualization and includes the political and educational spectrums within GCE-related theory. I intend this section to provide a reference point for GCE and to position my consideration of GCE in terms of the potential for contributing to a project of decolonizing education.

Scholars researching and theorizing a global approach to citizenship education recognize that urgent and troubling issues are global in scope: for example, poverty, global warming, AIDS, racism, wars (Nussbaum 2002a; Banks 2004a; Noddings 2004a; Richardson 2008; Ghosh 2008). Thus, there is a moral imperative for extending a notion of citizenship to those outside of our national borders (Noddings 2004a; Basile 2005). Through GCE approaches, students can gain a sense of agency and action that goes beyond charity and includes structural critiques of social issues (Ladson-Billings 2004; Davies 2006; Shultz 2007; Pike 2008). Pike (2008) theorizes that GCE "challenge[s] educators to acknowledge the ever-changing patterns of relationships among human communities, and between humans and their environments, and to help students explore the implications of such trends in terms of their rights and responsibilities, their allegiances and loyalties, and their opportunities for meaningful participation"

(45–46). A main rationale for a global approach to citizenship education is the fact that educational materials are overwhelmingly Western-American-Global North-centric and emphasize neoliberal values of consumerism over critical democratic engagement while celebrating globalization from above (Talbert 2005; Pike 2008; Kachur 2008). At the same time, schooling is positioned as a central place for promoting social justice (Glass 2000; White 2005; Pike 2008, 2008a)[2] and for developing a global sense of community: "Schools are places where people learn inclusiveness, civil courage, and how to live in communities encompassing diverse relationships" (Abdi and Shultz 2008, 8–9). The concept of global citizenship recognizes that contemporary processes of globalization problematize homogenous notions of national citizenship. Increases in the mobility and movements of peoples who spend parts of their lives in different nation-states and who have multiple loyalties and commitments challenge previously taken-for-granted notions of the monolithic nation-state. Therefore, through global citizenship education, schooling can engage with contemporary complex experiences of citizenship and identity (Scott and Lawson 2002; Guilherme 2002; Osler and Starkey 2003; McIntosh 2004; Castles 2004; Banks 2004b, 2009; Davies 2006; Pike 2008). By overtly recognizing that there are multiple epistemological understandings of both the global context and local issues, GCE concepts and pedagogies can promote engagement with "the links between conflict and interpretations of culture" (Davies 2006) and an understanding of how different topics and disciplines of study are interrelated (Basile 2005). In this sense, GCE represents a possible space for creating new "legends" of the relationship between individual citizens and between certain groups of citizens and the world (Pike 2008a). Significantly, GCE aims to empower individuals to think differently and to reflect critically on the legacies and processes of their own cultures and contexts so that they can imagine different futures and take responsibility for their actions and decisions (Andreotti 2006).

WORKING TO DEFINE IMPERIALISM AND COLONIALISM IN THE CONTEMPORARY CONTEXT

In order to examine how the theorization and practice of GCE might be implicated in a colonial project, it is necessary to set out a working definition of imperialism and colonialism. Said (1994) notes that at a basic understanding, imperialism refers to settlement on and control of a distant land possessed by and lived on by others. In this sense, he defines the relationship and distinction between imperialism and colonialism: "'[I]mperialism' means the practice, the theory, and the attitudes of a dominating metropolitan center ruling a distant territory; 'colonialism,' which is almost always a consequence of imperialism, is the implanting of settlements on distant territory" (9). Similarly, Smith (1999) notes that historically speaking "[c]olonialism became imperialism's outpost, the fort and the port of imperial outreach. . . . Colonialism was, in part, an image of imperialism, a particular realization of the imperial imagination" (23). Willinsky (1998) adds that 'imperialism' operates "as a loosely conceived historical phenomenon that covers a myriad of ventures directed at extending the dominion of Europe around the globe" (10). Therefore, in a historical understanding, imperialism is about dominating lands from afar, and colonization is ruling a foreign land on that land. Both concepts involve overt, direct measures as well as less obvious discursive modes of power that work at the level of 'imagination' to govern powerfully both on a level of physical and social institutions and on an epistemological level by enforcing a particular worldview.

Within the current global context, the term 'new imperialism' acknowledges the continued influence of more powerful nations on 'distant land that is possessed by and lived on by others.' Tikly (2004) argues that the contemporary global moment is marked by the emergence of a new form of Western imperialism. Although former 'colonies' are officially 'independent,' Tikly (2004) observes that within a discourse of development, so-called Second and Third World populations are incorporated into "a regime of global government" (173). In this sense, the 'new imperialism' speaks more to a subtle, 'unofficial' form of power and control than that of earlier imperialism, and 'neocolonialism' functions through a powerful discourse that gives former colonies official 'sovereignty' while they are in fact still dominated by Western nations. Thus Tikly (2004) identifies two strands of the new imperialism: (a) a new context of Western domination through a sense of transnational movement and the emergence of a global elite, and (b) a poststructural and culturalist turn in social studies through which new frameworks emerge to understand and analyze this 'new imperialism.' In raising some critical questions for an agenda for GCE, this chapter attempts to work through and with the tensions inherent to how the latter strand seeks to recognize and critique the first strand but is always at risk of further implicating the study of colonialism in the very Western domination a poststructural turn seeks to reject.

Any sort of pedagogy that seeks to promote social justice on a world scale, such as GCE, will have to be based on a strong understanding of and articulation of imperialism in order to locate its rationales and initiatives within the hegemonic global forces it seeks to critique and to transform. By evoking a notion of 'citizenship education' as a vehicle for social justice, as an educational agenda, GCE ties a notion of global community to state membership and thus to a history of imperial nations determining who does and does not belong. Citizenship is itself a contested concept,[3] and GCE must do the difficult work of locating its own complicity within the colonial legacy of education.

THE COLONIAL LEGACY OF EDUCATION: TOWARDS A RECOGNITION OF COMPLICITY

Those of us scholars and educators working on GCE-based pedagogy will have to be very conscious of the ways in which the concept of GCE is implicated in the colonial legacy of education. Since fostering intercultural perspectives is a central principle, it is important to consider just how GCE theory will talk about and through 'difference.' Willinsky (1998) speaks to the double bind of education in this regard. He explains how schooling extends the meaning of difference by developing the ability to identify what distinguishes 'civilized' from 'primitive,' 'West' from 'East,' and 'first' from 'third' worlds so that "[w]e are educated in what we take to be the true nature of difference" (1). Yet, he also notes that "if education can turn a studied distance between people into a fact of nature, education can also help us appreciate how that distance has been constructed to the disadvantage of so many people" (1–2). Said (1994) also speaks to what can be seen as a double gesture in the study of difference when he notes that awareness of the lines between cultures allows us to discriminate but also "enables us to see the extent to which cultures are humanly made structures of both authority and participation, benevolent in what they include, incorporate, and validate, less benevolent in what they exclude and demote" (15).

The question of recognition amid difference is tied to the politics of diversity in schooling. Asad (2000) explains how in a European context a discourse of 'inclusion' creates conceptual and political tensions: "The idea of European identity, I say, is not merely a matter of how a more inclusive name can be made to claim loyalties that are attached to national or local ones. It concerns *exclusions* and the desire that those excluded recognize what is included in the name. It is a symptom of anxieties" (12). Defining a 'global citizenship identity' will also require an inclusion of multiple loyalties, and yet by being 'global' as opposed to 'European', the exclusion/inclusion dualism is not evident as presumably all inhabitants of the globe are included. Yet, citizenship is about loyalty and responsibility and infers a sense of common allegiances; therefore, the concept of global citizenship inherits the "anxieties" of citizenship. Indeed, the idea of citizenship is conceptualized within a matrix of inclusion, exclusion and loyalty. In the context of citizenship education, it is important to recognize how imperialistic discourses have constructed and continue to determine particular notions of identity within unequal power relations. Asad (2000) is concerned about how young people come to understand "the educational formation of worldly divisions that carry with them a profound sense of who belongs where. . . . Imperialism does not tell the whole of students' stories, but it does figure in what they will learn of the world" (8). GCE is conceptually complicit in the imperial legacy of schooling and in the politics of recognition inherent to citizenship; yet, it also provides a conceptual space to renegotiate and make visible those tensions.

Willinsky (1998) provokes a consideration of how imperialism has divided and instructed notions of 'belonging' and "the part that schooling has long played in defining who belongs where" (244). Indeed, his work acts as a caution for those theorizing GCE and pushes for an acknowledgment of how current ideas of education have been influenced by and contained within an imperial framework. He points to the way that forces of imperialism historically worked to 'possess' the world through 'displaying' and 'knowing' colonized cultures and peoples who were 'edified' by a Western worldview. This process was then tied into a project of schooling that served both colonial states and colonized natives (19). Thus, he establishes the difficulty inherent to determining clear distinctions between the metaphorical and literal associations of imperialism and education (253). Willinsky (1998) raises some important questions for the motivations behind GCE when he writes, "The Western thirst for learning in that earlier era [of imperialism] was supported by, where it was not simply an extension of, the desire for colonial acquisition and political domination exercised by the European powers" (252–253). In what ways could GCE, in its (American, Canadian, British, Australian, New Zealand) agenda for global awareness, be complicit with a 'new imperialism' that, without a careful interrogation of its good intentions, may actually reassert western domination?

A critical approach to schooling is an education for critical consciousness that works to overtly link a historical understanding of the configuration of social forms with the ways they work subjectively. Questions of the 'who' of global citizenship are paramount. Mohanty (1990) notes that "[the] issue of subjectivity represents a realization of the fact that who we are, how we act, what we think, and what stories we tell become more intelligible within an epistemological framework that begins by recognizing existing hegemonic histories" (185). Willinsky (1998) brings to light how a hidden curriculum has worked to colonize the processes of education. He observes that imperialism's educational project lives on as an 'unconscious aspect' of education: "After all, the great colonial empires came to a reluctant end only during the years when I and the rest of the postwar generation were being schooled. It may take generations to realize all that lies buried in this body of knowledge as a way of knowing the world" (3). A significant aspect of this colonial imagination is a colonial nostalgic: "Beyond the economic and political legacy of the colonial era, the West has also been busy producing a colonial nostalgic that speaks to the lost style and seeming grace of those heady days. . . . Walt Disney mak[es] it a specialty" (Willinsky 1998, 12). In what ways might GCE serve to reify or challenge the colonial nostalgic? How can we theorize an approach to GCE that makes visible and/or attends to the unconscious aspects of education?

Willinsky (1998) insists that education has already constructed much of what we understand as difference and diversity in terms of race, culture and nation. In this sense, imperialism is alive and well in liberal democratic schooling: "What might be written off as the remote history of imperial adventures and misfortunes has to be considered as still working on the educated imagination" (244). It is important to consider how those 'far away' and 'not here' are 'imagined' in educational projects such as GCE. Von Wright (2002) responds to Nussbaum's (2002) notion of cosmopolitan citizenship and the development of a narrative imagination among liberal arts studies in U.S. colleges. 'Narrative imagination' fosters an engagement with the perspectives of global others through a general literary education and one that focuses on the study of often ignored global others. In an interview with Nussbaum, she poses an important question around how concepts of space and distance affect a transformative notion of diversity and citizenship identity in the global imperative:

> It seems easier to understand and include somebody who is different elsewhere, than to recognize differences in our own context and accept the otherness of one's neighbor. . . . Visiting other people does not necessarily confront your values and make you a citizen of the world unless you are willing to make changes in your own life as well. (414)[4]

Therefore, in a GCE framework, approaches to difference must recognize the extent to which those educational initiatives seeking to raise awareness about and learn about 'others' are implicated in power relations and colonial ways of knowing.

The selection and framing of 'global' issues themselves is therefore also a significant process for GCE theorists to consider. Tikly (2004) warns of a possible lack of acknowledgment of the complicity of 'the West' in what are being constructed as 'global' problems but which are being understood as 'Third World' problems. He articulates this poignantly when he notes that within the context of the new imperialism there is a

> resurgence of bio-political racism that uses cultural differences to explain social problems and in so doing obscures the role of the West in relation to issues such as high fertility rates and the spread of diseases such as HIV. These discourses also avoid dealing with the effects of high levels of consumption by western populations and the effects of economic globalization on poverty and the local environment. (185)

In the context of the 'new imperialism,' a postcolonial frame pushes an agenda for GCE to interrogate carefully its motivations and to identify the ways in which it is complicit in the reproduction of colonial power imbalances in terms of how it takes up notions of difference and how it frames the selection and content of global issues.

EDUCATION FOR DECOLONIZATION: (RE)LEARNING, (RE)KNOWING AND THE PROBLEM OF HISTORY

With a more complex understanding of the ways in which schooling is both complicit in the imperial legacy and considered a main site for the dissemination of new, potentially postcolonial understandings, much is demanded of schooling in the contemporary global moment. In this context, GCE, as a pedagogy and theory, may be a way for citizenship education to reposition itself as a 'decolonizing' project. As Mohanty (1990) remarks, "[T]he task at hand is to decolonize our disciplinary and pedagogical practices. The crucial question is how we teach about the West and its Others so that education becomes the practice of liberation" (191). She notes that such a transformation will have to take seriously the relations between knowledge and learning as well as between student and teacher experiences. Mohanty (1990) insists that "the theorization and politicization of experience is imperative if pedagogical practices are to focus on more than the mere management, systematization, and the consumption of disciplinary knowledge" (192). This point raises some significant questions for GCE theorists: Whose experience/knowledge/ways of knowing are at the center of GCE pedagogy? Who is the imagined subject of GCE initiatives, who is the object of study, and how is experience understood within a 'global' frame?

While questions of subjectivity and objectification are central to a critical engagement with GCE theory, its potential in terms of taking up a decolonizing view of global relations remains significant. Indeed, a project of decolonization cannot step completely outside the colonial imagination nor can it claim to be free of ethnocentrism. As Smith (1999) reminds us, "[d]ecolonization does not mean and has not meant a total rejection of all theory or research or Western knowledge. Rather, it is about centring our concerns and world views and then coming to know and understand theory and research from our own perspectives and for our own purposes" (39). Tikly (2004) defines the challenge for anti-imperial activists and intellectuals to work away at core assumptions within the Western episteme by confronting the normalized discourse and binaries of the development problematic in order to open up spaces for debate and contention. Fundamentally, Tikly (2004) urges educationalists to "'re-colonize' the terrain currently occupied by development economics and to begin to open up the black box of educational processes and the links between these and wider issues of inequality and social change" (194).

Central to a project of decolonization is a notion of 'relearning' that is promoted by Willinsky (1998) when he urges a "rethinking [of] what we have inherited" (258). He asserts that "we" need to "learn again" how five centuries of studying, classifying and ordering produced enduring and powerful ideas of race, culture and nation "that were, in effect, concepts that the West used both to divide up and to educate the world" (3). Much is at stake in such a project, but there is much also to be achieved through a critical pedagogical approach that acknowledges and unpacks the colonial legacy of education. This is articulated by Said (1994):

> Domination and inequities of power and wealth are perennial facts of human society. But in today's global setting they are also interpretable as having something to do with imperialism, its history, its new forms. . . . What we need to do is to look at these matters as a network of interdependent histories that it would be inaccurate and senseless to repress, useful and interesting to understand. (19)

A significant factor in a decolonizing project in education includes taking up the problem of history as a problem of the present. In Willinsky's (1998) view, "[t]he past is not forgotten, but it is used to invest the present with meaning" (246). He poses the question "What does it mean to be held in the throes of a past that we can no longer trust or be comforted by?" (49). In order to work towards a meaning for the present that might change the course of geopolitical power relations for the future, Willinsky (1998) insists we must return to history with a critical eye:

> The idea of returning with a critical eye to the history that we have inherited is not only about what has gone missing in the story of the past, but also about a history that has remained all too present as a force in our lives; which is to say that more or better history teaching, including the history of imperialism, does not in itself point the way forward. (245)

In such a project, Chow (1993) reminds us to be very careful about "[t]he danger of historical contextualization turning into cultural corporation" (38). Said (1994) articulates a warning in this regard:

> Appeals to the past are among the commonest of strategies in interpretations of the present. What animates such appeals is not only disagreement about what happened in the past and what the past was, but uncertainty about whether the past really is past, over and concluded, or whether it continues, albeit in different forms, perhaps. This problem animates all sorts of discussions—about influence, about blame and judgement, about preset actualities and future priorities. (3)

Smith (1999) adds that revisiting history has been very significant to decolonization because in the intersection of (a) indigenous approaches to history, (b) the modernist project, and (c) the strategies of resistance that have been employed, it becomes clear that "[o]ur colonial experience traps us in the project of modernity. . . . [T]here is unfinished business, that we are still being colonized (and know it), and that we are still searching for justice" (34). If GCE can be theorized as an educational project of decolonization, those theorizing it will need to be very aware of the discourses it takes up and employs. A review of writings on the relationship between colonization and schooling raises some important questions regarding how GCE might be positioned as a project of *de*colonization or *re*colonization.

GCE: BY WHOM, FOR WHOM?

There is a presumption in the concept of 'global citizenship' that there exists a global community to which all can belong and in which all can participate. Yet, citizenship itself is defined by who does and who does not belong.

Given that most citizenship education is based in state-sponsored and state-run schooling systems, global citizenship is predominantly understood as extending out from a national citizenship education project (Pashby 2008). Therefore, from a decolonizing approach, the concept of global citizenship must be theorized in a way that pushes beyond the extant common notions of political and social spaces and of citizenship education activity in order to enable agency and resistance within a global orientation. Silverstone (2001) raises the idea of global community as related to new media. He highlights the struggle of groups and cultures who have been displaced and/or are "on the move" for participation in new media "on their own terms." He raises the political importance of a 'global politics' for minorities who "recently or less recently, displaced, are seeking, and seeking to defend, not just the right to exist materially but the right to maintain their own culture, their own identity" (21). Willinsky's (1998) question of 'where is here,' or, phrased differently, 'where is home' is echoed in Silverstone's (2001) work on the intersection of 'the local' and 'the global':

> The populations that are involved are both local and global at the same time: they are local insofar as they are minority cultures living in particular places, but they are global in their range and reach. Not so much communities, more like networks: networks linking members in different spaces, in different cities, networks linking the dispersed with those who have remained, in some sense of the term, at home. (21)

These 'networks' represent spaces of much potential for pushing at existing hegemonic discourses of community and opening up possibilities for new ways of imagining a sense of being connected to others and having agency within global power dynamics. However, Silverstone (2001) notes that globalization is multifaceted and very much a contested process that is implicated in complex social relations steeped in both established traditions and new trends: "Not the exclusive preserve of elites, nor of the global media, but a to-ing and fro-ing of identities and interests, mobilized and articulated through an increasingly electronic space, but still dependent on, and vulnerable to, the real movements of diverse populations through space and time" (22). Indeed, speaking to indigenous issues, Smith (1999) insists the concept of globalization as ushering in a 'new world order' does not solve colonial problems for indigenous peoples but rather results in the emergence of new problems: "While being on the margins of the world has had dire consequences, being incorporated within the world's marketplace has different implications and in turn requires the mounting of new forms of resistance. Similarly, postcolonial discussions have also stirred some indigenous resistance . . . to the idea that colonialism is over, finished business" (24).

Thus another important question arises: Global citizenship education *by* whom *for* whom (Pashby, in press)? *Who* is the assumed student of a decolonizing project of GCE? *Where* is GCE conceived and practiced? Will a framework called 'global' citizenship education be a universal pedagogical approach, or does the fact the a bulk of the writing comes from particular Northern, Western contexts speak as much about what needs to be resisted or 'relearned' in those contexts as it does about what needs to be changed globally? Is there a particular geopolitical student-subject in mind? Willinsky (1998) insists that in terms of the colonial legacy of education, "the globalization of Western understanding was always about a relative positioning of the West by a set of coordinates defined by race, culture, and nation" (253). Is GCE a repositioning of the West, and if so, does it meet its 'good' intentions around a social-justice orientation to global issues by repositioning citizenship education in a postcolonial frame or is it inevitably lodged within the 'new imperialism'?

The question of who might resist an agenda for GCE and for what significant reasons might the conceptualization of a global commons be opposed is a significant concern. Smith (1999) explains how many indigenous intellectuals resist discourses of postcoloniality: "This is because post-colonialism is viewed as the convenient invention of Western intellectuals which reinscribes their power to define the world" (14). And similarly, while it is extremely important to hold the question of 'whose project' is GCE, Mohanty (1990) asserts that a postcolonial project must "be an active, oppositional, and collective voice which takes seriously the current commodification and domestication of Third World people in the academy. And this is a task open to all—people of color as well as progressive white people in the academy" (208). In what ways is the theoretical work on GCE open to a critique of its own (varying and consistent) epistemological assumptions and good intentions? How can those theorizing GCE, myself included, make visible the underlying power imbalances of contemporary global relations while acknowledging the complicity both of schooling and of Western concepts of 'the global' in those very inequities? Given the significant attention being given to GCE in particular Western democracies, is *global* citizenship education essentially an add-on to national citizenship education? Starting from a critical national citizenship and extending to a notion of global citizenship can be an important strategy in terms of interrogating the unconscious imperialistic roots still persisting through the hidden curriculum in Northern/Western schools. If so, in what ways can GCE theoretically and pedagogically serve to reformulate a notion of citizenship that includes a critical and decolonizing view of relations among individuals and groups from within such a national frame? To what extent is it also appropriate as a pedagogical theory in schools in non-Western contexts and/or in the Global South?

GCE theorists must consider an ethic of educational accountability that acknowledges education's and scholarship's role in establishing such divides as East and West and primitive and civilized. Willinsky (1998) calls for an educational agenda that will take to task "how the world has been constructed around centers and margins, and how these divisions were bolstered through forms of scholarship supported by imperialism" (16). In this sense, it will be essential for GCE theorists to confront the notion of educational complicity. A decolonizing GCE approach would take up both the institutional complicity of education in the legacy of colonialism and the personal complicity of individuals and groups who are implicated in its continued hegemonic privileging as perpetuated through education. GCE theorists in any global context will have particular work to do in acknowledging 'global' notions of privilege. As Chow (1993) asserts, this is a global phenomenon:

> The difficulty facing us, it seems to me, is no longer simply the 'first world' Orientalist who mourns the rusting away of his treasures, but also students from privileged backgrounds Western *and* non-Western, who conform behaviorally in every respect with the elitism of their social origins . . . but who nonetheless *proclaim* dedication to 'vindicating the subalterns'. My point is not that they should be blamed for the accident of their birth, nor that they cannot marry rich, pursue fame, or even be arrogant. Rather, it is that they choose to see in others' powerlessness an idealized image of themselves and refuse to hear in the dissonance between the content and manner of their speech their own complicity with violence. (14)

Therefore, a decolonizing project of GCE raises important questions around the subjects of global citizenship education and the objects of global citizenship learning. Smith (1999) explicates on the sense of violence raised by Chow that is an inherent danger of even 'well-intended' global studies:

> It galls us that Western researchers and intellectuals can assume to know all that it is possible to know of us, on the basis of their brief encounters with some of us. It appalls us that the West can desire, extract and claim ownership of our ways of knowing, our imagery, the things we create and produce, and then simultaneously reject the people who created and developed those ideas and seeks to deny them further opportunities to be creators of their own culture and own nation. (1)

Mohanty's (1990) notion of 'co-implication' is useful here. She refers to the idea that "all of us" (those identified as belonging to so-called First and to Third worlds) share both histories and responsibilities in that "ideologies of race define both white and black peoples, just as gender ideologies define both women and men" (195). She promotes a pedagogy that works to explicitly understand the "experience" of those positioned in any of those identity spaces as "historical, contingent, and the result of interpretation[; otherwise,] it can coagulate into frozen, binary, psychologistic positions" (195). Ultimately, the question of 'who' is the subject of GCE is implicated in the complex task schooling is set out to do. As Derrida (2002) reminds us, "One of the problems with school is that it occupies only a limited time and space in the experience of the subject, citizen or not, who has access to the image outside school, at home, or anywhere. This critical imperative is obligatory in school and to a large extent outside it" (60).

Related to the question of 'whose project' and how to encourage a critical and nuanced understanding of complicity is the need for a critical theorization of 'knowledge' within an agenda for GCE. The question of whose and what 'knowledge' is strongly connected to the power of having and representing identity; and in drawing on the concept of citizenship, questions of identity and belonging are integral to GCE. Willinsky (1998) notes that "imperialism of another sort lives on in how each of us is known and how each of us comes to know" (262), for, as Mohanty (1990) insists, "knowledge, the very act of knowing, is related to the power of self-definition" (184). However, Mohanty (1990) warns again of the constant risk of the co-optation of a transformatory theory of knowledge within an academic project:

> [N]ew academic analytic spaces have been opened up in the academy, spaces that make possible thinking of knowledge as praxis, of knowledge as embodying the very seeds of transformation and change. The appropriation of these analytic spaces and the challenge of radical educational practices are thus to involve the development of critical knowledges (what women's, black, and ethnic studies attempt), and simultaneously, to critique knowledge itself. (85)

Indeed, if GCE theory wishes to promote a decolonizing notion of justice within the context of the new imperialism, it must answer Tikly's (2004) basic question: "[I]s it possible to conceive of a critical social theory and epistemology on which an alternative to western hegemony can be built, and what ought the role of education to be in the endeavor assuming it were possible?" (192). Yet, as educationalists, though some of us theorizing GCE work hard to recognize the double bind wherein education is both an apparatus of colonial power and the tool to move the masses to resist and to open up new discourses and political spaces, we cannot rest our hands or our minds. As Willinsky (1998) notes, "How far can we go in seeing the world other than as we have inherited it, I do not yet know. The educational project always lies ahead" (262).

GCE: USING OUR "THINKING HATS" TO STRATEGIZE THROUGH THE "MESSY" WORK

This chapter has engaged in a process of formulating a framework through which to interrogate the 'good intentions' of global citizenship education within a commitment to decolonizing education in general and citizenship education specifically. I have begun to set out a working definition of 'new imperialism' in order to recognize the colonial legacy of education and its implication for contemporary educational agendas in the contemporary global context. Any type of schooling for decolonization is implicated in a paradox whereby schooling is a vehicle of colonization and a tool for attempting to dismantle hegemonic colonial discourses. There is a lack of certainty inherent to a project of decolonization, for it challenges many of the ways of knowing that are fundamental to Western schooling traditions, and it pushes for an engagement with complexity. Any attempt to implement a global approach to citizenship education will have much critical theorizing to do in order to work into a framework of citizenship education a sense of complicity and accountability for the colonial legacy of education. As Willinsky suggests, this work requires a resistance to and rejection of much of the 'certainty' on which the current paradigm of schooling relies:

> I am not at all sure whether we can un-install the mammoth program of Westernization that the world has absorbed, nor would I want to decide that this is the best course of action on behalf of others. When it comes to the world we know, the best we can hope for is to supplement what we know, to learn again, rather than to imagine walking away from being the educated subjects that we have become. (262)

Therefore, this discussion promotes a theorization of GCE pedagogy that is rooted in learning global relations "again" and makes a notion of Westernization and colonialism explicit in its conceptualization of both 'the global' and 'citizenship.' Fundamentally, GCE theory must take up explicitly the question of 'for whom' is global citizenship and 'by whom' will its pedagogy and concepts be determined in order to make overt its positioning within the geopolitical power relations defining the new imperialism.

The literature on GCE that I have studied closely and that I summarized at the beginning of this essay represents a broad conceptual and political spectrum (Barr 2005). I would like to highlight the work of a few theorists whose work engages the tensions I have raised in this chapter. Richardson (2008) traces the conceptual roots of GCE in Canada back to a particular "imperial imaginary" which continues to frame the concept of learning about "the global." And in her critique of the Make Poverty History (MPH) campaign in the UK, Andreotti (2006) brings explicit attention to the tendency towards a 'soft' version of GCE. Drawing on Spivak, she speaks to the potential for "sanctioned ignorances." Andreotti also observes that while a 'critical' approach to GCE opens up spaces for interrogating privileged assumptions and value systems and to promote changes in the hegemonic systems that continue to reinscribe inequities, the extent to which educators engaging in GCE are prepared to do the difficult work of acknowledging the complicity of and limitations of their own approaches is not clear. Her critique of MPH resists the implicit 'colonial nostalgia' of many global studies approaches. Pike's (2008) work responds to the question of global citizenship as a concept for the elite and to the question of 'for whom' is GCE relevant. He argues for the importance of highlighting "the elitism that can easily suffuse the rhetoric of global citizenship education: for the countless millions of people worldwide who daily struggle for survival and satisfaction of basic human rights, or for recognition of their cultural identity, global citizenship is not even on the agenda" (Pike, 2008, 44). In recent work, Andreotti (2010) argues that the role of GCE "is one of decolonization" and articulates the importance of acknowledging the "complex, diverse, changing, uncertain and deeply unequal" nature of contemporary societies (249). While these scholars' work, among others, provides evidence of a building momentum within GCE scholarship towards what could be considered a decolonizing project or at least one that works to interrogate the 'new imperialism,' Pike (2008a) acknowledges the "sparse activity on the ground" (225).

Therefore, while this chapter has used a working framework of education's complicity with colonialism to articulate some questions important in order to interrogate the rationales and assumptions inherent to theorizing global citizenship education, I do not do so to suggest that there is not important work already being done in this area. The questions and tensions I have raised do push for continued momentum in the more "critical" (Andreotti 2006) end of the GCE spectrum as we continue the challenging work of promoting a transformation in global studies and citizenship education while being explicit about the implications and limitations of our own approaches. A particular limitation at this point in time is the translation of the theoretical work into classroom practice. The work will be complex and "messy," but Smith (1999) reminds us of the importance of strategic thinking. When asked about the potential contradiction between a strong focus on "thinking" and "any sense of a transformative, truly postcolonial agenda," she promotes the link between strategic thinking and transformative action:

I think people theorise themselves and they end up in a position of not acting because to act can be very messy. There is no purity in it, and it is about thinking much more strategically about social change and what we have learned is that change is going to happen anyway. But you can influence change if you act. It is just the sense of agency; you grab it, you use it, but you don't leave your thinking hat behind when you act. You do try to mobilise the two together . . . Part of learning to act, is learning that when you act things happen, and so thinking about acting is simply thinking about what the likely possibilities are going to be and preparing for that. . . . (184–185)

Thus, I call on those of us theorizing, researching and practicing global citizenship education to continue to think strategically about change and to

24   *Karen Pashby*

use our agency to push for the decolonizing potential in GCE. The chapters
in this book point to a growing critical mass of educators and scholars
working to think critically and act strategically, and the essays in this collection will help to identify "the likely possibilities" and to prepare for the
inevitable tensions and complexities inherent to this important work.

NOTES

1. See, for example, Nussbaum 2002; Osler & Starkey 2003; Banks 2004; Golmohamad 2004; Davies 2006; Davies, Evans & Reid 2005; Openshaw and
   White 2005; Andreotti 2006; Shultz 2007; O'Sullivan and Pashby 2008;
   Abdi and Shultz 2008; Pike 2008; Andreotti et al. 2010.
2. For example: "The global economy (really meaning the U.S. idea of free-trade)
   is expanding at the expense of human rights and environmental protection.
   And where else but in social education lays the foundation for an alternative
   to this dehumanizing, demeaning, and homogenizing movement?" (White
   2005, 79).
3. See Pashby 2008 and also Scott and Lawson 2002, Delanty 2000, and Isin
   and Wood (1999), among others.

REFERENCES

Abdi, A. and Shultz, L. (eds.) (2008) *Educating for Human Rights and Global
Citizenship*. Albany, NY: State University of New York Press.
Andreotti, V. (2006) 'Soft vs. Critical Global Citizenship Education', *Policy and
Practice: A Development Education Review*, 3: 40–51.
———. (2010) 'Postcolonial and Post-critical Global Citizenship Education', in
G. Elliott, C. Fourali & S. Issler, *Education & Social Change*. London, Con-
tinuum, 238–250.
Andreotti, V., Jeferess, D., Pashby, K., Rowe, C., Tarc, P. and Taylor, L. (2010) 'Differ-
ence and Conflict in Global Citizenship in Higher Education in Canada', *Interna-
tional Journal of Development Education and Global Learning*, 2(3): 5–24.
Asad, T. 2000. "Muslim and European Identity. Can Europe Represent Islam?" in
E. Hallam and B. Street (eds.), *Cultural Encounters—Representing 'Otherness'*,
New York: Routledge, 11–28.
Banks, J. A. (ed.) (2004) *Diversity and Citizenship Education: Global Perspec-
tives*, San Francisco: John Wiley and Sons, Inc.
———. (2004a) 'Introduction: Democratic Citizenship Education in Multicultural
Societies', in J. A. Banks (ed.), *Diversity and Citizenship Education: Global
Perspectives*, San Francisco: John Wiley & Sons, Inc, 3–15.
———. (2009) 'Diversity, Group Identity, and Citizenship Education in a Global
Age', in J. A. Banks (ed.), *The Routledge International Companion to Multicul-
tural Education*, New York: Routledge, 303–322.
Barr, H. (2005) 'Toward a Model of Citizenship Education: Coping with Differ-
ences in Definition', in C. White and R. Openshaw (eds.), *Democracy at the
Crossroads: International Perspectives on Critical Global Citizenship Educa-
tion*, Lanham, MD: Lexington Books, 55–75.
Basile, C. (2005) 'Jefferson County Open School: Voices of Global Citizenship', in
C. White and R. Openshaw (eds.), *Democracy at the Crossroads: International*

Perspectives on Critical Global Citizenship Education, Lanham, MD: Lexington Books, 347–363.

Castles, S. (2004) 'Migration, Citizenship, and Education', in James A. Banks (ed.), *Diversity and Citizenship Education: Global Perspectives*, San Francisco: John Wiley & Sons, Inc., 17–48.

Chow, R. (1993) 'Excerpts from "Writing Diaspora: Tactics of Intervention in Contemporary Cultural Studies", in *Writing Diaspora: Tactics of Intervention in Contemporary Cultural Studies*, John Wiley & Sons, 1–54.

Davies, L. (2006) 'Global Citizenship: Abstraction or Framework for Action?', *Educational Review*, 58(1): 5–25.

Davies, I., Evans, M. and Reid, A. (2005) 'Globalizing Citizenship Education? A Critique of Global Education' and 'Citizenship Education', *British Journal of Educational Studies*, 53(1): 66–89.

Delanty, G. (2000) *Citizenship in a Global Age: Society, Culture, Politics*, Buckingham, UK: Open University Press.

Derrida, J. (in conversation with Bernard Stiegler) (2002) 'Right of Inspection' and 'Acts of Memory: Topolitics and Teletechnology' ", in *Echographies of Television*, Cambridge, Polity Press and Oxford, UK; Malden, MA: Blackwell Publishers, 31–67.

Ghosh, R. (2008) 'The Short History of Women, Human Rights, and Global Citizenship', in Ali A. Abdi and Lynette Shultz (eds.), *Educating for Human Rights and Global Citizenship*, Albany, NY: State University of New York Press, 81–95.

Glass, R. D. (2000) 'Education and the Ethics of Democratic Citizenship', *Studies in Philosophy of Education*, 19: 275–296.

Golmohamad, M. (2004) 'World Citizenship, Identity and the Notion of an Integrated Self', *Studies in Philosophy and Education*, 23: 131–148.

Guilherme, M. (2002) *Critical Citizens for an Intercultural World: Foreign Language Education as Cultural Politics*, London: Multilingual Matters Ltd.

Isin, E. F. and Wood, P. K. (1999) *Citizenship and identity*, London: Sage.

Kachur, J. L. (2008) 'Human Rights Imperialism: Third Way Education as the New Cultural Imperialism', in Ali A. Abdi and Lynette Shultz (eds.), *Educating for Human Rights and Global Citizenship*, Albany, NY: State University of New York Press, 177–192.

Ladson-Billings, G. (2004) 'Differing Concepts of Citizenship: Schools and Communities as Sites of Civic Development', in Nel Noddings (ed.), *Educating Citizens for Global Awareness*, New York: Teachers College Press, 69–80.

McIntosh, P. (2004) 'Gender Perspectives on Educating for Global Citizenship', in Nel Noddings (ed.), *Educating Citizens for Global Awareness*, New York: Teachers College Press, 22–39.

Mohanty, C. T. (1990) 'On Race and Voice: Challenges for Liberal Education in the 1990s', *Cultural Critique*, Winter 1989–90: 179–208.

Noddings, N. (ed.) (2004). *Educating Citizens for Global Awareness*, New York: Teachers College Press.

———. (2004a) 'Global Citizenship: Promises and Problems' and 'Conclusion: What Have We Learned?', in N. Noddings (ed.), *Educating Citizens for Global Awareness*, New York: Teachers College Press, 1–21, 122–135.

Nussbaum, M. (2002) 'Education for Citizenship in an Era of Global Connection', *Studies in Philosophy and Education*, 21: 289–303.

Openshaw, R. and White, C. (eds.) (2005) *Democracy at the Crossroads: International Perspectives on Critical GCE*, Lanham, MD: Lexington Books.

Osler, A. and Starkey, H. (2003) 'Learning for Cosmopolitan Citizenship: Theoretical Debates and Young People's Experiences', *Educational Review*, 55(3): 243–254.

O'Sullivan, M and Pashby, K. (eds.) (2008) *Citizenship education in the era of globalization: Canadian perspectives.* Rotterdam: Sense Publishing, 53–70.

Pashby, K. (2006) *Citizenship and Diversity in the Global Imperative: What Does Global Citizenship Education Mean for Multiculturalism?* Master's thesis, York University.

———. (2008) 'Demands on and of Citizenship and Schooling: "Belonging" and "Diversity" in the Global Imperative', in M. O'Sullivan & K. Pashby (eds.), *Citizenship Education in the Era of Globalization: Canadian Perspectives*, Rotterdam: Sense Publishers B. V., 9–26.

———. (2009) 'The Stephen Lewis Foundation's Grandmothers-to-Grandmothers Campaign: A Model for Critical Global Citizenship Learning?', *Critical Literacy: Theories and Practices*, 3(1): 59–70.

———. (2011) 'Cultivating Global Citizens: Planting New Seeds or Pruning the Perennials? Looking for the Citizen-Subject in Global Citizenship Education Theory', *Globalisation, Society and Education.*

Pike, G. (2008) 'Citizenship Education in Global Context', *Brock Education*, 17: 38–49.

———. (2008a) 'Reconstructing the Legend: Educating for Global Citizenship', in Ali A. Abdi and Lynette Shultz (eds.), *Educating for Human Rights and Global Citizenship*, Albany, NY: State University of New York Press, 223–237.

Richardson, G. (2008) 'Conflicting Imaginaries: Global Citizenship Education in Canada as a Site of Contestation', in M. O'Sullivan & K. Pashby (eds.), *Citizenship Education in the Era of Globalization: Canadian Perspectives*. Rotterdam: Sense Publishing, 53–70.

Said, E. (1994) *Culture and Imperialism*, New York: Knopf.

Scott, D. and Lawson, H. (eds.) (2002) "Introduction", *Citizenship Education and the Curriculum*, Westport, CT: Ablex Publishing, 1–6.

Shultz, L. (2007) 'Educating for Global Citizenship: Conflicting Agendas and Understandings', *Alberta Journal of Educational Research*, 53(3): 248–258.

Silverstone, R. (2001) 'Finding a Voice: Minorities, Media and the Global Commons', *Emergences*, 11(1): 13–27.

Smith, L. (1999) *Decolonizing Methodologies: Research and Indigenous Peoples*, London: Zed Books.

———. (2002) As quoted in Battiste, M., Bell, L. and Findlay, L. M., 'An interview with Linda Tuhiwai Te Rina Smith', *Canadian Journal of Native Education*, 26(2): 169–201.

Talbert, T. L. (2005) 'Freedom or French Fries: Packaged Democracy for World Consumption', in Cameron White and Roger Openshaw (eds.), *Democracy at the Crossroads: International Perspectives on Critical Global Citizenship Education*, Lanham, MD: Lexington Books, 31–54.

Tikly, L. (2004) 'Education and the New Imperialism', *Comparative Education*, 40(2): 173–198.

White, C. (2005) 'Critical Democratic Education for Social Efficacy', in Cameron White and Roger Openshaw (eds.), *Democracy at the Crossroads: International Perspectives on Critical Global Citizenship Education*, Lanham, MD: Lexington Books, 77–104.

Willinsky, J. (1998) *Learning to Divide the World: Education at Empire's End.* Minneapolis: University of Minnesota Press.

Von Wright, M. (2002) "Narrative Imagination and Taking the Perspective of Others" *Studies in Philosophy and Education*, 21: 407–416.

2   Unsettling Cosmopolitanism
Global Citizenship and the
Cultural Politics of Benevolence[1]

David Jefferess

As part of the "Stand Up and Speak" campaign to raise awareness of the UN Millennium Campaign to "make poverty history," the Canadian coalition of volunteer cooperation agencies Global Citizens for Change mailed out flyers to thousands of Canadians addressed: "Dear Global Citizen" ("An End to Poverty" 2007). Such an address presumes both an identity position and an ethical position of the addressee. The global citizen is one who identifies not (only) with their local or national community but as a member of a global community. Global citizenship, however, marks not simply a conception of belonging but an ethics of being: The global citizen is one who "Stands Up and Speaks" and who works to "make poverty history." To be addressed as a global citizen seemingly marks the transcendence of national identity and other exclusionary modes of affiliation, such as race, ethnicity, gender or religion. Yet, the context of this address suggests that not everyone can be a global citizen.

Global citizenship seems to mark an attitude of being in the world, and a transnational or universal identity, but as an ethics of action the global citizen is defined as one who helps an unfortunate Other. So, for instance, the Global Citizens for Change coalition is comprised of Canada's "9 leading volunteer cooperation agencies," development-focused organizations which send Canadians to "volunteer" (work) in states in the Global South. The presumptions that underlie the address, "Dear Global Citizen," reflect what Raymond Williams (1961) calls a society's structure of feeling, or what Edward Said (1993) calls the structures of attitude and reference of European imperialism, as a project of humanitarian benevolence. The form of imperialism has changed: Race discourse and the language of inferiority and dependence have been replaced by that of cultural diversity, nation-building and global citizenship. The notion of aid, responsibility and poverty alleviation, however, retain the Other as an object of benevolence.

The address, "Dear Global Citizen," which hails the subject into a global social imaginary, seems specifically anti- or postcolonial, in that it calls upon the subject to conceive of, and perform, a citizenship that is antithetical to the specifically national and legal notion of citizenship; global citizenship seems marked by inclusion, rather than exclusion, pluralism and tolerance. As such, it seems to repudiate the European imperial project of economic exploitation which has been rationalized by race thinking. Yet, as this collection contends, such a conception of global citizenship is indebted to and embedded in (neo)colonial discourse, and specifically that of imperial humanitarianism. By providing a postcolonial critique of specific examples of the dominant discourse of global citizenship in Canada, I want to position my analysis in terms of a politics of decolonization that understands global material inequality in relational terms and as a product of a continuing process. Decolonization, from this perspective, reflects not so much a desire for resolution and closure—which, from a Euro-American epistemological position the prefix of *post* in postcolonialism seems to affirm—but a critical praxis that foregrounds dynamism, process and critical self-reflection.

Having said this, postcolonialism, as a decolonizing process, should not be understood as an empty deconstructive practice. My analysis focuses upon deconstructing the discursive and cultural aspects of a neoimperial project that continues to be shaped by, and for the benefit of, Europe and European-dominated settler nations (the U.S., Canada, Australia, New Zealand), or, more broadly, the G8 or Organization of Economic Cooperation and Development (OECD) states; yet, I intend this analysis to further the postcolonial project of fostering intercultural understanding, egalitarian material social relations and peaceful coexistence.[2] As Gayatri Chakravorty Spivak describes this, deconstruction constitutes "a persistent critique of what one cannot not want" (Spivak 1994, 278). As a white, economically privileged male Canadian citizen, I also want to acknowledge the way in which my critique of these projects of global citizenship is not situated outside the cultural politics of benevolence I critique. Making a similar acknowledgment, Daniel Coleman describes his critique of Canada's "white civility" as a project of "wry civility": "Wry in the sense of remaining ironically aware of the pretentiousness of the civility that we nonetheless aspire to, and also of the pretentiousness in trying to be self-aware" (2006, 43).

In this chapter I critically examine the discourse of global citizenship specifically as theorized by Nigel Dower (2003) and Kwame Anthony Appiah (2006), and I draw upon the example of the university where I teach, the University of British Columbia (UBC), for which fostering global citizenship has become a primary mandate of the academic plan. While I am sympathetic to the desire for a way of imagining community that transcends the legacy of European colonialism and hence transcends the material and symbolic borders of nation, race, religion and so on, I believe that the unselfconsciously celebratory appeals to global citizenship that currently circulate in OECD states are indebted to earlier European, and specifically Eurocentric, formulations of humanity, civilization and peace. While global citizenship purports simply to identify an ethical philosophy and a politics of identity, the discourse produces the global citizen as a particular subject that is constituted by the ability to act, and specifically to "make a better world" *for*, rather than *with*, others. The emphasis upon global citizenship as an ethically framed identity functions to sanction ignorance of the history and structures of global material inequality and normalize the conditions of privilege that allow some to be in the position to help or "make a difference."

However, I do not want to simply reject the notion of global citizenship, or a global ethics. Appiah's reworking of the notion of cosmopolitanism, for instance, provides the beginnings of a theory of global ethics that engages with structures of inequality, both material and cultural. For Appiah, the cosmopolitan seeks to understand the interrelationships among all of the people on the planet, specifically in a way that values human diversity. Cosmopolitanism is an ethical philosophy that is concerned with understanding the role of the individual in the work of transforming ideologies and structures that produce and maintain inequality and injustice. While articulations of global citizenship reiterate this ideal of a universal humanity, the dominant articulations and uses of the concept seem to elide the positioning of the global citizen within a material history of global social relations. I want to reaffirm the ideals of Appiah's cosmopolitan ethics, but I also want to challenge the way in which this ethics is easily translated into popular discourses of global citizenship as simply an identity position that is formulated through, and rationalized by, benevolence and pity. To this end, in the closing section of the chapter, I suggest how global citizenship education might be practiced in states like Canada through a pedagogy of unsettling, or, in other words, wry—rather than white—civility.

AN IMAGINED GLOBAL COMMUNITY AND ETHICS

Since the late 1990s, global citizenship, as a concept which signifies the way in which one's identity and ethical responsibility are not limited to their "local" community (i.e., family, nation), has increasingly become a conceptual mantra for international development and humanitarian agencies, and a primary mandate of the institution of the North American university. The emergence of the concept of global citizenship in popular discourses of globalization and humanitarian ethics, at least in Europe and North America, reflects, and is reflected in, historical conceptions of cosmopolitanism, such as that articulated by the Stoics, as well as the return to the hope of humanism in the fields of political philosophy and critical and cultural theory. For instance, in the wake of the Cold War, Euro-American political philosophers such as Nigel Dower, Peter Singer, John Rawls and Michael Ignatieff have all argued for a particular responsibility *for* the Other that is either explicitly or implicitly theorized as an expression of cosmopolitanism. Rawls (1999) has argued for the West's "duty of assistance to burdened societies," and Ignatieff was influential in the development of the notion of the responsibility to protect. Dower (2003) contends that global citizenship is "premised on the belief that agents have global responsibilities to help make a better world and that they are part of large-scale networks of concern" (vii). Dower's theorizing of global citizenship fails to recognize the way in which agency is shaped or limited by social relations of privilege and power. Global citizenship functions as an ethical stance or political philosophy that an individual adopts; it does not identify a particular political subjectivity, it would seem. As I will argue, however, theories of global ethics, such as that presented by Dower, echo in their rhetoric the imperial project of civilization. More importantly, the discourse of global citizenship, while it represents the idea of universal inclusivity, produces insiders and outsiders: not everyone can be a global citizen.

While Appiah's conception of cosmopolitanism can be easily appropriated into the sorts of global citizenship as humanitarian benevolence I critique, Appiah's work is informed by a specifically postcolonial approach to understanding global relations of power. Appiah's father—who was a leader in the movement to end the British colonial dispensation of the Gold Coast and create the independent state of Ghana—reminded his children that they are "citizens of the world" (2006, xviii). Appiah explains that such recognition need not supplant local or national conceptions of belonging and identity. Indeed, it is important to differentiate cosmopolitanism from a notion of world citizenship, for, as Appiah notes, "The exercise of citizenship requires the capacity to participate in the public discussion of the polity" (2005, 101). As Dower concedes, because the institutional structures associated with citizenship do not exist at a global level, "citizenship" within the notion of global citizenship functions metaphorically (23); while various international frameworks of human and social rights exist, there is no global state apparatus that can ensure these rights. A global polity does not exist, as the United Nations, for instance, is comprised of nation-state representatives and is not a world federalist level of governance; the vast majority of the people in the world have little ability to officially participate in the governance of their lives, whether locally or globally. Without such a global polity of which to be a citizen, the discourse of global citizenship is, to this point, primarily concerned with identity and not with political subjectivity. Hence, citizenship, in this formulation, cannot (yet) mean participation and inclusion, rights and responsibilities.

More importantly, for Appiah cosmopolitanism need not be understood in terms of citizenship, and does not require a global system of governance modeled on the modern nation-state. As Chandra Talpade Mohanty (2003)—who has been influential in theorizing ideas of transnational solidarity—has argued, citizenship is a concept of subjectivity that has developed within liberal patriarchal capitalism, and, as a result, is associated with particular conceptions of rationality, order, and civility (65). Further, citizenship has historically served to produce a particular kind of community marked by its difference from others: insiders and outsiders, those who belong and those who do not, those who have rights and those who do not. Here, then, Appiah's theory of the cosmopolitan is distinct from the notion of the global citizen. As Dower's (2003) argument for global citizenship reveals, the concept is very much indebted to Western notions of the state, the citizen and agency as free will. For Dower, global citizenship reflects the aspiration for a global form of state apparatus that can constitute and secure *individual* human rights and provide for greater political participation for individuals (124).

In a sense, then, the emergence of the concept of global citizenship either elides the history of the concept of citizenship that Mohanty identifies or works to transform the ideological underpinnings of the notion of citizenship; global citizenship would seem to provide the conceptual framework for transcending the nation or the barriers of ethnic, religious or racial difference to include all within a global community. For instance, Martha Piper, former president of UBC and the initiator of global citizenship on the university's campuses, states that "our goal must be to educate global citizens who see themselves not simply as citizens of a local region, but also as human beings bound to all other human beings by ties of concern and understanding" (qtd. in Boothroyd 2005, 1). In this way, global citizenship provides a means of imagining the world as a global community in much the way Benedict Anderson (1991) argues that the nation is an imagined political community. So, where Anderson argues that the printing press and the standardization of national languages allowed for the development of communal affinity in the form of European nationalisms, we might say that the development of the Internet or satellite television has allowed for increasing awareness of the world as a complex and interrelated social community. However, we must also remember that only a limited group of people on the planet yet have regular access to, or the capability to use, these means of technology and these people are disproportionally based in OECD states.

The academic plan of UBC Okanagan (2006) defines the global citizen as one who is "willing to think beyond boundaries of place, identity and category and recognize all human beings as their equals while respecting humanity's inherent diversity. Within their own sphere of influence, global citizens seek to imagine and work towards a better world" (12). Hence, global citizenship connotes an identity and an ethical philosophy rather than the specific role and set of responsibilities associated with the citizen-subject of a democratic state. To be a global citizen is to adopt a global perspective that allows one to see oneself as interconnected with the experiences of others around the world. As Dower explains: "A global citizen may also accept an ethic of more extensive benevolence. She does not merely help those in front of her, she accepts a general responsibility and seeks out appropriate ways of helping, including helping at a distance" (92). Significantly, this 'identity' is described not through the discourse of political participation and responsibility but through a rhetoric of affiliation, obligation and moral goodness. While such a stance potentially provides an alternative—and perhaps a challenge—to the normativity of national identity, it also frames the only possible 'solution' to poverty as philanthropy.

Appiah's theory of cosmopolitanism echoes this emphasis upon identity. It does not mark one's belonging to a formal, global community in the way that national citizenship marks a particular kind of belonging experienced through a system of rights and responsibilities, but a way of understanding one's place in the world. He contends that cosmopolitanism connotes the idea that we have ethical obligations to those whom we do not know and to whom we are seemingly not tied by particular communal relationships or identities. As well, cosmopolitanism requires that we value particular human lives, and not just an abstract notion of humanity; hence, Appiah contends that we must take an interest in the specific practices, values and beliefs that lend those lives significance (2006, xv). Cosmopolitanism, Appiah argues, holds to the truth that everybody matters: Every human being has obligations to every other. Yet, he argues that beyond this little can be certain; cosmopolitanism is committed to pluralism, or the idea "that there are many values worth living by and that you cannot live by all of them" and to "fallibism," or the acknowledgment that "knowledge is imperfect, provisional, subject to revision in the face of new evidence" (144). Hence, unlike global citizenship, I would argue, cosmopolitanism does not seek to universalize human experience as a means of producing affinity or ethical regard; rather, it constitutes an obligation to the Other despite perceived differences. In this way, while Appiah's conception of cosmopolitanism seems to echo some of the central tenets of Western liberal humanism, unlike earlier formulations of humanism which paradoxically serve to rationalize and justify the "white man's burden" of the European colonial project or contemporary formulations of liberal "color blindness," the cosmopolitan commitment to diversity, self-awareness and an openness to new ideas seems particularly anti-imperial. But the framing of global citizenship, particularly in the address of Global Citizens for Change or in the academic plan of UBC, while it imagines a global human community, paradoxically limits who can perform global citizenship.

Both global citizenship, as defined by Dower, and cosmopolitanism, as defined by Appiah, serve to identify an affiliation among human beings beyond the established categories of communal difference—family, village, religion, language group and so on—and hence each is articulated not simply as an "identity" but a way of being in the world: an ethics of action. Yet, it is in the articulation of ethical obligation to the Other that I think a seemingly subtle, but crucial, difference between the two concepts exists.

Global citizenship is defined in the UBC Okanagan academic plan (2006) as a way of understanding one's place in the world, and valuing difference. The institution describes itself as having the role of modeling civility, sustainability and responsibility, which it characterizes as the foundations of citizenship (6). Further, the university identifies the need to create programming and opportunities for research on these themes, specifically in a way that comprehensively "internationalizes" the campus and its purpose. Ironically, however, Martha Piper (2005) contends that the need for global citizenship stems from interconnections that place the nation at risk in a world system. For instance, she quotes former Canadian Prime Minister Lester Pearson, from a 1946 speech, as saying that suspicion engendered in Iran can "bedevil economic developments" in Canada. Similarly, she contends, the "war on terror" reveals the way in which Canadians are part of a world system: instability in the Middle East can threaten Canadian security and prosperity (3). Such a conception of global "interdependence," coupled with the assertions of a specifically Canadian "civility" and "responsibility," echo the paradoxical rationale for the European colonial project: control/uplift of a savage/primitive Other. In this articulation of global citizenship, the distinction—and indeed presumed moral superiority—of Canadian nationalism and citizenship is paradoxically reinforced. From such a standpoint, we must be concerned with the insecurities of others insofar as they might threaten our own (national) security, as if global relations of power have not helped to produce "our security" and "their incivility."

Anderson describes the imagined community of the nation as a horizontal comradeship that masks the vertical "differences" in experience of members of a national community, based for instance on class, gender, race, religion, language or sexual orientation. In the global frame, Mohanty notes the stark differences in experience between the one-third world and the two-thirds world: the minority of the world's population, or the one-third world that is materially privileged, and the majority two-thirds world who are marginalized, disenfranchised or lacking basic needs. Global citizenship provides the framework, or imaginary, for a horizontal comradeship; yet it nonetheless reinforces the distinction between the one-third and the two-thirds world. For Dower, the active global citizen is one who works to produce a better world; yet his examples, like the example of global citizenship as a mandate of UBC Okanagan, figure this action as requiring an Other who needs to be known, understood and ultimately uplifted or saved. As such, the ethical framework of global citizenship masks the material relationships that produce some as privileged, and hence capable of being active global citizens, and some as in need of support, care, "aid."

Such a framework for conceiving of global interrelationships and responsibility is ahistorical in that it elides the history of imperial politics that has shaped the current world system, from the transatlantic slave trade, to European exploitation of the resources and people of its colonies, to the requirements of structural adjustment that are tied to Euro-

American development "aid." Pheng Cheah argues that the promise of freedom of cosmopolitanism

> is not only inaccessible to the majority of the world's population, who inhabit the other side of the international division of labor and are unable to move to OECD countries and the top-tier global cities. It is also severely undermined by the fact that the efficacy of these new cosmopolitanisms is generated by, and structurally dependent on, the active exploitation and impoverishment of the peripheral majorities. (2006, 11)

In contrast to the UBC academic plan, and to Dower's theorization of a global ethics in which global poverty is defined as a problem to be remedied, Appiah's articulation of cosmopolitanism specifically seeks to theorize an ethics of action in the context of such structures of global inequality, as I will elaborate below.

BENEVOLENCE AS A STRUCTURE OF ATTITUDE AND REFERENCE

The primary and most visible ways in which global citizenship is articulated on the campuses of UBC all but ignore material relations of global power and presume the privileged place of UBC students and faculty to "make a difference." Global citizenship, as an action, is defined in terms of how the UBC community can "help" others around the world. For instance, on the UBC Okanagan campus, Project GROW (Ghana Rural Opportunities for Women) has been a prominent project enacting the global citizenship ethic. In 2007 students and faculty raised more than $40,000 for the nursing program project to visit two villages in northern Ghana to donate six donkeys and carts, a small herd of goats, mosquito nets for 120 women and their children, and seed money for opening bank accounts ("Project Grow" 2008). The next stage of the project plans a microfinancing system for women in two villages. In March of 2008 nursing students presented stories and photos of their humanitarian trip to Ghana as part of events commemorating International Women's Day on the university's campus.

Similarly, the "Go Global" (2008) program provides opportunities for students to study at other universities around the world, but also to volunteer with educational and community-based projects outside of Canada. Significantly, of the forty countries where students can study, 60 percent are member states of the OECD, or the richest nations of the world. In contrast, just five of the fourteen states where students can volunteer are OECD countries, with many placements in the United Kingdom and Australia, for instance, working with services for refugee, aboriginal and other marginalized communities ("Go Global"). The Web site for these programs does not utilize an overtly humanitarian rhetoric, such as that utilized in the institution's academic plan. Rather, as Talya Zemach-Bersin argues in her critique of similar programs at U.S. universities, these programs "surreptitiously reproduce the logic of colonialism" (2007, 17); the most privileged students (the programs have hefty "program fees" for participants, in addition to costs for flights, etc.) utilize the knowledge, and indeed lives, of others as objects of their own knowledge production and skills development.[3] At the University of British Columbia, the volunteer program's initial name, "YouLead," I think reflects the presumption that underlies such formulations of global citizenship; the act of being a global citizen means working to create a "better world" for others by "helping" them. Why Canadians, and specifically economically privileged Canadians, are in the position to "Go Global" or "Lead" is not interrogated.

In the late 1990s I "volunteered" in Malawi with a Canadian development agency that is now a member of Global Citizens for Change. This experience was foundational in the development of my thinking around questions of identity, nation and race, economic and cultural globalizations and postcolonialism; hence, the opportunity to live and work in Malawi has helped to shape the very analysis I am presenting in this chapter.[4] The sort of analysis that I am making here, however, is often received as simply mean-spirited; there seems little to criticize in a framework that promotes the performance of a civic duty to one's neighbor in a way that transcends the socially constructed differences of nation, race or religion which have informed so much of the violence of the past few centuries. The Golden Rule that underwrites volunteerism, and that provides the common core for the Parliament of the World's Religions' 1993 *Declaration toward a Global Ethic*, which is cited as an important framework for global citizenship by Dower (31), seems an uncontroversial "good"; the only problem, it would seem, is that it does not normally inform ethical relations.

Yet, I think global citizenship, as the ethical framework for particular kinds of action—or "helping"—serves to mask the structural violence of contemporary global relations. Appiah argues that the Golden Rule, in its variety of versions in different religions, requires not simply doing unto others as one would wish done to oneself, which is the way it is typically represented. Indeed, acting upon such a tenet, in that simple form, might lead to various forms of violence; because I would wish something done to me does not mean that someone else would as well. Appiah suggests that to fulfill this ethical tenet one must understand the reasons for one's actions towards others, and, more importantly, seek to know how those actions will be understood by those others (2006, 61–63). Here, Appiah is engaging with what it means to truly value and understand difference. The ethical obligation to others requires learning about their interests and situation; cosmopolitans endorse this way of being, he argues, but they also understand that "we can't claim the way is easy" (63).

Global citizenship is theorized by Dower and many others as a global ethics enacted primarily through a responsibility *for* the Other.

Interestingly, Dower focuses almost exclusively on British or North Atlantic examples of the global citizenship ethic, including British-based struggles for an end to nuclear arms or environmental degradation and international nongovernmental organizations based in Europe or North America. He justifies his reliance upon examples of Europeans "helping" others by arguing that the vast majority of work that seeks to alleviate global poverty, promote democracy and end conflict is based in Europe and North America. He writes: "Though the amount of activism in poorer countries is, of course, less than in rich countries—and this itself ought to be and is to some extent a matter of concern to NGOs themselves—it is important to remember that it happens" (100). Dower's lone non-OECD example in *An Introduction to Global Citizenship* of the global ethic he is theorizing is a very brief description of the Chipko movement in India, which he presents via uncited Internet sources and as if the movement was obscure. It would not take much effort for Dower to identify dozens of books and articles on the Chipko movement or to identify hundreds of prominent struggles, initiatives or local organizations throughout Latin America, Africa, Asia and the indigenous communities of Turtle Island (North America), Australia or Aotearoa/New Zealand that are working for social justice, peace and decolonization. Indeed, despite the fact that people in the Global South must devote more time and energy to survival than the majority of citizens of OECD states, its fairly safe to contend that there is more—and/or more politically challenging—activism in the Global South than in the nation-state members of the OECD. I am thinking, here, of the Narmada Bachao Andolan movement in India; the Zapatista in Chiapas, Mexico; South Africa's antiapartheid movement or more current antiprivatization and AIDS activism; the World Social Forum; or the work of the Penticton Indian Band in British Columbia to utilize the Syilx decision-making process, Enowkinwixw, to name just a few. Each of these various movements and organizations has been influential in the development of both a transnational politics of identity and solidarity but also in providing the conceptual framework for thinking beyond race and nation; the conception of subjectivity articulated through the southern African concept of *ubuntu*, the Zapatista concern with understanding the interconnections of human beings or the Narmada struggle's focus on the relationship of humans to other animals and the environment all provide alternative epistemologies to the European Enlightenment thought of Kant, Locke and Hobbes, which provides the framework for so much of global citizenship philosophy. Significantly, as well, these movements and projects have been understood in their various locales not as "development" initiatives, or practices of benevolence, but initiatives seeking economic and social justice.

The global citizenship activism directed towards the environment or against war that Dower identifies focuses primarily on eliciting structural and cultural transformation, or at least significant policy changes, in Britain and Europe. Such examples, however, contrast starkly with the examples of global citizenship action he cites that are concerned with poverty; these initiatives are specifically Other-directed and presented as a problem of ethics. Global poverty is, according to Dower, a "distant concern" for those living in Europe (137). The "evil" of poverty must be "tackled" by those in positions of privilege: "Rich people and rich countries are keen, to the extent that they are, to do something about world poverty largely because extreme poverty is an evil they feel *they ought to tackle*. It is a global problem not primarily because it affects our 'non-moral' interests but because, given our moral values, it is something that ought to be alleviated by our collective efforts" (original emphasis, p. 19). As a problem of ethics and moral responsibility and action, at the individual or governmental level, poverty is conceived of as natural or outside of history and material relations of power. To frame global poverty in such a way is to disregard both the colonial history that I would contend produces "their" poverty and "our" prosperity as well as to mask the way in which recognizing the "interrelationships" of humans on this planet is not simply an ethical tenet but a material reality: If "we" were to carefully look in our cell phones and computers, our coffee and tea cups, our pantries and our closets, or our gas tanks, we would find that "our" convenience continues to be largely dependent on "their" exploitation. Global poverty is not distant; it is a part of everyone's daily existence.[5]

The inability of Dower to recognize tactics, strategies and epistemological frameworks for fostering social change and peace outside of the North Atlantic nation-states, and the presumption that poverty is a "problem" to be alleviated by those who are "rich" because they "ought" to, is both indicative of, and can be explained by, the way in which global citizenship reflects what Edward Said calls a structure of attitude and reference, in this case, of humanitarian benevolence. Said introduced this term as a way of illuminating how imperial presumptions are embedded in and reaffirmed by English literature of the nineteenth century, such as the work of Jane Austen. He draws upon and extends Raymond Williams (1961) definition of a structure of feeling: "The social character—a valued system of behavior and attitudes—is taught, formally and informally; it is both an ideal and a mode. The 'pattern of culture' is a selection and configuration of interests and activities, and a particular valuation of them, producing a distinct organization, a 'way of life' " (47). Manipulating Said's terminology, I want to suggest that the examples of global citizenship—both practices or initiatives and overt articulations in theory, university academic plans and development agency marketing—reflect a structure of attitude and reference which, paradoxically, normalizes the economic inequality and cultural hierarchy that global citizenship purports to transcend and redress. So benevolence reflects an unselfconscious attitude that is articulated through a complex repertoire of references: us/them, capable and incapable, normal/lacking, helper/ helped, present as distinct from the past, here as distinct from there and global poverty or human-rights abuses as problems to be solved. The most prominent ethical and philosophical arguments for a global ethics, to which the notion of global citizenship seems linked, all—to a greater or lesser degree—uncritically presume a specifically Western responsibility to "help"; I use the term *help* purposefully, for this structure of attitude and reference informs this philosophy and actions done in its name, and it is quite distinct from the responsibility of "redress," "compensation" or the transformation of the material structures of colonial inequality that the anticolonial activist Frantz Fanon (1961) demanded in his argument for a (re)new(ed) humanism.

Appiah contends that a cosmopolitan response to the suffering of the Other does not begin with identifying what we can do to help, which I would suggest is the starting point for initiatives such as those at UBC, but with understanding the problem: The question we must ask, he argues, is "Why is the child dying" (2006, 168)? Hence, charitable acts like providing clean water, medication and other humanitarian aid to children who are suffering and dying from diarrhea is not necessarily an absolute "good"; it may be a means of helping but it does little to transform the situation which produces the child's suffering. He writes: "I know, gentle reader, that you will pay to send food to starving children. Will you pay to promote reform in the design and execution of the land policies that help keep their families poor" (170)? Appiah identifies a number of the policy and structural problems that produce poverty, malnutrition or create the conditions for diarrhea to be both prevalent and deadly. Most significantly, for my analysis of global citizenship, Appiah identifies the way in which poverty in many African states, for instance, has increased over the past twenty or so years because of the way in which OECD governments—often through international organizations like the International Monetary Fund, World Bank and World Trade Organization—have imposed tariffs on African exports or imposed programs of structural adjustment that have limited the provision of education or health care. He notes: "If you 'save' the children by dumping free grain into the local economy and putting the local farmers out of business—who can compete with free?—you may, indeed, be doing more harm than good" (170). By focusing on what the global citizen must do *to* or *for* the Other, rather than conceiving a global ethics in terms of understanding our relationships *with* others, the focus of this ethical obligation seems to be the symptoms of global inequality and not the causes. Why can the Ghanaian government not provide the services and structures to enable rural Ghanaians to live a happy and healthy life? What are the systems and structures that produce poverty and suffering? Why are women and children particularly vulnerable? To pose these questions, in the critical way that I do, is not to condemn development aid and presume that microloans, for instance, might not be of benefit. However, questions such as these are not contended with if we presume—and are to maintain the presumption of—our benevolence in "helping" them.

I worry, then, that while the rhetoric of global citizenship sounds similar to the terms of Appiah's cosmopolitan ethics, its practice reveals the way in which it is indebted to the rhetoric and politics of pity and benevolence as a structure of attitude and reference. Over the past decade, at least, a great number of researchers and former humanitarian and development workers have provided compelling critiques of international aid.[6] As a cultural critic, my interest is specifically with the way in which humanitarian aid discourses continue to rely upon benevolence in a way that is reminiscent of the colonial "white man's burden." During the age of European colonialism, difference (from the European) was typically described either in terms of threat and security or pity and charity. The "native" was either a savage to be tamed or eradicated or an unfortunate soul to be educated and civilized. Global citizenship has emerged, it would seem, as a counterdiscourse to contemporary narratives of global cultural conflict, articulated by Samuel P. Huntington (1997) as a "clash of civilizations" (i.e., the West vs. Islam) and enacted through the regimes of security that mark the so-called war on terror. Global citizenship is abstractly defined in terms of the ideals of diversity, multiculturalism and mutual regard; hence it appears specifically anti-imperial and as an antidote to the polarizing rhetoric of contemporary global conflict.

The identity politics of this transnational communal identity, however, masks the politics of the ethical imperative which requires those who help and those who require help: indeed, the question presumed within Western humanitarian discourse is "How can we help?" And the relationship between the West and its Others seems to begin with the aid. However, individuals are not connected to others simply through a discourse of affiliation—or an imagined global community—but through economic and political structures that allow some to have more access and opportunities than others not only to employment, fresh water or material goods but to speaking and acting. I believe that global citizenship must also acknowledge, and provide the ethical framework for dismantling, the way in which benevolence functions as the presumed social character of the North Atlantic and continues to inform the ethical philosophy of the West towards its Others. We must ask why the child is dying, but I believe we must also ask: Why is it that certain people (and I recognize my position among this group), or institutions (such as the university of which I am a part), are in the position to help or "make a difference" and how is that position related to the reasons why the child is dying? I have asserted some responses to these questions, and my ideological position and critique of neoliberalism, I hope, is clear; however, I do not presume that these are the (only) approaches or responses. I do not want to assert another solution so much as suggest a reframing of the problem. Without posing and responding honestly to these questions, I believe, we continue to reproduce the familiar narrative of benevolence in which our privilege, and the social conditions of that privilege, remain invisible and continue to be reinforced.

REFLECTIONS ON THE PEDAGOGY OF UNSETTLING COSMOPOLITANISM

I close, then, with some reflections on my teaching of postcolonial studies in undergraduate classrooms at UBC Okanagan. I mean these reflections to perform a wry civility; while the pedagogical practice of unsettling I describe in this final section seeks to trouble the presumptions of global citizenship I have sought to deconstruct/decolonize, it nonetheless seeks to open spaces for an alternative cosmopolitanism. These reflections situate the global citizen as a one-third world subject; this is not to presume, as I think Dower and others do, that only a privileged few can undertake the responsibility of global citizenship, but that people are situated differently within the global social and, so, those privileged within this global order must perform a cosmopolitan ethic differently than those who are less privileged, or marginalized within it. I want to define global citizenship as a process of unlearning the structures of attitude and reference of benevolence which informs humanitarian discourses of aid, philanthropy or help.

The main classroom example I want to reflect upon regards responses to Ward Churchill's essay "I Am Indigenist: Notes on the Ideology of the Fourth World," in which, among other arguments, he outlines a case for the redistribution of land and population in the western U.S. to create a geographically significant "Buffalo Commons" or homeland for indigenous people. Specifically, he contends that 35 percent of the U.S. land mass is unceded indigenous territory, and that the federal and state governments hold in trust approximately 45 percent of the nation's land mass, meaning, in effect, that a territory the size of that unceded could be designated as indigenous territory. Citing research on land use and the agricultural economy, he argues that most of the counties of the Plains region (North and South Dakota, Nebraska, Kansas, Oklahoma, etc.) are fiscally insolvent and that the federal government must subsidize in perpetuity the services and industry of these counties to serve a relatively small nonindigenous population in a geographically enormous area: "Put bluntly, the pretense of bringing Euroamerican 'civilization' to the Plains represents nothing more than a massive economic burden on the rest of the United States" (2003: 289). Churchill proposes multilateral negotiations between the U.S. and a variety of indigenous nations, including the Crow, Cheyenne, Comanche and Kiowa, to exchange lands for the creation of a sovereign indigenous territory stretching from the Canadian to the Mexican borders, and constituting fully one-third of the current continental U.S. When I have had nonindigenous students read this essay, it is this argument that sparks consternation, if not outrage. Surely, Churchill must be joking. How can he argue for the appropriation of the land of these people? He is simply asserting an indigenous colonialism, no?

The first time I used this essay I hadn't intended for this particular argument to be the focus, and, to be honest, was not prepared for the frustration and resistance of students who were otherwise very eager to explore theories and examples of struggles for decolonization and social justice. After letting the students vent, we began to work through the argument and identify their various concerns. Churchill was making the case that since the land is not being effectively or efficiently used by the people on it, that they abdicated their right to it and others should be able to take it. He was contending that because there were few people, their interests might be sacrificed. He was arguing for the mass dislocation of people. He was describing the peoples of a large and diverse region in simplistic and homogenizing terms. He was arguing that a significant area of land should be given up, or given back, by the dominant American culture. Ultimately, we came to the troubling realization that while students had expressed anger towards Churchill's seemingly colonial ideology, we, as nonindigenous people living in unceded Syilx territory in the Canadian province of British Columbia, are the beneficiaries of a nearly identical process of colonial expropriation and dislocation to that proposed by Churchill and that the students had found so objectionable. Of course, an important distinction between Churchill's proposal and our experience as beneficiaries of a historical process is that Churchill's proposal in part seeks redress for colonial violence, a colonial violence constituted by our naturalization as citizens of Canada. The settler narratives of the history of the Okanagan region contend that white settlement brought civilization to an area that had previously been "underutilized" or used "inefficiently" by a primitive indigenous population, or, indeed, was an unpeopled wasteland made bountiful through European ingenuity. Of course, the history of settlement/conquest in Canada's west was— and continues to be—much more violent than the multilateral negotiated settlement Churchill suggests.

The sense of unsettlement that these nonindigenous students, and myself, experienced was, I think, very productive for making visible the structures of attitude and reference of benevolence that underwrite our understanding of global social justice. The curriculum became an encounter rather than a thing (a text to be understood), and the way we were implicated with the structures of power the reading identified became acutely visible (see den Heyer 2009). Working through our anxiety about Churchill's proposal reveals the inadequacy of the presumption of the need to "help" which presupposes much discussion of social justice in the one-third world. It reveals the way in which the alleviation of inequality and the redress of historical and present injustice require both a structural and relational analysis and require not a gift from those who are "fortunate" to those who are "less fortunate" but a transformation of relationships which require changes in material and conceptual positioning; in other words, a sacrificing of social and material privilege, as well as ideals that are established and comforting (cultural superiority, white supremacy, etc.). Further, I would suggest, such a sacrifice needs to be understood not as loss. It also reflects the ways in which the local *is* the historical (history is not in the past) and the elsewhere; to imagine the local as present and distinct, as I think we tend to do, sanctions the ignorance that allows injustice to persist. A key gap in theories of global citizenship is the way the local of the privileged, or the global citizen, is for the most part unmarked. Here, then, my analysis is indebted to critical analyses of white or male privilege wherein the self is dependent upon, at the same time that it is invisible against, the Other.

This pedagogy of cosmopolitan unsettling, as I conceive of it at this moment, is linked specifically to Paul Gilroy's musings on cultural estrangement and Shari Stone-Mediatore's postcolonial standpoint theory. Gilroy, describing an alternative "demotic" cosmopolitanism, contends that while the opportunity for self-knowledge is "worthwhile," "it must take second place behind the principled and methodical cultivation of a degree of estrangement from one's own culture and history" (2005, 67). He recognizes that often the opportunities for such estrangement are confined to members of an elite group, such as myself, as reflected in my own experience as a development "volunteer," or those UBC Okanagan students who are afforded the opportunity to "experience" rural Ghana. "Encounters with difference," however, are not necessarily experienced as "becoming estranged from the cultural habits one is born to" (70). Often the intercultural encounter, particularly within the framework of international development, reaffirms one's own cultural identity rather than unsettles it.[7] Yet, such moments—often linked with one entering into the community and culture of an Other—can provide an unsettling of one's experience as normative, revealing the way in which one's identity reflects a social positioning with a particular history.

Shari Stone-Mediatore describes this experience of coming to understand the self differently through engagement with the experience of others, "enlarged thought." Focusing upon a postcolonial reading practice, she defines enlarged thought as the "extent to which a narrative helps readers to test and revise their community's taken-for-granted narrative paradigms and to anticipate communication with differently situated others" (2003, 185). The key to this theory of unsettling, however, is not just that the reader becomes discomforted but that this unsettlement can be translated into new knowledge and attitudes, with the expectation that this will foster an ideological and material transformation. In the post-colonial literature and culture classroom, this involves critically reading texts like Erna Brodber's *Myal* (1988) not as "magic realism"—in a way that reaffirms the "real" of Western constructions of the rational and the autonomy of the material subject—but in a way that seeks to contend with the narrative as reflecting an alternate way of knowing to that of the dominant culture in Canada; in other words, by reading it as reflecting knowledge rather than "culture" or tradition, a standpoint approach to *Myal* brings into relief that the standard reading practice of the literature classroom is constituted by a particular, and historically situated epistemology itself. Again, an Other (of culture, place, etc.) is required for the readers' enlightenment to their own identity and privileged social positioning. To be a productive pedagogical tool of global citizenship education (in Canada), and one that gets past the question "How can we help?" to the questions I pose, must there not be ways to foster this unsettling that do not require an Other (always in ways, I recognize, where the consequences of this unsettling cannot be planned and may very well reinforce the benevolent cosmopolitanism I have critiqued as much as provide an alternative to it)? Stone-Mediatore's analysis of Howard Zinn's *A People's History of the United States* (2005) may provide such an example. She contends that Zinn's text uses "experience to challenge and transform the discourses of experience and writing that have organized experience" and that the potentially disruptive discursive practice of his work "include[s] unofficial, uncodified reactions to ruling discourses and thus belie[s] the violent effects of those discourses on our daily lives" (2003, 120).

I close with the discomfort I feel reading Slavoj Žižek's contention—in response to the argument that critical analyses such as his (and mine) provide "no 'practical' advice on what to do" (2008, 7)—that the only "practical" response to what he calls the "fake urgency" of humanitarian discourse is to do nothing. Rather than act hastily, for the sake of acting, and to fulfill our identities as benevolent helpers, Žižek contends that "we need to 'learn, learn, and learn' what causes this violence" (8). What makes this argument so unsettling? It's not that Žižek contends that people in the one-third world, or global citizens, must stop presuming they have the solutions for others' poverty and must stop "helping." Rather, I think it is the idea of sitting and reading and thinking as a response to global violence and inequality that I find unsatisfactory (largely, I suspect, because this is, for the most part, my response). While I agree with his critique of the false urgency of humanitarian rhetoric, people are suffering, now, and people are benefiting from that suffering now (Jefferess 2002). The pedagogy of unsettling I put forth here seeks to emphasize the need to alter our material and conceptual positions with regard to others rather than come to "know" them or acknowledge their humanity, in some abstract sense. This unsettling is pretentious, in that it reaffirms the need of the one-third world subject to act, to do, in the interest of all; it reflects, I fear, a structure of attitude and reference of benevolence, but I hope it aspires to a new, wry cosmopolitanism.

NOTES

1. Portions of the research for this chapter have been supported through a research grant from the Social Sciences and Humanities Research Council of Canada
2. See, for instance, Fanon (1961), Gilroy (2005), Spivak (2003).
3. For instance, the "Go Global" volunteer program assures participants that they will gain practical knowledge of cultural diversity, experience for a competitive job market, independence and maturity, as well as a sense of their capacity as individuals to effect change. See: http://www.students.ubc.ca/global/volunteer/.
4. For a more developed self-reflection on my experience "volunteering" in Malawi, see Jefferess (2001).
5. While I would hope that these oblique references to coffee, chocolate, sweatshop labor and oil provide fairly obvious examples of the way in which the conveniences and pleasures of OECD culture depend upon exploitative labor practices in the Global South, readers may be less aware of the way in which the demand for tantalum, or refined coltan, which powers cell phones and computers, helped to fuel the civil war in Congo.
6. See, for instance, Moyo (2009), Bond (2006), Anderson (1999).
7. The blog entries for participants from the UBC Okanagan nursing project in rural Ghana, for instance, are notably unselfconscious of the participants' social positioning in any political or historical way and often utilize language and structures of narration common to colonial representations of the exotic, primitive Other. The brief practicum in Ghana is described by many participants as an "adventure" into, paradoxically, a beautiful, welcoming place and a strange, "chaotic," "insane" "hell." Power outages are described as a natural fact of life for Ghanaians, and so unrelated to histories and structures of political economy. My purpose here is not to criticize these descriptions so much as identify the way in which they reflect the particular structure of attitude and reference of global citizenship I have outlined (http://weblogs.elearning.ubc.ca/nursing_in_ghana/—see also Heron 2007 and Cook in this volume).

REFERENCES

Anderson, B. (1991) *Imagined Communities: Reflections on the Origin and Spread of Nationalism,* revised edition, London: Verso.

"An End to Poverty" (2007) Global Citizens for Change. Retrieved April 16, 2008, from http://www.cciorg.ca/images/CCI_en2.pdf.

Anderson, M. (1999) *Do No Harm: How Aid Can Support Peace—Or War,* Boulder, CO: Lynne Rienner.

Appiah, K. (2005) *The Ethics of Identity,* Princeton, NJ: Princeton University Press.

———. (2006) *Cosmopolitanism: Ethics in a World of Strangers,* New York: W.W. Norton.

Bond, P. (2006) *Looting Africa: The Economics of Exploitation*, London: Zed.
Boothroyd, P. (2005, March 10) 'Global Citizenship and UBC' Lecture. Retrieved April 16, 2008, from http://www.trek2000.ubc.ca/Peter%20Boothroyd%20%20%20 Global%20Citizenship%20.pdf.
Brodber, E. (1988) *Myal*, London: New Beacon.
Cheah, P. (2006) *Inhuman Conditions: On Cosmopolitanism and Human Rights*, Cambridge, MA: Harvard University Press.
Churchill, W. (2003). 'I am Indigenist: Notes on the Ideology of the Fourth World.' In *Acts of Rebellion: The Ward Churchill Reader*. London: Routledge.
Coleman, D.(2006) *White Civility: The Literary Project of English Canada*, Toronto: University of Toronto Press.
den Heyer, K. (2009) 'Implicated and Called Upon: Challenging an Educated Position of Self, Others, Knowledge and Knowing as Things to Acquire', *Critical Literacy: Theories and Practices*, 3(1): 26–35.
Dower, N. (2003) *An Introduction to Global Citizenship*, Edinburgh: Edinburgh University Press.
Fanon, F. (1961) *The Wretched of the Earth*, trans. Constance Farrington, New York: Grove.
Gilroy, P. (2005) *Postcolonial Melancholia*, New York: Columbia University Press.
"Go Global." (2008) University of British Columbia, http://www.students.ubc.ca/global/.
Heron, B. (2007) *Desire for Development: Whiteness, Gender, and the Helping Imperative*, Waterloo, Canada: Wilfrid Laurier University Press.
Huntington, S. (1997) *Clash of Civilizations and the Remaking of World Order*, New York: Touchstone.
Jefferess, D. (2001) 'What's My Name? Or, Developing in Linga', *Jouvert: A Journal of Postcolonial Studies*, 6(1–2), http://social.chass.ncsu.edu/jouvert/v6i1-2/davidj.htm.
———. (2002) 'For Sale—Peace of Mind: (Neo)Colonial Discourse and the Commodification of Third World Poverty in World Vision's "Telethons." ', *Critical Arts: A Journal of South-North Cultural and Media Studies*, 16(1): 1–21.
Mohanty, C. (2003) *Feminism without Borders: Decolonizing Theory, Practicing Solidarity*, Durham, NC: Duke University Press.
Moyo, D. (2009) *Dead Aid: Why Aid Is Not Working and How There Is a Better Way for Africa*, New York: Farrar, Straus, and Giroux.
Piper, M. (2005, September 18) 'Internalizing Internationalism: Creating a University Global Culture'. An address to the Chancellor's Fall Conference, University of California Davis, retrieved April 16, 2008, from chancellor.ucdavis.edu/events/FallConf/2005/Martha%20Piper%20speech%202005%20Fall%20Conference.doc.
'Project Grow Valentine's Day Cards to Fund Mosquito Nets for African Villages' (2008, February 1) Media Release. Retrieved April 16, 2008, from http://web.ubc.ca/okanagan/publicaffairs/mediareleases/2008/mr-08-008.html.
Rawls, J. (1999) *The Laws of Peoples*, Cambridge, MA: Harvard University Press.
Said, E. (1993) *Culture and Imperialism*, New York: Vintage.
Spivak, G. (1994) 'Bonding in Difference', in A. Arteaga (ed.), *An Other Tongue: Nation and Ethnicity in the Linguistic Borderlands*, Durham, NC: Duke University Press, 273–285.
———. (2003) *Death of a Discipline*, Cambridge: Cambridge University Press.
Stone-Mediatore, S. (2003) *Reading across Borders: Storytelling and Knowledges of Resistance*, New York: Palgrave Macmillan.

46 *David Jefferess*

UBC Okanagan (2006) A community of excellence: at all times and in all things. Retrieved, April 16, 2008, from http://www.ubc.ca/okanagan/dvc/__shared/assets/academic-plan956.pdf.

Williams, R. (1961) *The Long Revolution*, London: Chatto and Windus.

Zemach-Bersin, T. (2007) 'Global Citizenship & Study Abroad: It's All about U.S.' *Critical Literacy: Theories and Practices*, 1(2): 16–28.

Zinn, H. (2005). *A People's History of the United States*. Harper Perennial.

Žižek, S. (2008) *Violence*, New York: Picador.

3 Postcolonial Cosmopolitanisms
Towards a Global Citizenship Education Based on 'Divisive Universalism'

Colin Wright

This chapter explores the contributions postcolonial theory can make to mainstream global citizenship education. It does so by interrogating the forms of universalism implicit in the turn to a new cosmopolitanism behind many contemporary conceptualizations of global citizenship. It is argued that postcolonial theory has been invaluable in identifying the violence of Eurocentric forms of universalism and in challenging the narrative of a single Western modernity. However, it is also argued that, in its emphasis on the ethical importance of difference, postcolonial theory has largely failed to tap the emancipatory potential of universalism. An alternative approach to global citizenship education based upon a notion of 'divisive universalism' and the generic cosmopolitanism it implies is then elaborated with reference to critical pedagogy.

GLOBAL CITIZENSHIP: THE EMPIRE'S NEW CLOTHES?

The notion of 'global citizenship' is fiercely contested. At the level of its rhetoric, however, its core principles seem uncontroversial. Among these are:

- an ethical emphasis on the responsibility stemming from our increasingly interconnected lives;
- an ideal of active, informed participation in an emerging global public sphere;
- an assertion of the need for a transnational system of individual and human rights;
- often a call for structures of world governance robust enough to enable a form of democracy exceeding the boundaries of the nation-state.

Implicit in all of these is an appeal to a community of co-constitutive belonging that transcends the local. As such, global citizenship draws much of its inspiration from the ancient Stoic ideal of cosmopolitanism. Ever since Diogenes replied to the particularizing question 'Where are you from?' with the universalizing declaration 'I am a citizen of the world,' the idea of a universal (*cosmos*) moral community (*polis*) has attracted those dissatisfied with the injustices of national, religious, racial, gender and class divisions. Kant reformulated this cosmopolitan ideal for the era of the Enlightenment by including all human beings in a potentially peaceful, law-bound community by dint of their shared rationality (Kant 1991). Indeed, it was this broadly Kantian vision of cosmopolitanism that underscored the push for a truly international human-rights law in the wake of the horrors of Auschwitz. Hannah Arendt, reflecting on the nation-state's capacity for totalitarianism, famously crystallized the cosmopolitan ideal when she invoked a fundamental 'right to have rights' (Arendt 1973). Today we see ambitious proposals for a cosmopolitan world democracy supported by a commonwealth of citizens emerging from the ever-dampening networks of globalization (Archibugi 2008).

In true Enlightenment style, a key institution in cultivating global citizens is education: It is in the classroom that values of tolerance and compassion as well as techniques of debate and participation initiate members into the projected world polity. For example, in its implementation of the Millennium Development Goals agreed at the UN Summit of 2000, the UK's Department for Education and Skills (DfES) published a document for educators entitled *Developing a Global Dimension in the School Curriculum* (DfES 2000). Eight key concepts of the 'global dimension' are identified. The first and most important is global citizenship, which is defined as: "Gaining the knowledge, skills and understanding of concepts and institutions necessary to become informed, active, responsible citizens" (DfID 2000, 8). Another key concept of the global dimension is diversity, focusing on "[u]nderstanding and respecting differences and relating these to our common humanity" (ibid.). In the explicit aim of inculcating a positive valuation of diversity, global citizenship education in fact takes its place in a long line of policy attempts to deal with the key issue of *difference*, the exponential significance of which over the last half-century is due to the patterns of economic migration intensified by globalization itself.

In the UK context, then, the policy response to the 'Windrush Generation' of Afro-Caribbean and other immigrants to Britain was initially an ideal of 'assimilation' which today smacks of out-and-out epistemic violence. Subsequent, more politically correct appeals to 'integration,' 'multiculturalism,' 'cultural diversity' and most recently 'community cohesion' have all been explicit reactions to the social and racial stratifications observable in postwar British society (Chen and Belgeonne 2008). The newest category of *global* citizenship, however, separates itself from such narrowly national concerns: It now enjoins schools, colleges and universities with the difficult task of preparing young people for the cultural diversity they will encounter abroad as well as at home. It is not simply that global citizenship education must confront the issue of cultural diversity, then (this is nothing particularly new), but that the parameters of citizenship itself are expanding beyond those of the nation-state. Global citizenship education thus responds to both local notions of *social* mobility and to the 'global' mobility of capital itself (scare quotes because, in truth, its mobility is restricted to the Northern Hemisphere). Specifically, global citizenship education responds to the convergence of both social and global mobility in producing highly educated people invested with actual, symbolic and cultural capital (see Bourdieu 1996). This begins to resemble the colloquial meaning of 'cosmopolitan' as a level of cultural refinement and 'worldliness' operating as a form of class 'distinction' in Pierre Bourdieu's sense (Bourdieu 1984).

Examined more closely, then, the benevolent rhetoric of global citizenship disguises a number of potential problems. Firstly, despite the generic placelessness of the original Stoic sentiment, the dominant version of cosmopolitanism today remains trapped within the model of a bounded nation-state that most commentators agree is being fundamentally reconfigured: The move from 'methodological nationalism' to 'methodological cosmopolitanism' advocated by Ulrich Beck for the social sciences has not yet been fully implemented in political or legal institutions (Beck 2000). The image of a planetary parliament seems embedded especially in cosmopolitan ideals of international relations, human-rights law and democratic governance.[1] The persistence of this image can lead to the addition of the word *global* to citizenship becoming an empty gesture, merely transposing the old national model to the supranational level as if such a global democratic government actually existed (whereas in their different ways, both the partisan strength of the IMF and the multilateral weakness of the UN demonstrate that it does not). Secondly, the combination of the appeal to both an ethical universality and a need for institutional structures to enforce it is all too easily appropriated by a *Pax Americana* that justifies military interventionism precisely through the declared superiority of Western humanitarianism and liberal democracy. It is a problematically small step from 'global citizen' to 'world police.' Thirdly and relatedly, even when presented as hand-wringing concern at global social injustice, many of the representations of the favellas and famines of the global South within education and wider media discourse are marked by a mixture of compassion and condescension that ultimately shores up an image of the 'victims' of globalization. This image can then validate the very discourse of development that is, arguably, victimizing those upon whom such representations are imposed. Fourthly, then, the category of 'global citizen' appears dangerously intertwined with neoliberalism, and perhaps even neoconservatism: the former, because a schooling in difference can serve as preparation for the demonstrably color-coded international division of labor, the latter, because if 'failed' or 'rogue' states are defined by anything, it is their inability to avail their citizens of the *human right* to participate in the free-market global village. Rights have always been entangled in the liberal tradition with property rights, from Hobbes to Lock, but something like a complete inversion takes place when Arendt's dictum becomes the 'right to have property rights.' Being extremely polemical, then, one could argue that global citizenship education is the smiling face of human capital theory.

WHOSE UNIVERSAL?

The crux of this debate about contemporary cosmopolitanisms surely revolves around the thorny question of *universality*. For without a commitment to some notion of a moral commonality beneath all of the borders and barriers that carve up the human experience, cosmopolitanism simply cannot get underway. Whether this rests on an a priori obligation to act on the international stage in conformity with a rational Idea of perpetual peace, as in Kant, or on an emergent 'risk society' whose threats (ecological, terrorist) dwarf what nation-states alone can respond to, as in Ulrich Beck, or on the communicative rationality embedded in the very structure of language, as in Habermas and Benhabib, every cosmopolitanism necessarily asserts a bond linking all human beings that may therefore be termed 'universal.' As the globalized world gets experientially smaller, and as its 'complex connectivity' (Tomlinson 2000) intensifies the relational nature of our existence, a *cosmos* of universal co-belonging does indeed start to become an imaginative and perhaps even practical possibility.

Far from answering the question 'what kind of universal?' however, globalization only poses it more acutely. After all, on the theoretical level, the 'linguistic turn' has led to postmodern, deconstructive and—as we shall explore in a moment—postcolonial critiques of the Eurocentric origins and effects of the concept of the universal. All of these in one way or another lay bare its violent side. Claims of privileged access to transcendent Truths—be they religious, scientific, economic or political—have legitimated all imperial projects, from ancient Rome to the British Empire and beyond. The instrumental rationality of Western modernity has specialized in steamrollering indigenous knowledges and cosmologies under the banner of a fundamentally Euro-American 'universality.' Suspicion of the universal goes back much further than the so-called 'linguistic turn,' however: Critiques have been mounted across the humanities and social sciences ever since Marx effectively cautioned us to ask, always, *whose* universal, and what interests does it conceal. It would be easy to forget this lesson when the universality being claimed is the warm and fuzzy one of moral commonality, except that we have the lesson of the deadly nexus between the worst excesses of colonial oppression on the one hand and the pious moralizing of the 'civilizing mission,' reliant upon Christian universalism, on the other.

Despite this suspicion regarding claims of universality however, it remains valid and even essential to point out their progressive, emancipatory power too. The generic ontological substrate of human existence the universal assertion reveals—or posits—can challenge the stratifying, *divide et impera* tactics of oppressive power by means of which hierarchies of race, class, gender and sexuality enforce and reproduce an iniquitous status quo. Every significant revolution has carried within it its own axiom of universality, whether that be the rights of man (Thomas Payne), of woman (Mary Wollstonecraft), of slaves (Toussaint L'Ouverture), of workers (Marx, Lenin) or of peasants (Mao). The universal can counter rather than consolidate poisonous patriotisms and negative nationalisms. It can create a 'space of appearance' in Hannah Arendt's phrase, institutional but also phenomenological, in which ethical reciprocity can be both instituted and felt.

In fact, the turn to a new cosmopolitanism, of which I am arguing global citizenship education is symptomatic, is predicated on the *articulation* of particular and universal, local and global. Kwame Anthony Appiah (2007) calls for a 'cosmopolitan patriotism' that will paradoxically protect national minorities, while Beck's similar call for 'cosmopolitan nationalism'—also attempts to integrate the building blocks of national identity into a transnational *sensus communis*. Even Hardt and Negri's analysis of the new empire runs counter to its broadly Marxist critique of bourgeois universalism insofar as their Deleuzian vision of an emergent 'multitude' is characterized by a plurality that no national elite could particularize and control, a sort of 'swarm universality' (Hardt and Negri 2000).

In the mainstream discourse of global citizenship education, it is also clear that the appeal of the cosmopolitan vision today lies not in a 'clean,' abstract philosophical universalism that transcends the local, but rather in one that confronts the multiplicity of 'structures of feeling' of belonging arising from heterogeneous interactions between local and global. For example, DfID advise teachers that students at Key Stage 1 should, through the citizenship strand of the curriculum, "develop an understanding of the universality of human rights, and begin to appreciate that they belong to a wider community" (DfID 2000, 5). By Key Stage 2, however, progress in this citizenship strand is measured by a student's capacity to think universality *with* particularity: They should "develop a sense of themselves as members of a world-wide community in which there exists *a wide range of cultures and identities but a common humanity*" (ibid., 7, my emphasis). Precisely because of this cosmopolitan appeal to a new universality that cleaves together sameness and difference, unity and plurality, the necessity of rigorously distinguishing between progressive and reactionary forms of universalism becomes an urgent theoretical but also political task.

To sketch a conceptual framework for doing so, I will now focus on a set of debates in which the issue of the universal is explored in all its ambivalence, namely, postcolonial theory and its related dalliance with the cosmopolitan ideal.

POSTCOLONIAL COSMOPOLITANISMS: EXPOSING THE EMPIRE

Of all the critical theories of the last half-century, it has arguably been post-colonial theory that has situated an engaged politics of difference within the political economy of emerging global power structures. Deriving its theories of difference not, or not only, from the play of literary or philosophical signifiers in predominantly Western texts, but rather from the felt (and fought) cultural dislocations of colonial oppression and postcolonial marginalization, it has 'written back' to the empire. In so doing, it has shaken the very foundations of many of its academic disciplines by exposing their complicity in what Foucault called the 'knowledge-power nexus.' Its early home in departments of English and comparative literature must be seen against the backdrop of, firstly, a critique of the canonized cultural superiority nourished by nineteenth-century novels, poems and travel writing and so on, and secondly, a commitment to a radical pedagogy making room for other(ed) voices offering other(ed) perspectives. It strikes me that postcolonial theory is now ideally suited for providing an alternative account of the version of globalization driving global citizenship education, precisely through its engagement with the question of the universal and the related ideal of cosmopolitanism. And because of its investment in radical pedagogy, it offers many lessons in how better to teach such a thing.

Although there is great disagreement about the meaning of the term *postcolonial*, some relation to colonialism is obviously intrinsic. Focusing on the meaning of the prefix, I would suggest three main ways of conceptualizing this relation distinguished by their respective temporal orientations. Firstly, taking it literally, the term *postcolonial* can refer to the complex historical, cultural and psychological *legacy* of an extended period under colonial rule. Such work is fundamentally oriented to the past, much of it focusing on the mode of political but also cultural decolonization. The implicit assumption here is that colonialism itself is over, but we continue to live with its residual effects. Secondly, however, and I think more often, the term *postcolonial* actually asserts a central *continuity* running from this colonial past and extending into the heart of a present described as neocolonial. Far from being ahistorical, work under this heading often utilizes historical methods in order to carve out alternate, politically motivated genealogies of the injustices of the present. This can range from demonstrating the indispensable role of the superexploitation of slavery in the earliest phases of European capitalist accumulation (Williams 1994) and its 'underdeveloping' impact on the African continent (Rodney 1974), to laying bare the hypocrisy of the conditions attached to IMF loans given in the name of development today (see Manley 1983 for the cautionary tale of Jamaica). Thus, the relation to colonialism in this second use of the term is emphatically not analogical, as if economic forms of hegemonic control are merely *like* the direct forms of governmental administrative control of the colonial era. Rather, the claim is that there has been a historical evolution of the former out of the latter. Indeed, in the form of dependency theory (Amin 1998) and world systems theory (Wallerstein 2004), the neocolonial description of the current global conjuncture is given an economic basis. In its fundamentally descriptive mode of analysis, this second sense of 'postcolonial' remains oriented to the present. The third definition of the 'post' in 'postcolonialism,' however, unites the temporal orientations of the previous two with a utopian vision of the future:

> [T]he prefix in postcoloniality is not meant to signal the end of the previous period but to stand for the sign of an emancipatory project, that is, it announces a goal yet to be realized: that of dismantling the economic, political and social structures and values, the attitudes and ideas that appeared with European colonialism. (Venn 2006, 4)

It is this emancipatory commitment that founds the kind of democratic imaginary needed to insist, as the World Social Forum movement does, that 'another world is possible.' I would suggest that there are three main areas of debate within postcolonial theory that, if taken on in some form in global citizenship education, might go some way towards such an imaginative reworking:

1. The critique of Western modernity and the Cartesian subject;
2. The critique of Eurocentric notions of universality and culture;
3. The positive exploration of postcolonial cosmopolitanisms.

Firstly, then, postcolonial theory has long contested the teleological narrative of Western modernity with its contemporary avatar in development discourse. The conceptual schema here involves a Darwinian line of ascent, with Europe at the highest evolutionary stage, and so-called developing nations occupying lower rungs of the ladder of progress. This image has done tremendous legitimizing work for European colonialism and now U.S.-led imperialism. Like all good ideologies, it has one foot in reality: By acknowledging the gap between rich and poor, developed and less so, it has empirical purchase, and by indulging a discourse of humanity and compassion, it raises hopes and salves consciences; but by ultimately administering more-better-faster modernity as the supposed cure for global inequalities, it effectively treats the disease through the intensification of its causes. Educators need to explore alternative etiologies of the maladies of the present.

Western modernity also presupposes, and *im*poses, a particular kind of subjectivity: rational, autonomous, self-identical, essentially Cartesian (the birth of philosophical modernity is of course enmeshed with that of its political side). It is this Cartesian subject that becomes the subject of *private* property with the emergence of mercantilism and then primitive capitalism, as well as providing the foundation for the alienated subject of the wage contract that props up the former to the extent that the industrial worker is separated from communal forms of labor and sociality. Furthermore, in a chilling recolonization of the ground won by the labor movement in turning class antagonism into a battle of rights rather than might, this atomized, rational, informed and jurisprudential subject of Western modernity has mutated into the subject of *individual* human rights. Mainstream metropolitan education threatens to interpolate such egocentric subjects who view themselves as somehow deserving the world and as 'knowing their rights' when the whole world is not surrendered.

Postcolonial theory has two interlocking ways of undermining this teleology of Western modernity and its mode of subjectivity. Firstly, it fractures and pluralizes the narrative of modernity itself. It shows that modernity has been differentially and unevenly implemented from Latin America to Africa, from the Indian subcontinent to East Asia. Just as globalization is always really globalization, so the yawning chasm that separates the processes of modernization in, say, Japan as opposed to India, caution us against any monolithic notion of modernity. Immediately, however, the implication of modern*ities*, plural, challenges the monopoly that Europe insists upon, as well as the linear temporality which is the form of this insistence. Such a challenge has been mounted by postcolonial categories like 'transmodernity' (Venn 2006), 'multiple modernities' (Bhambra 2007), 'alternative modernities' (Gilroy 1993), 'co-eval modernities' (Harootunian 2000) and 'vernacular modernity,' as well as Walter Mignolo's notion of 'global coloniality' as a polemical redescription of (post)modernity (Mignolo 2000). It is vital that modernity is pluralized in this way if the Western model of development is to be disentangled from neoliberal assumptions about the efficacy of currency devaluation, privatization of public services and dissolution of 'protectionist' trade barriers. This also allows one to question the related notion of a unified 'globalization' all too often assumed in discussions of global citizenship. There are economic, political, cultural and technological levels of globalization, and scrutiny of any one of these will quickly reveal a far from even playing field. If we *do not* actually live in a homogenously globalized world, all the more reason to examine the locations and motivations of the production of the discourse of global citizenship (Hutchings 2005).

Secondly, to the self-identical Cartesian subject of Western modernity corresponding to this vision of global citizenship, postcolonial theory opposes a hybrid, subalternized, diasporic, creolized subject. By drawing on the decentering effects of psychoanalysis and poststructuralism, but situating these effects in the co-constitutive play of (dis)identifying gazes between colonizer and colonized, and by linking these to collective forms of anticolonial resistance, the postcolonial theory of Homi Bhabha (to give only the most obvious example of this approach) manages to displace the cogito without ever giving up on agency (Bhabha 2003). Putting the philosophical core of Western individualism under erasure in this way also allows postcolonial theory to open a conceptual space for considering the different kinds of subjectivity—collective, spiritual, cosmologically integrated with the natural world—which the Enlightenment paradigm simply eliminates as premodern dogma. As M. Jacquie Alexander has argued (Alexander 2005), the category of the sacred represents a potentially rich resource in the ongoing project of decolonization precisely because it is unthinkable within the modernist reification of rationality. Related to this, protection of indigenous knowledges is one of the key terrains in the battle against the new 'tragedy of the commons' whereby the natural world, right down to its genetic encoding, is rapidly being transformed into corporate assets. Holistic, animist, vitalist cosmologies and the collective subjectivities they sustain also support notions of communal and even ecological wealth irreducible to monetary riches. While one must be very suspicious of the commodification of such alternative epistemologies in the repugnant form of 'new age' mysticisms and so on, the looming environmental crisis brought about by consumer individualism and the putative right to overconsumption demands that we try to take indigenous subjectivities seriously.

The second area of critical debate in postcolonial theory relevant to this discussion is the critique of Eurocentric universalism. Edward Said's famous analysis of 'orientalism' as the discursive construction of a knowable, and consequently a governable, object by Western forms of knowledge is seminal here (Said 2003). Said shows that behind the assumptions of dispassionate rationality and apolitical scholarship in disciplines as diverse as anthropology, geography and comparative philology, and behind also the aesthetic and experiential 'truths' in cultural forms of knowing such as travel writing, novels and landscape painting, lies the systematic eroticization of an Other against which the Occident can define itself. Here, the assumed universality of the rational pursuit of knowledge is placed in its proper European political and cultural economy. The key point about Said's (contested) use of Foucault in *Orientalism* is that despite being a discursive construct, the figure of the oriental had—and has—a very real material impact on the world: it informs policy and thus the technologies of control, administration and bureaucracy that shape and police 'oriental' societies, and individuate specific 'orientals' in constrained ways. Arguably, the contemporary cinematic but also journalistic stereotyping of young Arab men, particularly Muslims, as terrorists suggests that the trope of the passionate and uncontrollable oriental continues to circulate in the West, shaping the tortured geopolitics of the Middle East as well as the politics of security at 'home.'

A further, often underemphasized dimension of Said's critique is its attack on a Eurocentric notion of culture itself. He shows that the projection of an exotic orient relies on a conceptualization of culture as static, distinct and fully knowable—an attitude constitutive of the disciplines of colonial anthropology and ethnography. It is the idea that cultures can be pinned, like butterflies, into taxonomies open to the colonizer's gaze that enables orientalism to present a benevolent face. What might be called the 'museumization' of another's culture is an act of reductionism that can nonetheless be phrased in terms of 'preservation,' 'protection' and 'heritage.' This rhetoric is persuasive precisely when such cultures are threatened by the very hegemonic forces reducing them to objects of knowledge. Yet in being pinned down, butterflies die: The shimmering beauty of their erratic flight (culture in all its ephemeral complexity) is beyond such a necrophiliac epistemology. Part of the material impact of this culturalist discourse today is the double bind inherent in the struggle for cultural recognition in a globalized world dominated by the North. Consider the Native American forced to sell a bastardized 'dream-catcher' version of her culture, or the way in which Aboriginal claims to 'land rights' in Australia destroy, through the very terms in which they must be phrased, that intimate communion with the landscape at the core of Aboriginal culture. This is another crucial area in which postcolonial theory can supplement the more problematic aspects of global citizenship education: Cultural studies inspired by postcolonial theory have taken Said's lead in exploring the sites and conditions of possibility for the Eurocentric conception of culture itself, with the attendant political work done by the notion of 'authenticity' (Clifford 1988). Insofar as 'diversity' within global citizenship discourse is unreflexively envisaged as a precious essence that needs the protection of a system of rights, the violence intrinsic to cultural essentialism that Said brings out seems an important corrective to what I call 'happy clappy' multiculturalism, that is, a laissez-faire celebration of difference that imagines discrete but equal differences which need never clash. As has been noted recently in the UK, this sort of multiculturalism actually leads to social ghettoization and racial conflict.

If Said brings our attention to the calculated deployment of a figure of universality for imperial ends, Gayatri Chakravorty Spivak makes a crucial self-reflexive addition to this argument. In *A Critique of Postcolonial Reason* (Spivak 1999), Spivak updates Said's attack on Western academia to accommodate its extremely problematic incorporation of postcolonial theory itself in the 1980s and 1990s. She does so by laying bare the violence of Eurocentric universality within the very texts of the European tradition of critique upon which tenured academic 'postcolonialists' unthinkingly draw. For example, she finds in Kant's appeal to the aesthetic of the sublime in the *Third Critique* a key reference to the 'raw man' too uncultured to attain to such an elevated experience, even though it is the condition of access to the 'suprasensible realm of moral Ideas'; in Hegel's teleology of 'world' history she finds a distinctly Eurocentric snootiness about Indian art, deemed so ornamental as to be an obstacle to the realization of Absolute Knowledge; and in her sometime ally, Karl Marx, she finds a woefully undertheorized appeal to an 'Asiatic Mode of Production', a theoretical fiction that supports the same commitment to modernity that led Marx to demand more, not less, colonialism in India (see Chapter 1 in Spivak 1999). The other form of 'foreclosure' Spivak highlights, of course, is gender. What she describes as 'masculist universalism' (168) posits the "privileged male of the white race as a norm for universal humanity" (147). Little wonder, then, that the subaltern woman of the 'third world' largely drops beneath the radar of liberal universalism, even as her sweatshop labor puts cheap clothes on the backs of its advocates. The fundamental lesson to learn from Spivak is a structural exclusion built into Eurocentric universality: It is as if it has a need for a defining Other whose avatars cluster around race, class, sexuality and gender.

But is there any way in which the power of the universal can be deployed *against* this adversarial construction of otherness? I would argue that the history of anticolonial struggle itself demands that this question be asked. While there were serious flaws in the bourgeois nature of the various national independence movements in the mid-twentieth century, as Franz Fanon scathingly demonstrates (Fanon 2001), I would contend that anti-colonial nationalisms, as well as transnationalisms like the pan-Africanist movement, were also frameworks in which European universalism was turned against European hegemony. It was mutations in imperial forms of sovereignty that led to the outward extension of, precisely, principles of citizenship from the metropolitan centers to the colonial peripheries, opening up a discourse of universal rights that had progressive force. Now that the nation-state framework about which Fanon was rightly ambivalent has been somewhat attenuated by the forces of globalization, the importance of the same anticolonial deployment of the universal is renewed as a political strategy. We are therefore licensed to ask if the new talk of a 'global ethics' can be utilized for ends appropriate to the emancipatory project of post-colonialism. As postcolonial theory has begun to intersect in fascinating ways with theories of globalization (see the final chapter of Loomba 2005), the new cosmopolitanism starts to segue with ethico-political meditations originating from, or at least concerned with, the former colonies.

The Ghanaian philosopher Kwame Anthony Appiah, for example, charts a careful course between the violence of liberal universalism and the ethical vacuity of cultural relativism in order to propose a mode of cosmopolitanism that starts out from an assumption of difference (Appiah 2007). Contrary to the colonizer's view of difference as something to be overcome through the imposition of sameness (although note that Bhabha [2003] brings out the anxiety intrinsic to this dialectic), Appiah views difference as a source of richness and opportunity. In particular, he asserts a faith in what he calls 'conversation' as an intercultural process of negotiating reciprocal accommodations of difference. "Cosmopolitans," Appiah argues, "suppose that all cultures have enough overlap in their vocabulary of values to begin a conversation. But they don't suppose, like some universalists, that we could all come to agreement if only we have the same vocabulary" (Appiah 2007, 57). His emphasis is on living together as neighbors rather than as strangers, including all of the scope for disagreement that 'living together' affords as compared to demanding consensus and identity. In fact, Appiah's approach is not postcolonial in any systematic sense. *Cosmopolitanism: Ethics in a World of Strangers* traces the cosmopolitan ideal from the ancient Greek Cynics through Kant, the French and American revolutions, and on to the UN Declaration of Human Rights, thereby reinscribing an exclusively Eurocentric narrative of origins for the concept. However, in its emphasis on difference and dissensus within a framework of tolerance, the book does open up a wider ethical horizon. If Appiah lacks a postcolonial account of the origins and maintenance of *unequal* difference, he nonetheless insists on the need to reinvent our ethical repertoire. This seems to me salutary from a postcolonial perspective: A global ethics that does not fall back on the threadbare resources of European moral philosophy is less likely to be violently Eurocentric.

There are, however, major problems with Appiah's concept of cosmopolitanism. In its stress on conversation and tolerance and its celebration of the productive nature of difference, it is perfectly compatible with the liberal discourse of 'happy clappy' multiculturalism invoked above. This version of difference is fully embraced in global citizenship education in the ideal of diversity and, behind it, the essentialist conceptualization of discrete 'pockets' of culture that need protecting. The lack of an analysis of power relations, and specifically the deforming effects power has on communication (notions of competence, literacy and authority), leaves Appiah's pivotal concept of 'conversation' abstract and effete. The lack, too, of an interrogation of the notion of culture itself means that the very thing he believes he is protecting may already be a form of violence. Despite its promising title, his chapter 'Whose Culture Is It, Anyway?' actually concerns itself with the problem of world heritage and competing national claims to artifacts which might go under that heading, such as the Greek claim on the Elgin Marbles currently on display in the British Museum. Though nuanced and welcome, his critique of 'cultural patrimony' there touches only on 'high' culture. The more fundamental anthropological notion of culture as lived practices within frameworks of meaning and value is evaded. But what if cultural difference is not the result of an encounter between fully constituted identities at either that national or individual level, but internal to culture itself?

There is a much stronger sense of difference in more consistently postcolonial considerations of the new cosmopolitanism. As early as the late 1980s, James Clifford, for example, was already criticizing both the colonialist consequences of liberal universalist notions of a cosmopolitical culture, on the one hand, and the depoliticizing consequences of unconstrained cultural relativism on the other. More positively, however, he advocated a radical cosmopolitanism based upon a hybrid, antiessentialist understanding of culture and identity in which both are sites of an ongoing contestation (Clifford 1988). This is a cosmopolitanism that dispenses with the notion of a culturally fixed community in the bounded *polis*, and therefore with the poisoned chalice of the image of 'victim cultures' whose voices must be heard in the representative mechanisms of that *polis*.

Instead, Clifford insists on a discursive battle in which not rational conversation but agonistic contestation defines and redefines the parameters of identity in ways that overspill boundaries (hence his ongoing emphasis on diasporic identities).

Like Homi Bhabha's notion of hybridity, however, Clifford's dynamic sense of 'discrepant cosmopolitanism' rests on a model of language just as does Appiah's. In Clifford's case, it is a poststructuralist model in which the play of *différance*, rather than something like Habermasian communicative rationality, is structurally guaranteed. Pheng Cheah has offered a withering critique of Clifford's reliance on this model of language, which exemplifies what Cheah calls 'athropologistic culturalism' (Cheah 1997, 164). This rather inelegant phrase summarizes Cheah's argument that the Eurocentric anthropological assumption which defines human culture via language, and conceptualizes freedom as a freedom of expression rather than action, is transposed precisely within Clifford's (and Bhabha's) linguistic antihumanism onto a free play of the signifier in the enunciative split between colonizer and colonized, globalize and globalized. Both thinkers, then, in a normative gesture, end up presenting the aporetic structure of language as, in and of itself, a form of immanent resistance. It is well known that agency, traditionally conceived, does not survive this paradigm unscathed. As Peter Hallward has sardonically put it vis-à-vis Bhabha, "[i]t's as if apartheid, say, was overthrown by the *différance* of its own enunciation or *écriture*" (Hallward 2001, 26)—a proposition with which the ANC might have one or two problems! In its formalism, then, this appeal to language is overly divorced from questions of power.

Returning to the central issue of the possibility, indeed desirability, of a 'global ethics,' postcolonial theory has actually drawn more heavily on a quite different, Judaic tradition of ethical thought. This is typified in the esoteric work of Emmanuel Levinas to which Spivak, via Derrida, often appeals. For Levinas, the ethical relation to the absolutely Other is an almost traumatic primordial fact that preexists all socioculturally inflected value judgments: we encounter what Levinas calls the 'Face of the Other' and it hails us as ethical beings whether we like it or not (Llewelyn 1995). This has undoubted appeal today insofar as it grounds ethical reciprocity in a relation to otherness which is the opposite of the closed, antagonistic otherness Said shows at work within Eurocentric universality. As a kind of openness to the othering effect of the Other, and thus a grounding of (contingent) Sameness in (necessary) Difference, Levinasian ethics help to foreground a constitutive *relationality*. In an increasingly interconnected world, this seems valuable in bracketing out personal interests from ethical encounters as well as placing the otherwise insular Cartesian subject in its always interpersonal context. However, even this rich seam within postcolonial theory is flawed to the extent that Levinas's a priori gesture of ethical grounding is itself a paradigmatic strategy of Western philosophy (despite his appeal to an alternative non-Greek, Talmudic heritage). To this extent, it is potentially tied up in the very transcendentalism that nourishes imperial universality. Moreover, Alain Badiou has argued that this entanglement has led to a kind of pseudo-Levinasian ethics which ultimately supports the tropology of victimhood, which, as we have seen, undergirds the interlocking discourses of development and 'humanitarian intervention' (Badiou 2002).

TOWARDS A CRITICAL PEDAGOGY OF DIVISIVE UNIVERSALISM

Recent theorists who position themselves outside postcolonial theory—I am thinking of Alain Badiou's notion of the 'void of a situation,' Jacques Rancière's 'part of no part' and Slavoj Žižek's 'universal singular'—have elaborated a different universalism that I propose to call 'divisive' universalism. They are all inspired by a (post)Marxist perspective sustaining a form of politics that escapes the trap of representational democracy, national or supranational, thereby sidestepping some of the 'world parliament' problems inherent in the new cosmopolitanisms. Their avowed distance from, and in fact vehement critique of, certain tendencies within postcolonial theory is salutary for my own argument. For the primary target of their invective is culturalist identity politics, the area within postcolonial theory most amenable to appropriation by the version of 'cultural diversity' and 'cultural difference' circulating in mainstream global citizenship education.

    And yet the emphasis in Badiou, Rancière and Žižek on the invisible and marginalized, the *sans papiers*, economic refugees, and slumdwellers, is perfectly in keeping with the broader postcolonial project which focuses on the wretched of the newly globalized earth. Moreover, in its deliberate distance from state representation and its related emphasis on generic humanity, I would argue that 'divisive' universalism is much closer to the original Stoic principles behind cosmopolitanism than the Kantian variants. Perhaps it is helpful, then, to simply list the differences between these two kinds of universalism (see Table 3.1).

    Like most binaries, this opposition is fragile, and it is important to point out that a precondition for divisive universalism is the prior existence of its Eurocentric counterpart: no French Revolution, no Haitian Revolution. Although problematic in all the ways I have analyzed, then, the discourse of universal human rights and global ethics still paves the way for new deployments of divisive universalism.

    But how can global citizenship education support *this* universalism? No grand new pedagogical theory is required to address this question. We already have a body of work which proposes a practice of education well

Table 3.1 Differences between Eurocentric and Divisive Universalisms

Eurocentric Universalism	Divisive Universalism
• Exclusive and ultimately territorial	• Radically generic and irreducible to the nation
• Covertly instrumental for particular interests· Citizenship viewed as membership of an institutionally enforced system of individual/human rights	• Explicitly mobilized for particular interests but with universal implications
• Equality as a goal to be achieved by means of reform	• Citizenship viewed as intrinsic humanity (with humanity operating as a name for the generic collectivity)
• Reliance on mechanisms of representation	• Equality as an axiom asserted here and now
• Tendency toward identity politics	• Creation of alternate spaces of direct democratic participation
	• Tendency toward 'singular' politics subtracted from issues of identity

suited to challenging the effects of Eurocentric universalism within mainstream global citizenship education: critical pedagogy.

Theorists of critical pedagogy such as Paulo Freire (1974, 1996), Ivan Illich (1971), Henry Giroux (1983), Giroux and Shannon (1987), Michael Apple (1995), Peter McLaren (1995, 2005), bell hooks (1994), and Gayatri Chakravorty Spivak (1993) all emphasize a mode of pedagogy that equips students to do three main things:

1. question dominant values;
2. achieve an increased level of critical consciousness regarding the ideologies that impact on their lives;
3. place the discourse of education itself in its formative geo-socio-political context.

This last point is obviously crucial for our purposes here. Indeed, to the extent that the work of the Brazilian educator Paulo Freire has been inaugural for the entire field, critical pedagogy has always used a broadly non-Western, often postcolonial perspective in order to highlight the overlap between centers of power and the localized production of education discourse claiming universal worth. This makes critical pedagogy peculiarly well-'placed' to bring alternative perspectives to putatively *global* citizenship education.

Echoing Edward Said, critical pedagogy renders all education intrinsically political, giving the lie to the dream of neutral scholarship. From the spatial dynamics of classroom layouts, to the hierarchization of the teacher-student relation, from governmental agendas shaping national curricula, to the increasing privatization of education particularly at the tertiary level, critical pedagogy exposes the political basis of all learning. It does this in two senses: Firstly, it demonstrates the normative interests behind mainstream education, and secondly, it creates political spaces that encourage critical consideration of these interests. With the distance thereby achieved from 'common sense,' it interrogates the network of interests behind the validation of certain forms of knowledge itself (Western, often scientific, often linked to the corporate world) as well as the denigration of others (non-Western, indigenous, feminist and so on). The fundamental issue of what gets counted as knowledge at all, let alone worthwhile knowledge, is key in debates about globalization often oriented around descriptions of the 'knowledge economy.'

However, it is important to point out that critical pedagogy is motivated in this self-reflexive critical work by a commitment to grassroots democracy. Part of that commitment is indeed seeing education, in the same terms as the UK's Department for International Development, as crucial in enabling "informed, active, responsible citizens" (DfES 2000, 8). Far from the essentially conservative reflex within liberalism, however, critical pedagogy is invested in genuine social change. By 'learning to unlearn,' in Spivak's phrase, but also by learning that one already brings albeit marginalized forms of knowledge to the classroom, critical pedagogy privileges a mode of *experiential transformative learning*. It is experiential in that it is not based on integrally transmissible information but is a process of self-questioning one must go through. It is transformative in that it reconfigures the dominant value systems by which one's behavior is, often unconsciously, regulated. It is certainly a form of learning in that techniques, and more importantly dispositions, of critical thought are acquired, but also in that it opens up spaces in which new perspectives can be shared and challenged.

The usual critique of critical pedagogy is that it is a form of soapbox propaganda for various leftisms. This fundamentally misunderstands the process involved, which is one of ceaseless questioning rather than of reinforcing dogmatisms. While a humanist Marxism certainly influences the work of both Paulo Freire and Peter McLaren, and while anarchist themes definitely pervade Ivan Illich's proposal to 'de-school society' (Illich, 1971), these are but contingent theoretical tools. Critical pedagogy certainly does *not* aim to produce robotic Marxists or anarchists. Where critical pedagogy has allowed itself to become ossified in the ways sometimes imputed to it, it has been because of a reliance on a version of Marxism predicated on Eurocentric rather than divisive universalism: The orthodox model of class struggle has proved itself time and time again to be extremely unwieldy in colonial and postcolonial contexts. Yet Marxism remains a praxis of, precisely, critique, and one dialectically implicated in site-specific struggles. Critical pedagogy opens up a space in which this dialectic of knowledge and praxis can break down clunky epistemological constraints, including preexisting so-called Marxists ones imported from Europe. If the trope which has organized European modernity since the Enlightenment is that of sight (the light of reason, eradicating the shadows of ignorance, the gaze of knowledge etc.), critical pedagogy effectively replaces this with the trope of *listening*. This is listening not as a condescending process of gathering information from 'victims' so that you (the educated one) can represent their plight because they are incapable of doing so. On the contrary, it is listening to the Other as an active process of the *othering of the self*, an opening up to other epistemologies which challenge one's worldview. This is why, for example, the *Paulo and Nita Freire Project for Critical Pedagogy* hosted at McGill University in Canada is committed to dialogue with indigenous peoples and to free and full access to its resulting archives (see http://freire.mcgill.ca/).[2] This process of listening but also of making heard is already a practice of resistance against the academic co-optation that Spivak sees a certain version of postcolonial theory succumbing to.

So how can critical pedagogy support a new global citizenship education based upon what I have called divisive universalism? Firstly, the classroom must be turned into a self-reflexive space in which the locations and interests behind Eurocentric universalism within education discourse itself can be explored. Secondly, individual subjects must be taught in a way that is 'global' not in the sense of harmonizing with the dominant account of globalization, but in the sense of including nondominant perspectives in other than tokenistic ways. For example, the teaching of history must not only expand outwards from a national perspective to world perspectives as DfES already advise, but it must juxtapose antagonistic accounts of the same world historical events in order to lay bare the political nature of historical narrative itself (what is at stake, for example, when the 1857–1858 uprisings against British colonial power in India are referred to by Indian historians as the 'First War of Indian Independence,' but by British historians as the 'Indian Mutiny'). Secondly, citizenship education should question rather than assume the existence of a global public sphere and world polity, partly by exploring the hypocrisies of supranational entities such as the IMF, WTO and UN, but partly too by exploring grassroots activisms that do not restrict 'politics' to professionalized institutional spaces. Practices of *direct* rather than only parliamentary democracy should be validated.

Precisely because of the persistence of the uneven power of some nations over others, global citizenship education should emphasize a generic sense of 'citizenship' irreducible to qualifications of national belonging but also independent of the problematic paradigm of rights. Rather than squaring the circle of local and global as the new cosmopolitan universalism has attempted, this unashamedly generic notion of humanity gets back to the roots of Stoic cosmopolitanism in asserting a global commonality incompatible with borders. Thirdly, global citizenship education should approach the key problem of difference in two compatible ways. On the one hand, where issues of race, ethnicity and class are raised, students should be encouraged to reflect on their own essentializing gestures and be equipped with the hermeneutic tools to recognize this process in wider representations of such issues: The motivated construction of difference needs to replace embedded assumptions about difference as given or natural. On the other hand, *difference as constitutive exclusion* needs to be foregrounded by focusing classroom debates on those other figures of globalization such as economic migrants, political asylum seekers, undocumented workers, workers in export processing zones, the homeless and so on. While 'bleeding-heart' liberals always point to such figures, their eyes brimming with tears, it is invariably to refine the system of rights that supposedly protects them. What I am proposing, however, is that these figures, precisely as phenomena of the border and thus the logic of inclusion-exclusion, constitute both an indictment of Eurocentric universalism and an incitement to divisive universalism. Using global citizenship education to place such figures in their fully globalized context is a form of 'divisive universalism' in that they are shown to be structurally necessary products of the dominant neoliberal version of globalization. To paraphrase Marx, their suffering is universal and the wrong done to them is wrong in general.

But perhaps *the* model for citizenship which is in a position to mobilize divisive universalism today is that of 'environmental citizenship' (see Bell and Dobson, 2005). Arguably, while the figure of the economic refugee and his cousin the slumdweller do dramatize the human cost of neoliberal globalization, the true 'limit to capital' (to borrow David Harvey's phrase), the one that unites us all and yet simultaneously confronts us all with the necessity of change, is the finitude of the natural world. By most estimates, we are currently consuming 1.4 planets. The real challenge, then, the one that, if met, would truly divide consumer capitalism against itself, is to extend generic equality to the *nonhuman world*. If the Haitian Revolution extended the franchise of egalitarian human rights beyond Europe, we now need to push them beyond even human exploitation in order to encompass the exploitation of the earth fundamental to the expansive and exponentially intensive system of capital. This is what interconnectedness ultimately means. The potential intersections between critical pedagogy and ecological politics then seem to me to be crucial in thinking of a global citizenship education based upon 'divisive universalism.'

What is particularly valuable about divisive universalism, finally, is not only that it is still a universalism, but also that it maximizes universalism in a way that avoids the traps of relativism and identity politics into which postcolonial theory itself has fallen on occasion. But it is not a *given* universalism. It has to be posited as part of a different politics, as Alain Badiou has recently argued:

Confronted with the artificial and murderous division of the world into two—a disjunction named by the very term, 'the West'—we must affirm the existence of the single world right from the start, as axiom and principle. The simple phrase, 'there is only one world', is not an objective conclusion. It is performative: we are deciding that this is how it is for us. Faithful to this point, it is then a question of elucidating the consequences that follow from this simple declaration. (Badiou, 2008)

NOTES

1. For example, Seyla Benhabib proposes a form of 'democratic iteration' by means of which cosmopolitan ethical principles are, over time, incorporated into positive, enforceable national law via the democratic will of its citizens (Benhabib 2006). Kant's 'world citizen' here is really a national citizen with a cosmopolitan or worldly outlook: The problem of rights that cross borders is evaded because of the assumption that every demos must be bounded. Furthermore, this process of 'democratic iteration' has little purchase on reality, which furnishes us with multiple examples of democracies whose majorities are apathetic before decidedly unethical foreign policies. This was brutally exposed by the war in Iraq.
2. This project, and also Paolo Freire's own early work, has been criticized from an indigenous perspective precisely for cleaving too closely to a class-based model of a singularized, monolithic 'struggle' and, for that reason, to tokenistic forms of listening with regard to indigenous forms of knowledge and experience. This is a danger to which Spivak's work consistently alerts us. However, while one might have hesitations about the Eurocentric universalism that marks traditional critical pedagogy—a narrow humanism, a 'stagism' with regard to the modes of production that echoes development discourse, a tendency to see indigenous cultures as problematically 'premodern' etc.—these are, or should be, eradicated through the reflexive, horizontal processes of critical pedagogy as a *practice* rather than a coherent theory. I would insist, again, that because the same applies to Marxism, the latter remains a vital resource for critical pedagogy. It is for this reason that I have referred to the post-Marxism of Badiou, Rancière and Žižek.

REFERENCES

Alexander, J. M. (2005) *Pedagogies of Crossing: Meditations on Feminism, Sexual Politics, and the Sacred (Perverse Modernities)*, London: Duke University Press.
Amin, S. (1998) *Capitalism in the Age of Globalization*, London: Zed Books.
Appiah, K. A. (2007) *Cosmopolitanism: Ethics in a World of Strangers*, London: Penguin.
Apple, M. (1995) *Education and Power*, New York: Routledge.
Archibugi, D. (2008) *The Global Commonwealth of Citizens: Toward Cosmopolitan Democracy*, Princeton, NJ: Princeton University Press.
Arendt, H. (1973) *The Origins of Totalitarianism*, San Diego: Harcourt Brace Jovanovich.
Badiou, A. (2002) *Ethics: An Essay on the Understanding of Evil*, trans. Peter Hallward, London: Verso.
———. (2008) 'The Communist Hypothesis', in *New Left Review*, 49: January-February.

Beck, U. (2000) *The Brave New World of Work*, Cambridge: Polity.
Bell, D. and Dobson, A. (eds.) (2005) *Environmental Citizenship*, London: MIT Press.
Benhabib, S. (2006) *Another Cosmopolitanism*, Oxford: Oxford University Press.
Bhabha, H. (2003) *The Location of Culture*, London: Routledge.
Bhambra, G. K. (2007) *Rethinking Modernity: Postcolonialism and the Sociological Imagination*, London: Palgrave Macmillan.
Bourdieu, P. (1984) *Distinction: A Social Critique of the Judgement of Taste*, trans. Richard Nice, London: Routledge.
———. (1996) *The State Nobility: Elite Schools in the Field of Power*, trans. Loretta C. Clough, Oxford: Polity.
Cheah, P. (1997) 'Given Culture: Rethinking Cosmopolitical Freedom in Transnationalism', in *Boundary 2*, 24(22): 157–197.
Chen, L. and Belgeonne, C. (2008) 'Education for Community Cohesion: Lowest Common Denominator or Daring to be Different', in *Critical Literacies: Theories and Practices*, 1(2): 76–86.
Clifford, J. (1988) *The Predicament of Culture: Twentieth Century Ethnography, Literature and Art*, Cambridge: Harvard University Press.
Department for Education and Skills (DfES) (2000). *Curriculum and standards guidance: Developing a global dimension in the school curriculum.* London: Department for Education and Skills.
Fanon, F. (2001) *The Wretched of the Earth*, trans. Constance Farrington, London: Penguin.
Freire, P. (1974) *Education for Critical Consciousness*, London: Sheed & Ward.
———. (1996) *Pedagogy of the Oppressed*, trans. Maria Bergman Ramos, London: Penguin.
Gilroy, P. (1993) *The Black Atlantic: Modernity and Its Double Consciousness*, London: Verso.
Giroux, H. (1983) *Theory and Resistance in Education*, Westport, CT: Bergin & Garvey.
Giroux, H. and Shannon, P. (eds.) (1997) *Education and Cultural Studies: Toward a Performative Practice*, London: Routledge.
Kant, I. (1991) *Kant: Political Writings*, ed. Hans Reiss, Cambridge: Cambridge University Press.
Hallward, P. (2001) *Absolutely Postcolonial: Writing between the Singular and the Specific*, Manchester, UK: Manchester University Press.
Haroontunian, H. (2000) *Overcome by Modernity: History, Culture and Community in Interwar Japan*, Princeton, NJ: Princeton University Press.
Hardt, M. and Negri, A. (2000) *Empire*. Cambridge, MA: Harvard University Press.
hooks, b. (1994). *Teaching to Transgress: Education as the Practice of Freedom*, London: Routledge.
Hutchings, K. (2005) 'Subjects, Citizens or Pilgrims? Citizenship and Civil Society in a Global Context', in Randall Germain and Michael Kenny (eds.), *The Idea of Global Civil Society: Politics and Ethics in a Globalising Era*, London: Routledge, 84–99.
Illich, I. (1971) *Deschooling Society*, New York: Harper.
Llewelyn, J. (1995) *Emmanuel Levinas: The Genealogy of Ethics*, London: Routledge.
Loomba, A. (2005) *Colonialism/Postcolonialism*, London: Routledge.
Manley, M. (1983) *Jamaica: Struggle in the Periphery*, London: Third World Media Ltd.
McLaren, P. (1995) *Critical Pedagogy and Predatory Culture*, London: Routledge.

——. (2003) 'Revolutionary Pedagogy in Post-Revolutionary Times: Rethinking the Political Economy of Critical Education', in Darder et al. (eds.), *Critical Pedagogy Reader*, London: RoutledgeFalmer, 151–184.

——. (ed.) (2005) *Red Seminars: Radical Excursions into Educational Theory, Cultural Politics and Pedagogy*, Cresskill, NJ: Hampton.

Mignolo, W. (2000) *Local Histories/Global Designs: Coloniality, Subaltern Knowledges and Border Thinking*, Princeton, NJ: Princeton University Press.

Rodney, W. (1974) *How Europe Underdeveloped Africa*, Washington, DC: Howard University Press.

Said, E. (2003) *Orientalism*, London: Penguin.

Spivak, G. (1993) *Outside in the Teaching Machine*, London: Routledge.

——. (1999). *A critique of postcolonial reason: Toward a critique of the vanishing Present*. Cambridge, MA: Harvard University Press.

Tomlinson, J. (2000) *Globalization and Culture*, Oxford: Blackwell Publishers Ltd.

Venn, C. (2006) *The Postcolonial Challenge: Towards Alternative Worlds*, London: Sage.

Wallerstein, I. (2004) *World-Systems Analysis: An Introduction*, Durham, NC: Duke University Press.

Williams, E. (1994) *Capitalism and Slavery*, London: University of North Carolina Press.

4 Engaging the Global by Resituating the Local
(Dis)locating the Literate Global Subject and His View from Nowhere

Lynn Mario T. M. de Souza

> One has to persist in being indigenous in order to persist in becoming white. (Viveiros de Castro 2009, 158)

Although Street (1984) painstakingly showed that far from an abstract decontextualized cognitive code or 'knowledge,' literacy consisted of variable highly contextualized and situated social and semiotic practices; the notion of literacy as a homogeneous universal skill causally connected with development and progress persists in public policies worldwide (UNESCO, DfID, EFA, Torres 2000[1]). Moreover, it is generally assumed that such official policies for the stimulation of development through the dissemination of alphabetic literacy do just that: disseminate literacy. And where such policies do not yet exist or are not yet implemented, moves are taken, often by governmental and civil society organizations, to articulate the creation and/or implementation of alphabetic literacy policies. In this chapter, I explore the connections between global citizenship and the universalization of alphabetic literacy. I adopt the critical strategy of "worlding texts" suggested by the postcolonial critic Edward Said (1983)[2] and situate literacy policy documents in their sociohistoric contexts so that they may be seen as "a system of forces institutionalized by the reigning culture at some human cost to its various components" (53). I address the complexities embodied in such forces in the specific case of indigenous literacy education policies in Brazil.

FROM THE GLOBAL TO THE LOCAL: COMPLEXITIES AND CONTAMINATIONS

The problematic of global citizenship education revolves around a perceived need, in a globalized world of approximations, juxtapositions and flows of all sorts to negotiate difference—linguistic, cultural, racial and so on through an effective engagement in the school institution with various manifestations of this difference. This need may be phrased in terms of "intercultural understanding" and "intercultural dialogue" (as in the case of the so-called Istanbul Resolution of the EU in 2007) or in terms of "ensuring their own and others' well being" (as in the Oxfam educational proposal of 2006) or even in terms of being "taught about shared values and life" always at a supranational level.

Richardson and Blades (2006), however, warn that such proposals may privilege liberal-democratic abstract, normative and disembodied concepts of citizenship and civic engagement where difference, although evoked, is rapidly suppressed in favor of equality and symmetry. Andreotti et al. (2010) describe specific instances of what Richardson and Blades had anticipated, where GCE practice tends to be couched in "seemingly neutral notions of difference that generally fail to engage with conflicts and tensions inherent to processes of globalization and ideas of citizenship and nationhood" (20). In response to such practices, Abdi and Shultz (2008) propose an alternative, whereby GCE may be seen more relevantly as a product of (rather than a suppression of) diversity beyond any state or national boundaries.

From a postcolonial perspective, GCE, seen in these terms of 'intercultural engagement,' 'engagement with difference' or evocation/suppression of diversity, seems curiously and ironically reminiscent of what Said (1993) termed 'identity thought' or 'us-and-them' binary thinking which he considered to be typical of imperialist cultures as well as those cultures trying to resist the expansionism of Europe in the nineteenth and early twentieth centuries. Said sought to show that postcolonial theories went beyond such binaries and identified new, complex forms of alignments that "provoke and challenge the fundamentally static notion of *identity* that has been the core of cultural thought during the era of imperialism" (36). Said referred to the perspective taken by such challenges to binary imperialistic thinking and which sought to reveal the complex intertwined and often contradictory alignments as the 'contrapuntal perspective.' Leela Gandhi (2006, 4) called attention to how postcolonial critics in general took on board this contrapuntal perspective of revealing interconnections, interrelationships and complex contaminations in what once seemed to be purities on the side of the colonizing culture as well as on the side of the defenders of anticolonial nationalism.

It is against this backdrop of wishing to venture 'interculturally' beyond binary exclusions and suppressions but still being caught in an apparently unseen web of 'identity thought' that I examine below the problematic of intercultural policies of indigenous education in Brazil. According to the Indigenous Education Census of 2005, the indigenous population of Brazil was 600,000, less than 0.4 percent of the total Brazilian population and distributed in 227 peoples with 180 indigenous languages. Of this population, 174,000 were in official indigenous schools. Such schools were created in accordance with the precepts of the Constitution of 1988, which explicitly declare that indigenous education should be differentiated, specific, intercultural, bilingual and of quality. Article 210 of this constitution goes on to stipulate that "Regular fundamental education will be given in Portuguese, guaranteeing, however, to the indigenous communities, the right to use their own mother tongues and their own learning processes". The issue of what exactly was to be understood by the phrase "their own learning processes" was considered to be resolved by the later Law of Basic Education (LDB) of 1996 in its Articles 78 and 79, which stipulated that indigenous education should include the "recuperation of historical memory," the "reaffirmation of ethnic identity," the "valorization of indigenous languages" and the provision of "access to information and knowledges of mainstream society and of other indigenous societies" (78, 79).

In short, in contrast to previous assimilationist policies of indigenous education which required indigenous communities to be literate in the national language and to follow the national curriculum, and in apparent contrast to the literacy-as-pathway-to-development policies of international agencies, current Brazilian policy guarantees that indigenous communities, in official indigenous schools, have access to literacy and education in their own local "languages and knowledges." Moreover, legislation also permits indigenous communities to establish their own curricula, produce their own teaching materials and appoint their own teachers. However, against this apparently permissive, harmonious and respectful background of official policies for education and literacy in indigenous languages and cultures, significant discrepancies have been observed in actual practice: Many indigenous communities seem to prefer indigenous schools which adopt predominantly national-language literacies rather than schools using predominantly indigenous language literacies (Cavalcanti 1999). Recent research (Scaramuzzi 2008; Grupioni 2008) even points to how this preference for alphabetic writing and alphabetic literacy practices in Portuguese alter indigenous communities' conceptions of identity, culture, territory and local knowledges.

Scaramuzzi (2008), for example, shows how concepts of identity, intercommunity relations and land possession have been altered drastically by the introduction of alphabetic writing and alphabetic literacy practices in indigenous schools. Where these concepts were previously flexible and fluid, open to change, Scaramuzzi concludes that at present, through the influence of alphabetic literacy in Portuguese and the accompanying phonocentric notion of the fixity of the spoken word in writing, the concepts mentioned appear to have acquired an unprecedented fixity and homogeneity, even a certain unprecedented ethnocentricity and a clear resistance to change. Scaramuzzi makes clear his regret of the drastic change that this has brought to certain indigenous communities. Grupioni's (2008) research also shows how the introduction of formal education (and consequently, alphabetic literacy) introduced new concepts into indigenous communities, such as unprecedented concepts of 'culture.' Some of these communities apparently discovered the (nonindigenous) notion of culture for the first time; others, armed with this new notion, sought to recuperate the indigenous 'culture' they believed they had lost as a result of colonization. In either case, none of these indigenous communities escaped unscathed from the effects of the new fixing notion of 'culture' that came with formal schooling and alphabetic literacy. How should one interpret these discrepancies, which point to losses instead of gains on the part of indigenous communities, as a result of official formal education and alphabetic literacy policies which in fact sought to respect and benefit these communities with the preservation of their own languages and cultural values?

EPISTEMOLOGICAL CONFLICT: CONTAINMENT OF DIFFERENCE

From the perspective of the policymakers, in opting for national-language literacies and curricula, indigenous communities may be making unforeseen and uninformed interpretations of the concepts of culture, interculturality and identity which could prejudice their interests or survival as minority groups. An earlier version of this reading of the situation was that of the Brazilian educationalist and literacy specialist Paulo Freire, who suggested that the indigenous refusal of official policy may be understood as an uncritical appropriation of oppressive forms of thinking by the oppressed, capable of resulting in the appropriation of dominant models and practices and self-exclusion.

I suggest, however, that an alternative reading of the situation, from the contrapuntal perspective of the indigenous, may provide a different picture: The changes and apparent losses being lamented may be the result of an epistemological conflict where the nonindigenous players in the issues at stake have difficulty in perceiving and understanding the complexity of indigenous knowledges; thus, instead of the claim of official policy to be open to cultural difference and respectful of indigenous epistemologies, an official monocultural posture appears to predominate and perhaps inadvertently seeks to contain and suppress the very epistemological difference it purports to valorize. A posture of containment of difference in official policy becomes apparent in the fact that the proposals for "intercultural" education (as opposed to a previously assimilationist one) are aimed only and specifically at the indigenous minority and not at mainstream education in Brazil; this seems to presuppose that it is the minority that has to be "intercultural," whereas mainstream culture continues undisturbed on a monocultural course. As we shall see, this dominant official monocultural stance is a key to understand the epistemological conflicts involved in understanding the increasing indigenous option for national-language literacy to the detriment of indigenous-language literacy.

Postcolonial theories (Said 1983; Bhabha 1994; Spivak 1995; Gandhi 2006) have long since eloquently pointed out, in various terms, the colonial strategy of containing the difference of the colonized Other by reducing it to the sameness of the colonizing self whereby it could be read as comparatively deficient and inferior, always of course in the terms of the dominant epistemologies of the colonizer. Such binaries and hierarchies apparently should make no sense in the current Brazilian context of respectful official postassimilationist and postcolonial relations with its indigenous minority.

Unfortunately, judging by the cross-epistemological difficulties mentioned above, these binaries and hierarchies may be resurfacing as a result of developmentalist policies of education and literacy that ironically enunciate the preservation of marginalized cultures at the same time that they contribute to the further isolation and marginalization of indigenous communities. There seems to be a need for policymakers to self-critically examine their epistemological and cultural presuppositions even as they seek to implement what they see as intercultural education, albeit *indigenous* intercultural education. It is to a consideration of these epistemological differences that I shall now move to below.

BEYOND THE VIEW FROM NOWHERE: INDIGENOUS EPISTEMOLOGIES OF VISION, PERSPECTIVISM AND PREDATION

Many Brazilian indigenous cultures of the Amazon region and elsewhere are nonphonocentric and perceive knowledge as housed, expressed and accessed by *vision* rather than by verbal language (Lagrou 1996; Keifenheim 1999; de Souza 2003, 2005, 2006, 2008). Visions are ritually, collectively and conventionally defined and accessed as valued sources of individual and collective knowledge. In terms of literacy and writing practices, for these cultures, if writing is taken as a form of registering knowledge, and if knowledge is acquired through vision and not through verbal language, then it necessarily has to be visual writing (and not alphabetic writing, which presupposes sound and verbal language as the source of knowledge). Such visual writing takes the form of codified drawings and markings on ceramics, wood, textiles and bodies (as tattoos). These visual writing practices may be easily not seen as 'writing' to the unsuspecting monocultural, phonocentric, alphabetic eye of the nonindigenous policymaker, even when such a person may be critically aware of the postcolonial issues involved in epistemologically reducing the difference of the Other to the sameness of the dominant perceiving self.

In terms of the self-other dynamic commonly discussed in postcolonial theory, Brazilian indigenous cultures offer the intriguing epistemological alternative of what Castro (2000, 2009) has called 'indigenous perspectivism.' In this self-other dynamic, seeing and being seen are basic constitutive elements which define identity, personhood, culture and nature. In this indigenous epistemology, all living beings are seen to have not nature but *culture* in common (where 'culture' refers to the cognitive capacity of perceiving, knowing and understanding). Thus, visible (physical) differences between beings are considered to be differences of *nature* which mask a common shared *culture*. Such visible differences are seen as superficial and qualitative (different, other), not quantitative (inferior/superior) and perceived always from situated, specific locations or perspectives. There are thus only perspectives and never a privileged "God's-eye view" or a "view from nowhere" that may smooth over an infinite number of points of view. Counter to commonly held concepts of relativism, which presuppose a possibility of choice between different and multiple points of view, the relativism of perspectivism is based on the concept that nature or the body is absolute, not changeable, and is the locus of a perspective, which therefore cannot be chosen. The perspective one has is therefore defined by one's body or nature and is not contingent or plural. According to Castro, each perspective is an interpretation intricately connected to the local, situated, vital interests of each species: "What jaguars see as 'beer', humans see as 'blood;' where we see a muddy salt-lick on a river bank, tapirs see their big ceremonial house, and so on . . . not a plurality of views of a single world, mind you, but a single view of different worlds" (2004, 6).

In terms of intercultural (and we may add postcolonial) understanding, Castro emphasizes "equivocation" as perhaps the most important aspect of indigenous perspectivism: "An equivocation is not just a 'failure to understand', but a failure to understand that understandings are necessarily not the same, and that they are not related to imaginary ways of 'seeing the world' but to the real worlds which are being seen" (11). The real world in this sense varies according to the bodies and the natural species of the perceiver. What all perceivers have in common, as we have said, is 'culture' or the cognitive capacity of knowing and making sense of the world. Although interconnected, perspectives are not partial views of an external, unified existent point of view—a 'view from nowhere'; they are located and equivocal:

> Perspectivism is not the affirmation of equivalence—an indifference—between all points of view; it is the affirmation of an incompatibility with the notion of the "best perspective" . . . To put it differently: jaguars, like people, are humans and are subjects of a perspective as powerful as the human perspective. But jaguars and people cannot be humans at the same time, and for this reason they cannot agree on what is the true perspective. (Castro 2009, 110)

In this indigenous epistemology, the lack of an external referent (or "true perspective") against which conflicting perspectives may be evaluated as being "more correct" or "less deviant" results necessarily in equivocal, noncoincidental and unoverlapping perspectives. This in turn demands constant translation among subjects from different species. It is important to understand the concept of translation in such an epistemology: here, "to translate is to presume that an equivocation always exists; it is to communicate by differences, instead of silencing the Other by presuming a univocality—the essential similarity—between what the Other and We are saying" (Castro 2004, 10).

Given the nonexistence of an external referent or a point of convergence which could "ground" or guarantee a normative, stable, fixed and universal meaning, equivocation as the noncoincidence of meaning or the difficulty of understanding both guarantees and at the same time impedes communication and the possibility of mutual understanding. It guarantees communication in the sense that given the primacy of a state of nonunderstanding, communication becomes vital to attempt understanding. It is in these attempts at mutual understanding that the importance of translation arises, occupying the space of endemic equivocation:

> To translate is to situate oneself in the space of the equivocation and to dwell there. It is not to unmake the equivocation (since this would be to suppose it never existed in the first place) but precisely the opposite is true. To translate is to emphasize or potentialize the equivocation, that is, to open and widen the space imagined not to exist between the conceptual languages in contact, a space that the equivocation precisely concealed. (Castro 2004, 10)

Like communication in a state of primal misunderstanding, equivocation according to Castro is what founds and stimulates a relationship and not what impedes it. Equivocal translation then is to establish a relationship across differences and to communicate by and through differences, with no guarantee of mutual understanding.

The aim of perspectivist equivocal translation, then, is not to find a synonym of one's language in the language of the Other, so one may say that one is speaking of the "same thing" as the other; on the contrary, the aim is not to lose sight of the difference concealed within equivocal, apparently similar representations between one's own language and that of the Other, "since we and they are never talking about the same things" (11). For Castro, where European ethnocentrism consists in doubting the sameness of the Other, using sameness as the basis for judgment, indigenous ethnocentrism consists in doubting the sameness of the Other, using otherness as the basis for judgment (if they are different [in form] they are the same). It is worth recalling here that sameness in indigenous perspectivism involves the cognitive capacity to think and to make meaning, and as such it is a capacity that belongs equally to all forms of life. The equivocation that accompanies this shared capacity involves perceiving that though all species are equally capable of thinking and making meaning, this also guarantees that they will make meaning in the terms of their species and remain unintelligible to each other. Thus, in spite of the fact that misunderstandings exist, they will never be the *same* misunderstandings across the species. Similarity in this epistemology is then what founds difference and not what overcomes it. Castro is rightly at pains to add that this is not relativism as is commonly conceived, where varying representations or manifestations share a common, external referent against which they are "measured" (e.g. varying representations of gender, food, taboos, etc.); indigenous perspectivism, as explained above, sees radical diversity with no external referent; thus, "any species of subject perceives itself and its world in the same way we perceive ourselves and our world" (6). This epistemology thus sees different species as basically interconnected though characterized by perceptible and dynamically conflicting elements.

In terms of the relationship to literacy, from the cultural stance of indigenous perspectivism alphabetic and nonalphabetic writing are seen as visibly different but essentially interconnected, each portraying conflicting situated perspectives. If 'intercultural' is taken to mean an encounter with alterity and difference, perspectivism may be seen to indicate that indigenous communities with such epistemologies may already be 'intercultural' before the policies of official intercultural literacy and education. This would account for the reluctance of many indigenous communities to separate and isolate alphabetic and nonalphabetic, phonocentric and visual forms of writing, and the preference to interconnect them, each in their own contexts. This explains the complex coexistence between the newly acquired Portuguese-language alphabetic literacies and curricula of the indigenous community school and the visual nonalphabetic indigenous-language literacy practices still carried out *outside* the schoolhouse. However, to the unprepared nonindigenous eye, the new alphabetic national-language educational and literacy practices that occur *inside* the schoolhouse would seem to necessarily indicate the nonexistence of their indigenous-language correlates.

Developing and extending the concept of indigenous epistemologies of perspectivism and following Lévi-Strauss's (1995) description of Amerindian cultures as marked by an openness to alterity,[3] Fausto (1999, 2000) offers a useful account of what he calls the indigenous cultural *logic of predation*. Connected to perspectivism, this manifests itself as a dire need for newness and difference, where the Other, the apparently 'different,' is seen (as in perspectivism) as the locus of a perspective and qualities. In this logic, however, the perspective and qualities of a powerful Other may be seen to be desirable and not eliminable (as occurs in the colonial logic of assimilation). In the logic of predation, the self (individual and collective) is seen as constituted heterogeneously by differences acquired from the Other. As such, a need is felt to accede to and take possession of the perspective (hence the knowledge) of this desirable, stronger Other without allowing oneself to be captured by the perspective of the Other. Elaborating on the example given above, by Castro, in which jaguars, like people, are humans and are subjects of a perspective as powerful as the human perspective, but where jaguars and people cannot be humans at the same time (and for this reason they cannot agree on what is the true perspective), the predatory strategy would suggest that one should be careful not to be absorbed by the jaguar's perspective to the point of losing one's own humanity or, in short, to try to "capture" the jaguar's perspective without abdicating from one's own human perspective, and at the same time allowing one's human perspective to be modified by and enriched by the jaguar's perspective.

Here, what was left as unelaborated interconnectedness and conflict in the concept of perspectivism is now elaborated as perspectival hybridity, where *identity* is never a static purity to be 'preserved' (as in the colonial dynamic of reducing otherness to the sameness of the self). On the contrary, perspectival hybridity results from the acquisition of the perspective/knowledge of the Other, without losing one's own perspective; without being "captivated" by or assimilated to the perspective of the Other. Thus, instead of the purity and the preservation of an imagined sameness, the logic of predation values the translation and transformation of knowledges; paradoxically, 'sameness' and 'essence' in identity, culture and knowledge are seen to persist, but are never static and undergo constant change. When faced by an influx of new and conflicting perspectives and knowledges, 'resistance,' or the effort not to be assimilated to the Other, curiously takes the form of acceding to and acquiring the knowledge/perspective of the Other, without losing one's own perspective, yet having one's perspective transformed and translated, and as such, enriched. Thus the acquisition of new knowledges, literacies and languages is not seen as the "loss" of previous knowledges, literacies and languages, but as the "maintenance" of the 'same essence' in a process of constant renewal of vitality when confronted by the threatening newness of a stronger, mainstream Other. This cultural logic thus goes beyond standard Western, essentialist logics of maintenance and preservation of identities and values.[4]

The cultural logic of predation may explain the reluctance on the part of indigenous communities to replace already existing nonphonocentric indigenous literacies and nonformal education with phonocentric, alphabetic literacy and formal schooling either in indigenous languages (albeit using indigenous knowledges) or in Portuguese. From the perspective of the logic of predation, it is not a question of either/or, but both/neither (i.e., both translated and transformed) resulting in new, hybrid forms of language, literacy and educational practices. It is important to note that 'hybrid' here is not meant as something having lost its original purity but as something having gained from the contact with newness and alterity, and hence 'bettered' its chances of survival (where, following the nuances of the logic of predation, 'survival' is not to ever remain the same, but to constantly become different, although occupying the 'same' locus or perspective). In terms of literacy practices, it is not a question of moving linearly from 'preliterate' to 'literate' practices, but of 'maintaining' preliterate, nonphonocentric, visual literacy practices now translated and transformed but not eliminated or replaced by alphabetic literacy.

WORKING THROUGH EPISTEMOLOGICAL DIFFERENCE: TRANSLATION AND TRANSFORMATION AS REACTIONS TO OFFICIAL POLICY

Though it is clear that those involved with official policies of literacy and schooling in indigenous communities in Brazil may be aware of concepts of literacy as social practices, it is not at all clear that they are aware of the epistemologies of perspectivism, predation and vision. From a dominant, nonindigenous, Eurocentric perspective, visual literacy is still seen (Sampson 1990) as being reliant on and having less value than alphabetic literacy. This belief seems to be based, in turn, on the phonocentric presupposition (Derrida 1974) that alphabetic writing, allegedly permitting the reader to recuperate the voice (and, by implication, the intentions/meanings) of the writer, is self-sufficient for freeing the text from its context of origin, as if the text could always mean the same wherever and whenever it is read. In contrast, visual writing, not connected to verbal language, is considered to be dependent on local contextual knowledge in order to be understood and hence is not self-sufficient. However, just as the alleged 'recuperation' of the voice of the writer through the alphabet requires a previous knowledge of a code relating letters to sounds and sounds to words and words to meanings, visual literacy practices, as shared social practices, are also based on codes which relate visual elements in the visual texts to previously conventional-ized meanings. Such graphocentric ideologies of writing inhibit the perception and understanding of the various and complex forms of indigenous visual writing.

In light of the discussion so far of the indigenous epistemologies of vision, perspectivism and predation, the reactions of indigenous communities to the monocultural stance of official policies of literacy and schooling in indigenous communities cannot be seen in the simplistic binary terms of resistance or assimilation. As we have seen, the use of visual nonalphabetic literacy practices continues, informally, outside the school-house, as a repository for unwritten collective indigenous knowledges in the indigenous languages, and as the source of informal indigenous edu-cation and the continuity of indigenous culture. On the other hand, and simultaneously, alphabetic literacy, mainly in Portuguese, is preferred in contexts of formal schoolhouse education where the knowledge of the dominant nonindigenous community is accessed and taught by indigenous teachers from an indigenous perspective. This means that even though the same textbooks may be used as in the nonindigenous mainstream schools, the fact that they are taught by indigenous teachers, with their indigenous epistemologies of vision, perspectivism and predation, may mean that the contents of these mainstream textbooks may probably undergo cultural translation and transformation; the same may also occur with the literacy practices in which these textbooks are used, where, for example, indigenous perspectivism or vision may translate and transform the reading practices to which the alphabetic textbooks are subjected. Examples of such practices are the extensive use of drawing in indigenous schools, remembering that, from the perspective of a visual, nonphonocentric culture, 'drawing' is in fact 'writing.' Thus, instead of or together with the alphabetic writing of narratives or compositions, students produce drawn, colored visual texts.

WHAT DIFFERENCE DOES DIFFERENCE MAKE? LESSONS FOR LITERACY AND GLOBAL CITIZENSHIP EDUCATION

What are the lessons to be learned from the complexities of this situation for literacy and global citizenship education? Considering that the policies of indigenous literacy education in Brazil originated in innumerous ethnographic studies, and that much of present literacy research, especially in the New Literacies framework, is undertaken through ethnographies both in one's own culture—as the work of Barton and Hamilton (2000)—and in other cultures such as the work of Street (1995), it is worth recalling, with Said (2004), the trap of what I have called the monocultural stance mentioned above:

> This is what constitutes resistance: the capacity to differentiate between what is directly given and what can be denied . . . either because the circumstances of the humanist specialist can confine him into a limited space beyond which he dare not venture, or because he is indoctrinated to recognize only that which he was educated to see. Should he accept the predominant horizons and confinements or, as a humanist, attempt to defy them?[5] (Said 2004, 100–101)

Clifford (1994) refers to something similar when he problematizes ethnographic methodology, calling it the danger of "representational authority" of the ethnographer:

> What one sees in a coherent ethnographic account, the imagined construct of the other, is connected in a continuous double structure with what one understands. Strange behavior is portrayed as meaningful within a common network of symbols—a common ground of understandable activity valid for both observer and observed, and by implication, all human groups. Thus ethnography's narrative of specific differences presupposes, and always refers to, an absolute plane of similarity (208–209).

Like what happens in the monocultural trap, Clifford and Said both warn that in encounters with cultural difference one may unconsciously and uncritically assume one's own values as universal and as the yardstick against which difference is perceived and measured. This impedes one from seeing phenomena which are meaningless or do not occur in one's own culture; examples in the discussion above are the issues of vision, perspectivism and predation as perceived in Brazilian indigenous cultures.

In a similar vein, King (1999) also draws attention to the dangers of monocultural presuppositions at play in intercultural encounters, but refers to this, in no uncertain terms, as 'epistemic violence of the colonial encounter'; he pleads for intercultural analysts/ethnographers to "look beyond the Eurocentric foundations of [their] theories and contest the epistemic violence of the colonial encounter. This challenge requires engagement with the knowledge forms and histories of those cultures that have been colonized by the west" (199). Razack (2006) and Britzman (1997) further the argument by claiming that it may not be sufficient to be critically aware of one's own epistemic differences in intercultural encounters such as ethnographic studies:

> Making room for diversity and making diversity a room is not the same as exploring the tangles of implication. For, to explore the tangles of implication requires something more than the desire to know the other's rules and then act accordingly. One is also implicated in one's own response. Implication is not so easily acknowledged because the otherness that implicates the self is beyond rationality and consciousness. We are still grappling with what difference difference makes and with what makes a difference. The question at stake here is not so much that the voices are proliferating but that the rules of discourse and engagement cannot guarantee what they promise to deliver: the desire to know and be known without mediation and the desire to make insight from ignorance and identity. (Britzman 1997, 36)

Spivak (1994), in a similar context, emphasized the need for this perception of being implicated in the unequal violence of encounters with difference and also the need to undo this violence as "unlearning one's privilege."

In his later work, Freire (2005) emphasizes the importance, in epistemological conflicts in dialogue with an Other, of hearing oneself hearing the other. In intercultural contact, on both sides of the divide the interlocutors are both *in* the world and *with* the world. Freire here refers to the fact that as interpreting subjects in an encounter, one brings to the encounter the world or episteme that constitutes one. This occurs to both parties in an encounter. Thus it is not only the 'world' that constitutes one's knowledge that matters, but also the fact that this world is affected and transformed by the 'world' created by the encounter between one's world and that of the Other encountered. Thus Freire draws attention to the need for critical interpretation in such intercultural ethnographic encounters to avoid the monocultural traps of epistemic violence in which one can be easily implicated. Thus in 'reading critically' the difference of an Other, one needs to not only learn to listen but also to listen to oneself listening. Hoy (2005) perhaps sums up the dilemma by calling attention to the importance of learning to listen and reflect on how one understands and perceive how one's meanings may have come from one's social groups and not from oneself. As scholars looking at a community ethnographically, from the outside, in spite of our openness and critical self-consciousness in participant observation, we are still inevitably the products of our own cultures in terms of what we deem 'local,' 'universal,' 'human,' 'authentic.' Do we 'resist,' 'assimilate' or 'translate'?

Back to our dilemma with indigenous literacy practices in Brazil and their discrepancy with official policy: Do we change policy to accompany the changes in practices from a developmental stance to a postcolonial stance? Do we lament the loss of previous, 'authentic' literacy practices and decry the 'disorderly' appearance of new 'hybrid' practices? Do we attempt, with Castro, to perceive the "equivocations" and failures to understand? Or do we read policy documents as Rizvi and Lingard (2010) suggest by 'worlding' the text, unsilencing its silences and revealing the politics of policy production? Perhaps if we first abandon our tendency for universalistic perspectives—the view from nowhere, a risk even when we are doing critical ethnograph—if we learn to unlearn our privilege and listen to ourselves listen, we may then allow ourselves as scholars to engage in (self)critical translation, allowing ourselves to be equivocally translated in the process.

The implications of this for GCE are many. As discussed above, when GCE proposals are manifested in public policy they often tend to be normative, 'inclusive' and universalistic. In the light of the discussion of indigenous perspectivism and literacy education in Brazil, the danger which may arise in such proposals for GCE may be the very normative universalistic basis on which they are constructed, where concepts of knowledge, language, culture, nation and identity may be presumed to be given, homogeneous and unproblematic. Gandhi (2006) calls attention to how often uncritical universalistic concepts of community based on sameness result in the invisibility of anything that is radically different from the implicit and presupposed self. When such communities propose to open themselves to 'others' different from them, the only 'others' that are normally visible are those similar to the presupposed self.

This is reminiscent of Levinas's (1951) indictment of Western philosophy's incapacity to perceive and respect an 'Other' that is radically different, considering this an important ethical issue that needs to be addressed both ethically and pedagogically. He emphasized the need for openness to the Other and the nonreducibility of the difference of the Other to the sameness of the self. From this perspective, proposals and policies of GCE that focus on inclusion need to be critically examined to see if the 'Others' to be 'included' are merely those 'visible' because their differences (in knowledges, languages and culture) are deemed to be minor in relation to the dominant centre; if so, are other Others, whose differences to the dominant self are greater, also 'included' with the same enthusiasm? And does this 'inclusion' entail erasing the difference that equivocally separates, or does it seek to inhabit this very space of insuppressible equivocation?

NOTES

1. Even where discussion documents of international agencies point to notions of literacy as social practice and not as abstract codes leading necessarily to development, official disclaimers precede such documents identifying these opinions as those of their (often academic) proponents and not of the official agency; see, for example, UNESCO Document 1997 Literacy, Education and Social Development.
2. See also Rizvi and Lingard (2010, 61) and Rizvi (2009) for the relevance of Said's theories to contemporary educational policy.
3. For a related discussion of a strategies of anticolonial "relationality" as openness to difference, see Gandhi's (2006) and Butler's (2004) discussion of the "precariousness" of the Other and Derrida's (2000) concept of *philoxenia*, as a hospitable welcoming the unknown Other.
4. For an alternative nonessentialist, nonselfsame logic of relating to otherness, see Levinas (1984), Butler (2004) and Zylinska (2005)
5. My translation from the Portuguese edition.

REFERENCES

Abdi, A. and Shultz, L. (2008) *Educating for Human Rights and Global Citizenship*, Albany, NY: SUNY Press.

Andreotti, V., Jefferess, D., Pashby, K., Rowe, C., Tarc, P. and Taylor, L. (2010) 'Difference and Conflict in Global Citizenship in Higher Education in Canada', *International Journal of Development Education and Global Learning*, 2(3): 5–24.

Barton, D. and Hamilton, L. (2000) Literacy practices, in D. Barton, M. Hamilton, and R. Ivanic (eds.), *Situated literacies: Reading and writing in context*, New York: Routledge, 7–15.

Bhabha, H. (1994) *The Location of Culture*, London: Routledge.

Britzman, D. (1997) 'The Tangles of Implication', in *Qualitative Studies in Education*, 10(1): 31–37.

Butler, J. (2004) *Precarious Life: The Powers of Mourning and Violence*, London: Verso.

Castro, E. V. (2000) 'Cosmological Deixis and Amerindian Perspectivism', in M. Lambek (ed.), *Anthropology of Religion*, Oxford: Blackwell, 306–326.

———. (2004) 'Perspectival Anthropology and the Method of Controlled Equivocation', *Tipiti*, 2(1): 3–22.

———. (2009) *Eduardo Viveiros de Castro: Entrevistas*, Sao Paulo: Azougue.

Cavalcanti, R. A. S. (1999) 'Presente de branco, presente de grego? Escola e escrita em comunidades indígenas do Brasil Central', unpublished MA dissertation, Rio de Janeiro.

Clifford, J. (1994) 'On Ethnographic Allegory', in S. Seidman, *The PostModern Turn: New Perspectives on Social Theory*, Cambridge: Cambridge University Press, 205–228.

Derrida, J. (1974) *Of Grammatology*, Baltimore: Johns Hopkins University Press.

———. (2000) *Of Hospitality*, Stanford, CA: Stanford University Press.

de Souza, L. M. T. M. (2003) 'Voices on Paper: Multimodal Texts and Indigenous Literacy in Brazil', *Social Semiotics* 13(1): 29–42.

———. (2005) 'The Ecology of Writing among the Kashinawa: Indigenous Multimodality in Brazil', in A. Suresh Canagarajah. (ed.), *Reclaiming the Local in Language Policy and Practice*, Mahwah, NJ: Lawrence Erlbaum Associates, 73–95.

———. (2006) 'Entering a Culture Quietly: Writing and Cultural Survival in Indigenous Education in Brazil', in Sinfree Makoni and Alastair Pennycook (eds.), *Disinventing and Reconstituting Languages*, Clevedon, UK: Multilingual Matters, 135–169.

———. (2008) 'Going beyond "Here's a Culture, Here's a Literacy": Vision in Amerindian Literacies', in Prinsloo and Baynham (eds.), 2008, *Literacies, Global and Local*, Amsterdam: John Benjamins, 193–213.

DfID (2002) 'Improving Livelihoods for the Poor: The Role of Literacy', DfID Background Briefing. Retrieved July 2010 from www.dfid.gov.uk/pubs/files/bg-briefing-literacy.pdf.

Fausto, C. (1999) 'Da inimizade: forma e simbolismo da guerra indígena', in A. Novaes (ed.), *A Outra Margem do Ocidente*, Sao Paulo: Companhia das Letras, 251–283.

———. (2000) 'Of Enemies and Pets: Warfare and Shamanism in Amazonia', *American Ethnologist*, 26(4): 933–956.

Freire, P. (2005) *Pedagogia da Tolerancia*, Araraquara, Brazil: UNESP Editora.

Gandhi, L. (2006) *Affective Communities: Anti-Colonial Thought*, Durham, NC: Duke University Press

Grupioni, L. D. (2008) 'Olhar Longe porque o Futuro é Longe: cultura, escola e professores indígenas no Brasil', unpublished PhD thesis, University of São Paulo.

Hoy, D. (2005) *Critical Resistance: From Poststructuralism to Post-Critique*, Cambridge, MA: MIT Press.

Keifenheim, B. (1999) 'Concepts of Perception, Visual Practice and Pattern Art among the Cashinahua Indians (Peruvian Amazon Area)', *Visual Anthropology*, 12: 27–48.

King, R. (1999) 'Orientalism and Religion: Postcolonial Theory', *India and "The Mystic East"*, London: Routledge.

Lagrou, E. M. (1996) 'Xamanismo e Representação entre os Kaxinawá', in E. M. J. Langdon (ed.), *Xamanismo no Brasil: Novas Perspectivas*, Florianópolis, Brazil: Editora da UFSC, 197–231.

Lévi-Strauss, C. (1995) *The Story of Lynx*, Chicago: University of Chicago Press.

Levinas, E. (1951) 'Is Ontology Fundamental? Re-Published', in A. Peperzak, S. Critchley and R. Brenasconi (eds.), *Levinas: Basic Philosophical Writings*, Bloomington: Indiana University Press.

Levinas, E. (1984) Paix et Proximité in Emmanuel Levinas. *Les Cahiers de la nuit surveillée* No. 3, Paris, Editions Verdier, 340.

Oxfam (2006) *Education for Global Citizenship*. Retrieved February 2010 from http://www.oxfam.org.uk/education/gc/files/education_for_global_citizenship_a_guide_for_schools.pdf.

Razack, S. (2006) *Looking White People in the Eye: Gender, Race and Culture in Courtrooms*, Toronto: University of Toronto Press.

Richardson, G. and Blades, D. (2006) *Troubling the Canon of Citizenship Education*, New York: Peter Lang.

Rizvi, F. (2009) 'Towards Cosmopolitan Learning', *Discourse: Studies in the Cultural Politics of Education*, 30(3): 253–268.

Rizvi, F. and Lingard, B. (2010) *Globalizing Education Policy*, London: Routledge.

Said, E. (1983) *The World, the Text and the Critic*, London: Faber & Faber.

———. (1993) *Culture and Imperialism*, New York: Vintage.

———. (2004) *Humanismo e Crítica Democrática*, São Paulo: Companhia das Letras.

Sampson, G. (1990) *Writing Systems: a linguistic introduction*, Stanford: Stanford University Press.

Scaramuzzi, I. (2008) 'De Indios para Indios: a escrita indígena da História', unpublished PhD thesis, University of São Paulo.

Spivak, G. (1995) *The Spivak Reader*, London: Routledge.

Spivak, G. C. (1994). "Bonding in difference," in Alfred Arteaga (ed.), *An other tongue: Nation and ethnicity in the linguistic borderlands*. Durham, NC: Duke University Press, 273–85.

Street, B. (1984) *Literacy in Theory and Practice*, Cambridge: Cambridge University Press.

———. (1995) *Social Literacies*, London: Longman.

Taylor, M. (ed.) (1986) *Deconstruction in Context: Literature and Philosophy*, Chicago: Chicago University Press.

Torres, R. M. (2000) *Literacy for All: A United Nations Literacy Decade* (2003–2012), United Nations Literacy Decade Base Document, UNESCO. Retrieved July 2010 from http://www.fronesis.org/immagen/rmt/documentosrmt/UN_Literacy_Decade.pdf.

UNESCO Institute for Education (1997) *Literacy, Education and Social Development*. Retrieved July 2010 from http://www.unesco.org/education/uie/confintea/pdf/3c.pdf.

Zylinska, J. (2005) *The Ethics of Cultural Studies*, London and New York: Continuum.

Part II

Critiques of GCE Initiatives

Policies, Campaigns, Study Abroad
and Volunteering Schemes

5 Entitled to the World
The Rhetoric of U.S. Global Citizenship Education and Study Abroad

Talya Zemach-Bersin

On July 24, 2008, in the heat of an election cycle that captured the attention of people throughout the world, presidential candidate Barack Obama left the contested grounds of the United States and traveled to the symbolic "Victory Column" in Berlin to deliver a much-anticipated speech titled "A World that Stands as One." The speech was heard not only by the impressive 200,000 people in attendance, but was broadcast on all major TV news networks in the United States. Fox News (2008) reported that while the content of Barack Obama's speech may have captured the attention of Germans, it was a mere one sentence in the introduction of the speech that was "enough to catch attention back home" (para.1). Indeed, following the speech, news reports, headlines and the debates of political pundits and U.S. citizens alike focused primarily on how Barack Obama chose to introduce himself at the tiergarden rally: "Tonight, I speak to you not as a candidate for President," Obama (2008) had begun, "but as a citizen—a proud citizen of the United states, and a fellow citizen of the world." In many ways, the speech that followed did not stray far from its beginnings. Obama made repeated appeals to vague transnational ideals such as "common security," "common humanity," "shared sacrifice" and "shared destiny." New York Times op-ed columnist David Brooks (2008) aptly noted that Obama used the theme of walls coming down eleven times in the speech (para. 4). "No doubt there will be differences," Obama acquiesced, but because we live in a world in which challenges such as global warming, trade, AIDS and terrorism are not confined to national borders, "the burdens of global citizenship continue to bind us together." "This is the moment," Obama urgently sounded at the climax of the speech, "to stand as one."

Under the headline "Obama Casts Self as World Citizen, but Will It Play in America?" Fox news portrayed Obama's claim to world citizenship as a dramatic contrast to John McCain's campaign promise of "Country First." "While Barack Obama took a premature victory lap today in the heart of Berlin, proclaiming himself a 'citizen of the world' " McCain spokesman Tucker Bounds told Fox News (2008), "John McCain has dedicated his life to serving, improving and protecting America" (para. 10). Frank J. Gaffney Jr. (2008), assistant secretary of Defense for international security under the Reagan administration, joined the fray, charging that "global citizenship amounts to a code for subordinating American interests" (para. 6). Obama's vision of world citizenship, Gaffney laments, "could prove fatal to our sovereignty and constitutional form of government" (para. 11). The real choice for voters, he concludes, is between "a global citizen in the white house or a president of, by, and for the American people" (para. 13). Gaffney implies that it is not possible for a "world citizen" to be a true American. Similarly, an editorial in the *New York Sun* jousted, "We'd settle for a president who is a citizen of America, thank you very much" (para. 3). After Obama's speech in Germany, *Sun* correspondent Russell Berman (2008) explained that Republicans "are banking on a backlash at home" (para. 1).

Indeed, some liberals worried that Obama's "world citizen" rhetoric was "too post nationalist for the typical American swing-voter" (Scheiber 2008, para. 8). Obama supporters were anxious that their candidate had made a "huge mistake" by failing to present himself as "unambiguously nationalistic" (Comment Board 2008, para. 18). Concerned Democrats rushed to their candidate's defense, quickly pointing out that Obama had not introduced himself merely as a citizen of the world, but also as "a proud citizen of the United States." Writing for *The New Republic*, Noam Scheiber commented that the speech was "the exact right combination of love for America and plea for international cooperation." Obama supporters vociferously fought against the implication that as a world citizen, Obama could be expected to care less about America and American interests abroad than John McCain and his "country first" promise. When David Brooks (2008) lambasted Barack Obama's vision of world citizenship as merely a "saccharine show for the rock star masses" (para. 15), *The New York Times* published a slew of letters to the editor disagreeing vehemently with Brooks's critique (2008). One concerned reader charged that Brooks's pessimistic commentary "reveals just how far our national mind-set has sunk into the dark dichotomies" of "us" versus "them" (para. 1). Another reader lauded Obama for refusing to "cower to history, or to our traditional limitations" (para. 6). Many Americans argued that Obama's optimistic worldview of nations coming together cooperatively under what he called "the burdens of Global Citizenship" to combat shared problems is not "just Disney," as Brooks would have it, but the necessary politics for the future of an intimately interconnected world.

The ever-present tensions between national and global citizenship, between patriotism and solidarity with humankind, between bounded national identities and transnational affiliations, extend beyond political party lines and questions of who should be president of the U.S.. According to philosopher Joshua Cohen (2002), the conflict is "practical as well as theoretical, with important implications for contemporary debate about protectionism, immigration, human rights, foreign intervention, development assistance, and what we should teach in our schools" (viii). The debate that gathered in the aftermath of then presidential hopeful Barack Obama's speech is representative of the ways in which claims to global and national citizenship are widely imagined as irreconcilable and mutually exclusive. In this chapter I argue just the opposite; that the idea of global citizenship is not fundamentally in opposition to U.S.-American nationalism, but can be imagined instead in cooperation and conjunction with the priorities and concerns of powerful and expansionist nation-states. Uncritical and celebratory articulations of global citizenship potentially legitimize, enact and expand, rather than mitigate, the unfettered international power of the U.S.

One critical site in which U.S. nationalism and the rhetoric of global citizenship have a well-developed symbiotic relationship is the field of institutionalized international education for U.S. undergraduates. Through textual analysis of the widespread uses of global citizenship rhetoric in the U.S. commercial, institutional and governmental discourses of study abroad, it becomes clear that claims to global citizenship are often serviced in the interest of the nation. This is no minor contention, as the number of U.S. students studying abroad each year has more than quadrupled over the past two decades (Institute of International Education 2009). Institutions of higher learning increasingly describe "international experience" as a key component of undergraduate education, and more students study abroad in more places, with a greater variety of programs, than ever before. Among the privileged minority for whom travel is both institutionally accessible and financially feasible, spending time studying in a foreign country has become something of a rite of passage. As Jane Gordon announced in the *New York Times* (Gordon 2006), many "students now believe that studying abroad is an entitlement" (para. 6).

While scholars have subjected many forms of border-crossing travel to rigorous academic analysis, study abroad as a technology of knowledge production, citizenship education and cultural diplomacy has enjoyed a profoundly uncontested status. The vague language of "international understanding" and "cultural exchange" has allowed study abroad to remain protectively depoliticized and peripheral to cultural studies of U.S. empire. For nearly one hundred years, the common cause of promoting student travel has united U.S.-American progressive educators and academics, conservative policymakers, restless students, supportive families, business interests, religious organizations, leftist internationalists and the federal government in what could be termed an international education consensus. Regardless of changing rationales over time and a range of diversely articulated interests in any one moment, the impact of such a consensus has been to not only shield the politics of study abroad from sustained academic critique, but to mystify, dehistoricize, depoliticize, aestheticize and individualize the experience that is today served up to an ever-growing number of U.S. undergraduates. For many of these students, the political implications of their decision to spend a semester abroad are painted over by an entirely unchallenged discourse of personal growth, adventure, career advancement, multiculturalism and global citizenship. It is pressing, then, that educators and students together explore the historical and cultural politics of study abroad, so that the very attempt to imagine a more just and communicative world might challenge, rather than reproduce, the violences of empire and inequality.

Since its early formations in the interwar period, institutionalized U.S. American student travel has been a politically significant enterprise that reflects, reproduces, and participates in geopolitical arrangements and asymmetrical systems of power. Study abroad for academic credit began to gain legitimacy in the interwar period, and organizations such as the Institute of International Travel (IIE est. 1919), and the Experiment in International Living (est. 1932) sought to link student travel to the creation of a more peaceful world and understanding citizenry. In the aftermath of World War Two, and increasingly as the Cold War progressed, the U.S. government came to rely on students as "goodwill ambassadors," combating the spread of communism by exporting the desirability of the American way through their travels. Federal policies, including the Fulbright Act of 1946, the Smith-Mundt Act of 1948, The National Defense of Education Act of 1958, the Peace Corps of 1961, the International Education Act of 1966, the National Security Education Act of 1991 and more recently the Paul Simon Act of 2007, together illustrate not only the continuous politicization of student travel and international education, but the shifting meaning of study abroad in relation to twentieth-century geopolitics and various articulations of the "national interest."

The meaning-making activity of student travel has helped to frame deeply enmeshed ideas about nationality and worldliness throughout the twentieth century, as plural and often seemingly contradictory interests converge over the project of training privileged U.S. undergraduates in how to think about, care about, interact with, and imagine themselves in relation to, "the world." This chapter examines one particular contemporary strain of international education ideology: a powerful rationale that links the production of U.S.-American global citizens to the fashioning and maintenance of U.S. military, economic and cultural supremacy throughout the world in an age of globalization. Much of this argument hinges on the idea that the conditions of globalization present challenges to which educational institutions must respond. Despite the fact that the U.S. has largely been the "beneficiary and enforcer of this new world order" (Loomba 2005, 221), Americans have voiced a rising concern that globalization may be a threat to U.S. global hegemony and supremacy. Not only is the U.S. imagined to be increasingly vulnerable to foreign attack, but "anti-Americanism" is thought to be more prolific than ever before; nations such as China and India appear to be gaining international and economic strength; and the American citizenry is often declared fatally incompetent for its widespread ignorance of geography, international politics, foreign languages and cultural differences. U.S.-initiated study abroad is discussed today within a context of both anxiety about, and celebration of, global interconnectedness. While institutions of higher education are busy internationalizing their curriculums to meet the demanding cultural and economic conditions of globalization and endorsing study abroad under the depoliticized rhetoric of producing "global citizens," a long-held assumption that U.S. students who study abroad will actively endorse and advance U.S. interests (both 'abroad' and when back 'home') has gripped the hopes and imaginations of the U.S. government and nongovernmental organizations alike. Within this discourse, global citizens are described as extracting the resources necessary for the maintenance of U.S. power while simultaneously functioning as diplomatic envoys spreading pro-U.S. sentiment throughout the world. While the internationalization of higher education has long been connected to foreign-policy aims, study abroad today is articulated as a necessary national response to a new cultural, political and economic threat called "globalization."

"Like it or not," the American Council on Education (ACE) (2002) announced, "Americans are connected with people the world over" (7). ACE depicts a complex and challenging situation caused by "the rapid movement of people, goods, financial transactions, and ideas." The U.S. is seen as "unready," lacking the required "global competence of our people" to cope with such conditions (7). In this view, globalization is a threat to the United States largely because American citizens do not know how to succeed in a globalized world. ACE argues that without the cross-cultural skills needed to stay on top, Americans are a threat to the success and viability of their own country. Displaying a similar logic, The Lincoln Commission (2005), a federally appointed council of politicians and educators dedicated to promoting study abroad, gravely avers that because the U.S. is not globally competent, it "is not as well equipped to exercise its leadership role as it could be. The situation is dangerous. It threatens our capacity to defend our values. Above all, it threatens the national interest" (iii, 8). The Lincoln Commission indicates that unless the U.S. is in a position to generate and sustain international control and supremacy, the welfare of the nation is threatened. Educators and politicians have announced that an internationally ignorant citizenry is a risk the U.S. cannot afford to take in the globalized age. "What Nations don't know can hurt them," the Lincoln Commission (2005) warns; "the stakes involved in study abroad are that simple, that straightforward, and that important" (8).

Two months after the World Trade Center attacks of September 11, 2001, then President Bush (2001) released a statement in honor of International Education Week, sponsored by the U.S. Department of Education and the Department of State, in which he explained, "America's leadership and national security rest on our commitment to educate and prepare our youth for active engagement in the international community" (para. 4).

International education, President Bush argued, is necessary for the continuing prosperity, power and security of the U.S. ACE echoes President Bush's sentiments by asserting that study abroad produces the global competency necessary for national security. Using hyperbolic language that capitalizes on the trauma of 9/11, ACE (2002) writes, "The tragic events of September 11, 2001 crystallized in a single, terrible moment, the challenges of globalization and the importance of international research and education to our national security" (7). Surely current geopolitics and cultural conditions do require new educational approaches from higher education, yet within this nationalist discourse, education is serviced in the name of the very ideologies of national global supremacy that have participated in the construction of this violent and unequal world. When the urgency of the situation established this way, study abroad emerges as a solution to particular challenges of the globalized world *for the nation-state*, expected to buttress America's position of global power, advance economic interests and defend homeland security by producing a new generation of globally competent Americans.

The federal government and institutions of higher education alike have warmly lauded this cry for international education. The U.S. Senate declared 2006 the "Year of Study Abroad" on the grounds that "the security, stability, and economic vitality of the United States in an increasingly complex global age depend largely upon having a globally competent citizenry" (United States Senate 2005, para. 7). Senate resolution 308 affirms the belief that it is the responsibility of "the educational systems of the United States" to ensure, through the internationalization of education, "that the citizens of the United States are globally literate" (para. 1). As a bipartisan congressional effort, the Lincoln Commission (2005) established the goal of sending one million U.S. undergraduates abroad annually by the year 2017 "to study other lands, languages, and cultures" (iii). Institutions of higher education are rising to the challenge, "internationalizing" their campuses in part by increasing the accessibility and variety of study-abroad programs for their students. Study abroad has become more prominent and integrated into American higher education than ever before. Universities throughout the country are turning their attention to the values of "global citizenship education" and the development of "cross-culturally competent" and "globally literate" students.

The institutional discourse of international education found in the mission statements of colleges, universities and programs throughout the U.S. frequently employ the vague and depoliticized rhetoric of "global citizenship" to describe the goals of study abroad. Wesleyan University's Office of International Studies (2007) explains that study abroad is "integral to the University's efforts to internationalize the curriculum and prepare students for global citizenship" (para. 1). The president of Ithaca College has gone so far as to announce the school itself as "an innovative institutional global citizen" (Williams 2007, para. 9). Schools such as Macalester

College, Haverford College, Lehigh University, Drake University and Elizabethtown College have even established special centers and institutions for global citizenship education on their campuses. Even the theme of the U.S. Department of State's International Education Week 2007 was dedicated to "fostering global citizenship" (U.S. Department of State and U.S. Department of Education, 2007). NAFSA (2009), the National Association of International Educators, recently described the goal of international education as establishing the "mantle of global citizenship" as a "shared national compass" (2). From Temple University's Office of International Programs' (n.d.) mission statement "Prepare yourself to be a global citizen. Study abroad" (para. 2) to Colgate University Abroad's (2006) exclamatory statement "Become a global citizen and study abroad!" (para. 1), the rhetoric of global citizenship abounds.[1]

The romantic ideal of becoming a cosmopolitan citizen of the world is ancient and well established in Western moral and Enlightenment philosophy. But today's study-abroad discourse implements the idea of world citizenship in a way that veers from a philosophical tradition emphasizing the importance of transcendent moral concern. Instead of signifying a philosophical standpoint, global citizenship is frequently described as simply reflecting the "reality" of globalization. Globalization enthusiasts often describe the process of globalization as having created a deterritorialized and "seamlessly wired global village" (Shohat and Stam 1996, 146), or what Kwame Anthony Appiah (2006) calls a "global tribe" (xiii). Bruce Robbins (1999) insists on the recognition of actually and already existing everyday cosmopolitanisms forged by immigrants, diasporic communities, transnational religions, environmentalist, feminist and international workers' movements. Believing that boundaries and borders are weakened by the rapid mobility of people, ideas, technology, goods and media, some Americans conclude that global citizenship is not just the key to a peaceful and prosperous future but is an undeniable reflection of current affairs. Nicole Price Fasig (2007), editor of *Abroad View: The Global Education Magazine for Students*, writes, "The days of thinking of ourselves as Californians, as Midwesterners, as Americans, are drawing to a close" (6). The ubiquity of words like *globalization, transnationalism,* and *postnationalism* seem to challenge the status of the nation as a "viable economic unit, a politically sovereign territory, and a bounded cultural sphere" (Cheah 1998, 22). Increased communication across cultures, nations and borders has led to fantasies of a deterritorialized global community often evoked by the privileged of the "developed" world, who have access to internationalized forms of communication, media, mobility and cross-cultural consumption.

In *Imagined Communities,* Benedict Anderson (1996) explains that nationalism depends on the narrative construction of imagined political identities. Anderson understands the nation as an imagined brotherhood, a collective kinship that constructs an "us" and a "we," to which citizens belong and owe protection and loyalty. The building blocks of national identity are often mythologies or stories of a shared history and experience. If Anderson is correct in highlighting the importance of print culture in establishing nationalism and emotional connections to the nation, then might it be possible that globalized print cultures and transnational media make for feelings of global belongingness as opposed to national boundedness? Theorists such as Arjun Appadurai (1996) have ventured to argue that globalized media and mobility have provided people with the imaginative building blocks of a postnational political world. It is not enough, however, to identify that both nationalism and feelings of global solidarity are socially and historically constructed. Critics of nationalism have critiqued the ways in which nationalism is narrated in accordance with political agendas and dictated within structures of power. "National mythologies," write Stam and Shohat (2007), "provide warm and fuzzy fables of unity to 'cover over' what are actually extremely conflictual histories" (8) in an effort to construct a strategic understanding of shared commonality. Timothy Brennan (1990) similarly explains, "Nations . . . are imaginary constructs that depend for their existence on an apparatus of cultural fictions" (49). The cultural fiction of global citizenship can similarly be theorized as a "warm and fuzzy" fable, a feint of universality and belonging that often inadvertently obscures the severe inequalities, injustices and acts of violent exploitation that persist in the globalized age.

The interests of the nation are frequently and strategically executed under the rhetoric of universality, human rights and global citizenship. The U.S. in particular has a long history of describing itself in universalized terms in such a way as to legitimize foreign expansion and interventionist foreign policy (Hunt 1987). Pheng Cheah (1998) notes that "even official U.S. nationalism feels the need to put on nonnational costume now and then" in an effort to gain the power that comes with claims to cosmopolitanism or universality (20). Laying claim to a depoliticized universality is a powerful political tool, one particularly valuable to a nation whose international reputation is, like that of America, far from benign. While the rhetoric of global citizenship displays what Bruce Robbins (1999) describes as "morals and sentiments rather than agents and politics" (18), American students who study abroad cannot be removed from the political and national contexts from which they come. Global citizenship, to use Timothy Brennan's (2001) contention, is "a discourse of the universal that is inherently local—a locality that is always surreptitiously imperial" (81).

Like nations and national citizenship, global citizenship is not a predetermined or preexisting constant. Citizenship is a social construction strategically crafted and historically formed. Although people may be born into a particular institution of citizenship, the process of becoming a citizen goes beyond a birthright claim. In "Admission to Citizenship," Herman R. van Gunsteren (1988) identifies knowledge, defined as including "communicative competence, culture, [and] information" (733), as a condition for citizenship. Shared knowledge of culture, language and history creates a sense of community and belonging that has often been established as a prerequisite to citizenship. International educators likewise establish knowledge of another place, gained through a study-abroad experience, as a prerequisite for attaining the privilege of global citizenship. Despite the fantasy of the global village, individuals are not global citizens simply by virtue of living on planet Earth. There is no law of *Jus Soli* (birthright citizenship) when it comes to global citizenship. Rather, students must be constructed as global citizens through privileged and unequally distributed access to international education.

Many view it as the responsibility of educational institutions to produce competent citizens and to instill in them a sense of national belonging, or, in the case of global citizenship, a sense of naturalized access to the world. Ian Lister (1995) writes that since the nineteenth century,

> The school promoted a sense of nationhood through its rituals (such as flag ceremonies, national days, and even the layout of the world map on the classroom wall) and through its curriculum, which stressed the national language, the national literature, and the national history, in which history was related as the story of the making of the nation. (110–111)

Education works to socialize students into citizenship, transmitting particular worldviews and instilling in them knowledge of, and obedience to, cultural beliefs and practices. Education, then, is an assimilative force, attempting to construct—or imagine—shared understandings of national citizenship as determined by those in power. School systems develop loyalty to the nation and standardize education in an effort to produce the desired ideal of national citizens. Similarly, study-abroad programs and institutions of higher education socialize students into a national ideal of global citizenship.

The global-citizen license is granted to study-abroad students by institutions of higher education. Thus, the ability to become a global citizen is dependent on the extent to which an individual is able to attain international knowledge through preapproved and closely monitored educational channels that are institutionalized in the U.S. Furthermore, the idea that Americans are not already, but must be transformed into, individuals with international knowledge and cross-cultural skills renders invisible those Americans who have already developed such skills and experiences as an everyday necessity, such as immigrants, those with multicultural backgrounds, or the many Americans who do not have membership in dominant cultures and thus have no choice but to be "cross-culturally literate" on a daily basis. By describing Americans as a group lacking the ability to engage effectively with difference, both the invisibility and normativity of whiteness and class privilege are assumed. The study-abroad discourse of global citizenship privileges the attainment of particular forms of knowledge that are dependent on mobility, education, economic comfort and sociopolitical freedoms. Despite its ring of universal inclusiveness, global citizenship is an identity available and granted to some but not to others.

The relative privilege necessary for attaining institutionally sanctioned global citizenship is explicit in current statistics, which show that particular demographic groups study abroad far more than others.[2] Despite the fact that nearly 40 percent of all U.S. undergraduates attend community colleges, these students account for just 2.5 percent of those studying abroad (Lincoln Commission 2005, 15). Most students who study abroad are enrolled in liberal-arts colleges, and Lincoln Commission research shows that "just 108 institutions (out of over 4,200 American colleges and universities) account for 50 percent of all the students abroad" (ibid.). Moreover, students of color are significantly underrepresented in study-abroad programs (17). Data from the 2008–2009 academic year show that while African American students make up 13.5 percent of total student enrollment in higher education, only 4.2 percent of students who study abroad are placed in the "Black-non-Hispanic" category. Similarly, only 6 percent of those who study abroad are identified as Hispanic/Latino American, while that same group constitutes 11.9 percent of total student enrollment in U.S. educational institutions. Meanwhile, Caucasian students are overrepresented in study-abroad enrollment, constituting 80.5 percent of students who study abroad and making up 63.3 percent of postsecondary enrollment (Institute of International Education 2010).

Far from embodying universality, individuals are constructed into global citizens through their ability to access elite modes of attaining citizenship. In "Broken Promises," Arjun Appadurai (2002) criticizes the "international community" as "less a community than a club for the world's wealthiest nations" (43). Despite its "nonnational costume," the discourse of global citizenship does not, Himadeep Muppidi (2004) might say, "speak for 'citizens of the world, members of the human community' who are not Americans" (102, 73). The U.S. ideal of global citizenship is not directed in the study-abroad discourse to anyone other than Americans (and is only available to a small percentage), producing an understanding of the global that is bound primarily to elite understandings and the advancement of the U.S. "As a result," writes Muppidi (2004), "the global is consistently colonized by the American national" (74). Furthermore, despite a glaring lack of institutional legitimacy, the use of the term *citizen* itself implies certain rights, privileges and powers. Claiming global citizenship in the context of American students studying abroad can be read as representative of long-standing notions of U.S. entitlement and universality that have functioned hand in hand with assertions of power and control. Constructed as such, the American global citizen can refuse to be limited by nation-state borders. The global citizen is encouraged to assume the right to travel unhindered, to penetrate cultures without the hassle of boundaries, to extend his or her rights of citizenship transnationally and to unabashedly profit from this unequal global arrangement. While global citizenship is described in the cosmopolitan spirit of commonality and shared experience, it is actually an identity deeply invested in the advancement and development of American power and success.

Ania Loomba (2005) defines colonialism as a system under which "[i]n whichever direction human beings and materials traveled, the profits always flowed back into the so-called 'mother country' " (9). The metropolis extracting resources from the periphery has been used as a framework for understanding imperialism and the capitalist world system. Through study abroad, global citizens are expected to enact a similar process by harvesting the resource of international knowledge to strengthen and benefit America. In the case of a nationalist study-abroad ideology, knowledge is closely linked to power. ACE (2002) states that study-abroad programs "produce the core knowledge experts need for national security, economic competitiveness, and U.S. foreign policy leadership" (15). According to this logic, knowledge extracted through study abroad can move beyond the individual student and into the realm of national profit. As former U.S. Secretary of Education Margaret Spellings (2007) explains, "International education enlarges our perspective, as individuals and as a nation" (para. 4). Knowledge acquired by global citizens is expected to make the world beyond U.S. borders legible, readable, knowable and therefore both consumable and controllable. That which is exposed and understood through the acquisition of knowledge is no longer urgently perceived of as a mysterious threat to U.S. international strength and can be inserted and incorporated into national projects.

Increasing the "global competency" and "global literacy" (Lincoln Commission 2005, ix) of the U.S. citizenry is a project in the production of knowledge. By studying the context in which knowledge is produced, the political implications of such knowledge can be brought into view. In *Orientalism*, Edward Said (1979) addresses the relationship between academia and political projects of power. He identifies "the extent to which 'knowledge' about 'the Orient' . . . was an ideological accompaniment of colonial 'power' " (Loomba 2005, 42). Orientalism, Said (1979) explains,

> can be discussed and analyzed as the corporate institution for dealing with the Orient—dealing with it by making statements about it, authorizing views of it, describing it, by teaching it, settling it, ruling over it; in short, Orientalism is a Western style for dominating, restructuring, and having authority over the Orient. (3)

Educational institutions often enact such a task, as intellectuals are in the socially sanctioned position of claiming authority to produce knowledge about and over the Other. Mimicking the logic of Orientalism, ACE recognizes study abroad as a tool for producing knowledge connected to national, political and economic power. The group's executive summary states: "The United States must invest in an educational infrastructure [identified as study-abroad programs] that produces knowledge of language and cultures . . . to meet the needs of government agencies, the private sector, and education itself" (ACE 2002, 7). Ricardo Salvatore (1998) calls such quests the "enterprise of knowledge," a project often undertaken by intellectuals that is key to the construction of "arguments of economic interest, benevolence, moral reform, knowledge, and the 'national interest' " of empire (72).

Knowledge and global competency are continuously articulated within the discourse of study abroad as essential to U.S. "national interest" in world leadership, homeland security, economic achievements and foreign-policy success. Ulf Hannerz (1996) explains the relationship between knowledge and control, writing, "[c]ompetence with regard to alien cultures itself entails a sense of mastery, as an aspect of the self. One's understandings have expanded, a little more of the world is somehow under control" (103). The definition of global competency provided by ACE (2002) connects competency to leadership and power:

> Global competency is a broad term . . . It involves, among other things, foreign language proficiency and an ability to function effectively in other cultural environments and value systems, whether conducting business, implementing international development projects, or carrying out diplomatic missions. (7)

This definition of global competency highlights the importance of international education and its relationship to producing the knowledge systems that are expected to establish and maintain U.S. power, unhindered mobility and international strength. To "function effectively" here means the ability to fulfill one's desires, to achieve one's goals without the onerous limitations and barriers of cultural difference.

Study-abroad students join their historical predecessors: the ranks of missionaries, explorers, anthropologists and humanitarian aid workers who have served as "goodwill ambassadors," promoting the soft-power interests of the metropolis. The two-way flow of strategic information conducted by global citizens is illustrated by an article published by the *Online NewsHour* of PBS, which alerts the public to a "growing class of global citizens—voracious learners, cultural sponges, and unassuming ambassadors—who have chosen to take international detours for study, work and fun" (Wasey 2006, para. 6). PBS describes students as "voracious learners," alluding to the conviction with which global citizens produce knowledge, but also refers to students as "cultural sponges," open and passive vessels for resource extraction and transportation. Simultaneously, global citizens are identified in this article as "unassuming ambassadors," gently veiled champions of American diplomacy. In specific—although ultimately unpredictable—ways, U.S. students studying abroad are expected to change the beliefs of hosts throughout the globe.

A nationalist discourse of study abroad charges that student travelers ought to "promote knowledge and understanding of the United States in other countries" (ACE 2002, 19) that will better position the U.S. for international success. According to the U.S. Senate (2005), "Educating students internationally is an important way to share the values of the United States [and] to create goodwill for the United States around the world" (para. 2). Students studying abroad are often referred to as global ambassadors, described as one of America's most valuable foreign-policy assets. John O'Harney (2006), editor of *Connection: The Journal of the New England Board of Higher Education*, writes, "There's a better way to spread democracy around the world . . . and boost America's economic competitiveness at the same time" (5). Study-abroad goodwill ambassadors do not fight on battlefields, O'Harney notes, but they can fight for America abroad. As "unassuming ambassadors," O'Harney expects study-abroad students to be charming young people who make friends abroad and promote goodwill toward their home country through these relationships and patronages. Study-abroad students are assumed to actively combat anti-Americanism, disabusing foreign "natives" of their misconceptions and prejudices toward the U.S.

U.S. international strength is greatly aided by foreign consent and approval that may reduce resistance to the global extension of U.S. power. Many on all sides of the political spectrum have recently pointed out that resentment toward the U.S. "has become virtually universal" (Stam and Shohat 2007, xi). Stam and Shohat (2007) explain that while discussions of anti-Americanism "largely involved the Arab/Muslim world, recent times have seen a growing rift between the United States and its allies" (ibid.). Indeed, Stam and Shohat apprise, "The majorities in most countries in Europe, Asia, Africa and Latin America oppose American foreign policy and the U.S. role as self-appointed global 'leader' " (xiv). Joseph Nye (2007), the father of "soft-power" theory, argues that study abroad is essential to the replenishment of international pro-American sentiment that "has diminished in recent years" (4). Nye explains that that soft power, defined as the ability to "attract followers through the strength of a country's values and culture," decreases resistance to U.S. foreign policy and reduces the need for military action (ibid.). Manufacturing consent is indispensable to the global reach of the U.S. "The first task of Empire," write Michael Hardt and Antonio Negri (2000), "is to enlarge the realm of the consensuses that support its own power" (15). The nationalist discourse of study abroad asserts that American students are dispatched to become global citizens in an effort to produce a favorable climate for the globally encompassing extension of American power by spreading pro-U.S. values and ideals abroad, displaying for the world the innocence, youth and good-will of the nation.

A *Washington Post* editorial by foreign correspondent David Ignatius (2005) titled "Replant the American Dream" exemplifies the elements of cultural imperialism found in the discourse of study abroad. "America isn't just disliked or feared overseas—it's reviled," Ignatius explains, and so "[t]he United States must begin to replenish this stock of sup-port for America in the world" (A37). Ignatius alleges that the task of creating goodwill toward the U.S. falls "to the American public. It's a job that involves traveling, sharing, living our values, and encouraging our children to learn foreign languages and work and study abroad" (ibid.). Ignatius calls on students to "[r]eplant the American Dream" abroad. According to such a discourse, the very foreign policy that has inspired critiques of U.S. international behavior is allowed to persevere and perhaps escalate while students "soften" opposition through their travels, foster goodwill and weaken resistance to American economic, cultural and political advancements. Additionally, global citizens are positioned as smoke screens to the expansion of U.S. imperialism and military aggression. By lending a strategically friendly face to the vio-lence and arrogance of American foreign policy, study-abroad students are expected to distract from politics while simultaneously fortifying U.S. international power.

This specific discourse of study abroad appropriates the global to service the interests of the U.S. by renaming nationalistic projects with the rhetoric of "global understanding," "international education" and "global citizenship." The "globe" is something to be consumed, a com-modity that the privileged American student has the unchallenged and unquestioned right to obtain as an entitled citizen of the world. As Michael Byers (2005) asserts, "Words—and our choice of words—matter. Words provoke and shape social, political, and economic change" (para. 2). But language is also flexible, open to multiple meanings and vulnerable to counterhegemonic resistance and reclamation. Byers urges students to reclaim global citizenship from the likes of George W. Bush and cor-porate advertisers, to employ the term in such a way as to challenge the authority of existing power structures. Vanessa Andreotti (2010) has similarly made the case for a critical global citizenship education that would function as a decolonizing force, providing historical analysis of global inequalities and helping students develop the skills for "collab-orative but un-coercive" engagement with "complex, diverse, changing, uncertain and deeply unequal" (246) societies. Despite the strength of an international education consensus that has brought together a broad array of educators, politicians and professionals in common cause, the demands of Byers and Andreotti for a critical global citizenship educa-tion are fundamentally at odds with the sentiments of a discourse that prioritizes study abroad as necessary for economic competitiveness, national security and national greatness.

Global citizenship is not a neutral, new, universal or apolitical term. We cannot afford to assume that global citizenship is inherently benevolent or morally superior to national identification. The participation of institutions of higher education in vague and uncritical discourses of global citizenship raises serious concerns about the role of education in an interconnected and unequal world. Loomba (2005) writes, "[i]f universities are to remain sites of dissent and free intellectual inquiry, if scholarship is not to be at the service of American or any other power, critiques of past and ongoing empires are going to be more necessary than ever" (228). To do so, American institutions and American students must resist the urge to recede into an alluring yet erroneous discourse of the global. "Americans' most dangerous quality," writes Jedediah Purdy (2003), "is our belief in our own universality and innocence" (62). The nationalist discourse of study abroad embodies both such beliefs, allowing students to become global citizens while perpetuating systems of power and inequality under the rhetoric of universality and innocence. When presidential hopeful Obama introduced himself to the world as "a proud citizen of the United states, and a fellow citizen of the world," he was being perhaps less contradictory and unusual than both his supporters and critics believed. Those on the left were too quick to assume that a citizen of the world president was a harbinger of a new era, while those on the right were mistaken to expect that a citizen of the world would prioritize the needs of foreign countries over the U.S. Global citizenship, I have argued, is often imagined and described in explicitly nationalist terms. These terms draw from and perpetuate, rather than challenge or critique, fantasies of U.S. supremacy, entitlement, and global expansion. If global citizenship education is to be "reclaimed," as Byers suggests, it will require attention to the historical and cultural politics of global citizenship education, an ongoing process of identifying the possible ways in which claiming global citizenship is not an alternative to empire, but a form *of* empire. It is only by doing so that envisioning and making a different kind of world will become possible.

NOTES

1. Despite the frequency with which the term *global citizenship* is implemented in conversations about international education, rarely is a concrete definition presented or explored. Typically, the term is employed as a vague and flexible signifier of a kind of cosmopolitan global-mindedness that might involve empathy, knowledge and action.
2. One group that is overrepresented in study abroad is women. Nearly two-thirds of study abroad participants are female and only one-third is male. It is likely that this has more to do with academic interest, opportunity, gendered cultural assumptions and expectations and programs offered rather than relative levels of gendered privilege.

REFERENCES

American Council on Education (2002) *Beyond September 11: A Comprehensive National Policy on International Education*, Washington, DC: American Council on Education.

Andreotti, V. (2010) 'Postcolonial and Postcritical Global Citizenship Education', in G. Elliott, C. Fourali and S. Issler (eds.), *Education for Social Change*, London: Continuum, 223–245.

Anderson, B. (1996) *Imagined Communities: Reflections on the Origins and Spread of Nationalism*, revised edition, London: Verso.

Appadurai, A. (1996) *Modernity at Large: Cultural Dimensions of Globalization*, Minneapolis and London: University of Minnesota Press.

———. (2002) 'Broken Promises', *Foreign Policy*, 132: 41–44.

Appiah, K. A. (2006) *Cosmopolitanism: Ethics in a World of Strangers*, New York: W.W. Norton & Company.

Berman, R. 'McCain Camp Hopes for Backlash' (2008, July 25) *New York Sun*, http://www.nysun.com/national/mccain-camp-hopes-for-backlash/82626 (accessed December 16, 2008).

Brennan, T. (1990) 'The National Longing for Form', in H. Bhabha (ed.), *Nation and Narration*, London and New York: Routledge.

———. (2001) Cosmopolitanism and Internationalism, *New Left Review*, 7: 75–84.

Brooks, D. "Playing Innocent Abroad" (2008, July 25) *New York Times*, http://www.nytimes.com/2008/07/25/opinion/25brooks.html?ref=todayspaper (accessed).

Bush, G. (2001) International Education Week, http://exchanges.state.gov/iew2001/message.htm (accessed October 31, 2007).

Byers, M. (2005) "Are You a 'Global Citizen'?" *The Tyee: B.C.'s Home for News, Culture and Solutions*, http://thetyee.ca/views/2005/10/05/globalcitizen (accessed February 10, 2011).

Cheah, P. (1998) 'The Cosmopolitical—Today', in p. Cheah and B. Robbins (eds.), *Cosmopolitics: Thinking and Feeling beyond the Nation*, Minneapolis: University of Minnesota Press, 20–41.

Cohen, J. (2002) 'Editor's Preface', in *For Love of Country*, Boston: Beacon Press, viii.

Colgate University Abroad (2006) *About Colgate.* http://www.colgate.edu/DesktopDefault1.aspx?tabid=987&pgID=103 (accessed October 30, 2007).

Comment Board, "Obama's Berlin Speech." (2008, July 24) *The New* Republic, http://blogs.tnr.com/tnr/blogs/the_stump/archive/2008/07/24/obama-s-berlin-speech.aspx (accessed December 1, 2008).

Editorial, "Citizen of the World?" (2008, July 25) *New York Sun*, http://www.nysun.com/editorials/citizen-of-the-world/82644/ (accessed December 16, 2008).

Fasig, N. P. (2007) 'Thinking Globally', *Abroad View* 9(2): 6–12.

Fox News (2008) "Obama Casts Self as World Citizen, But Will it Play in America?" http://www.foxnews.com/politics/elections/2008/07/24/obama-casts-self-as-world-citizen/ (accessed December 10, 2008).

Frank J. Gaffney, Jr., "World Citizen Obama" (2008, July 29) *FrontPage Magazine*, http://frontpagemag.com/Articles/Read.aspx?GUID=8E0D6225-F23A-44A8-AEF5-3346149185A6 (accessed December 10, 2008).

Gordon, J. (2006) 'Studying Abroad, Safe or Not.' *The New York Times*, April 23.

Hannerz, U. (1996) *Transnational Connections: Culture, People, Places*, New York: Routledge.

Hardt, M., & Negri, A. (2000) *Empire*, Cambridge and London: Harvard University Press.

Hunt, M. (1987) *Ideology and U.S. Foreign Policy*, New Haven and London: Yale University Press.

Ignatius, D. (2005) 'Replant the American Dream', *The Washington Post*, A37 November 25, 2005.

Institute of International Education Open Doors Report (2009) 'Americans Study Abroad in Increasing Numbers', *The Institute of International Education*, http://opendoors.iienetwork.org/?p=150651 (accessed March 11, 2011).

—— (2010) http://www.iie.org/en/Research-and-Publications/Open-Doors/Data (accessed March 11, 2011).

Letters, "When Obama Spoke in Berlin" (2008, July 26) *New York Times*, http://www.nytimes.com/2008/07/26/opinion/l26brooks.html?scp=6&sq=barack%20obama%20berlin&st=cse (accessed December 1, 2008).

Lincoln Commission (2005) 'Global Competence & National Needs: One Million Americans Studying Abroad', Washington, DC: Commission on the Abraham Lincoln Study Abroad Fellowship Program.

Lister, I. (1995) 'Educating Beyond the Nation', *International Review of Education* 41(1/2): 110–111.

Loomba, A. (2005) *Colonialism/Postcolonialism*, New York: Routledge.

Muppidi, H. (2004) *The Politics of the Global*, London and Minneapolis: University of Minnesota Press.

NAFSA: Association of Foreign Educators (2009) "Renewing America's Leadership," Washington, DC: NAFSA.

Nye, J. (2007) 'Squandering the U.S. Soft Power Edge', *The International Educator* 4: 4–6.

Obama, Barack. "A World That Stands as One" (2008, July 24) Full text of the speech as prepared for delivery can be found at http://www.huffingtonpost.com/2008/07/24/obama-in-berlin-video-of_n_114771.html (accessed June 9, 2009).

O'Harney, J. (2006) 'An International Strategy', *Connection: The Journal of the New England Board of Higher Education* 2(XXI): 5.

Purdy, J. (2003) *Being America: Liberty, Commerce, and Violence in an American World*, New York: Knopf.

Robbins, B. (1999) *Feeling Global: Internationalism in Distress*, New York: New York University Press.

Said, E. (1979) *Orientalism*, New York: Vintage Books.

Salvatore, R. D. (1998) 'The Enterprise of Knowledge: Representational Machines of Informal Empire', in G. M. Joseph, C. C. Legrand and R. D. Salvatore (eds.), *Close Encounters of Empire*, Durham, NC: Duke University Press, 69–104.

Scheiber, N. "Obama's Berlin Speech" (2008, July 24) *The New Republic*, http://blogs.tnr.com/tnr/blogs/the_stump/archive/2008/07/24/obama-s-berlin-speech.aspx (accessed December 1, 2008).

Shohat, E. and Stam, R. (1996) 'From the Imperial Family to the Transnational Imaginary: Media Spectatorship in the Age of Globalization', in R. Wilson and W. Dissanayake (eds.), *Global Local: Cultural Production and the Transnational Imaginary*, Durham, NC: Duke University Press, 145–170.

Spellings, M. (2007) *Statement on International Education Week 2007*, http://iew.state.gov/statements/sec-ed.htm (accessed November 17, 2007).

Stam, R. and Shohat, E. (2007) *Flagging Patriotism: Crises of Narcissism and Anti-Americanism*, New York: Routledge.

Temple University Office of International Programs (n.d.). *Why Study Abroad?* http://www.temple.edu/studyabroad/students/index.html (accessed October 31, 2007).

U.S. Department of State and U.S. Department of Education (2007) International Education Week 2007, http://iew.state.gov (accessed November 18, 2007).

United States Senate, 109th Congress, 1st Session (2005) S. Res. 308 Designating 2006 as the 'Year of Study Abroad.' Washington, DC: U.S. Government Printing Office.

Van Gunsteren, H. R. (1998) 'Admission to Citizenship', *Ethics* 98(4): 731–741.

Wasey, A. (2006) 'Studying and Working Abroad a Growing Passion for Young Americans', *PBS Online NewsHour*, http://www.pbs.org/newshour/generation-next/demographic/abroad_10-25.html (accessed October 31, 2007).

Wesleyan University Office of International Studies (2007) *About Us*, http://www.wesleyan.edu/ois/aboutus.html (accessed April 2, 2007).

Williams, P. G. (2007). *President's Corner: Worldwide Web of Learning*, http://www.ithaca.edu/icview (accessed October 30, 2007).

6 How Does 'Global Citizenship Education' Construct Its Present?
The Crisis of International Education

Paul Tarc

> In my view, an adequate interrogation of the present (postcolonial or otherwise) depends upon identifying the difference between the questions that animated former presents and those that animate our own (Scott 2004, 3).

Under processes and imaginaries of an intensifying globalization, international education and its variants have increasing salience across multiple domains in the Anglo West. Indeed, since the end of the Cold War as capitalism was 'set loose' to become global, international education has also become less constrained along particular registers. At the end of the first decade of the twenty-first century, when 'performativity' continues to be a dominant organizing principle (Lyotard 1984), international education has become a fully fledged *expedient*. That is, various aspects of international education are increasingly recognized as desirable and useful by many students, employees, universities, businesses, think tanks and governments alike. For entrepreneurial universities, ministries of education, transnational corporations and NGOs, the subject position of the 'global citizen' is being advocated for and advanced (Andreotti, Jeferess, Pashby, Rowe, Tarc, and Taylor 2010). At the same time, academic theorizations of 'global citizenship' (Dower 2003; Held and McGrew 2003; Peters, Blee and Britton 2008) and cosmopolitanisms (Cheah and Robbins 1998; Appiah 2006; Nava 2007; Benhabib 2008; Pinar 2009; Todd 2010) have multiplied in attending to the increasing frequency and intensity of transnational connections, affiliations and flows operating both above and below the level of governments (Appadurai 1996). Global citizenship education (GCE) is a small but growing educational discourse oriented to these larger processes and theorizations of globalization and internationalization.

In this chapter, I read GCE as a twenty-first-century variant of international education, invoked as an intervention, at least partly, attuned to the altered conditions of global times. My work is less concerned with attempting to pin down an exact definition or idealization of the term, or in assessing its theoretical coherence—for example, the conceptual (in)stability of 'global citizenship' in the absence of political institutions of global governance (Davies 2006; Pike 2008; Wood 2008). Rather, as a loosely defined notion of 'global citizenship' intersects with imaginaries of educational practices and aims, 'global citizenship' can be viewed as a discursive intervention that constructs a historical present and set of (new) challenges to which an *'education* for global citizenship' is to respond. Although the meanings and uses of GCE will vary across contexts of practice and analytic registers, it is possible to sketch out a coalescing zeitgeist or present-day problem space (Scott 2004) in the (neo)liberal Anglo West in which GCE is to intervene. But to better understand the limits and possibilities of GCE and, if possible, strategically guide this intervention in the present, it is necessary to take up postcolonial scholar David Scott's call for attention to differentiate past and present historical moments, to situate and better understand this latest iteration of international education.

In his introduction to *Conscripts of Modernity*, Scott (2004) articulates an orientation to interrogating postcolonial objects of inquiry *within* the historical present. For Scott, fundamental to critical analysis is to historicize the underlying vision or *dream* central to a movement, rather than the outcomes or manifestations of the dream. For example, one can, in postcolonial fashion, remarks Scott, critique the *answers* to the animating questions of the "anticolonial dream" and trace how these answers have "withered into postcolonial nightmares" (2). However, the more useful approach for Scott is to focus on the *dream* or animating *questions* themselves. The present material conditions and attendant imaginaries need to be interrogated and differentiated from the past, so that new questions can be formulated. Scott claims that too much focus is placed on critiquing past answers and coming up with better answers to older (and thereby less consequential) questions. He suggests that one ought to examine the visions or longings for change that motivated a social movement, rather than only focus on the movement's outcomes. He writes:

> [The postcolonial critique] has been to assume that it is postcolonial answers—rather than postcolonial questions—that require historicization, deconstruction, and reformulation. My view is precisely the reverse of this: it is our postcolonial questions and not our answers that demand critical attention. (3)

To imagine new opportunities and challenges for international education in the present moment, thus, earlier manifestations of international education can be read as a set of answers, begging the uncovering of a set of longings or questions. And it is these questions, according to Scott, which need to be examined and then reformulated in the present.

A parallel approach, to which Scott credits Bernard Yack (1992), is to historicize the *discontents* producing the dream or the *obstacles* to the dream. Accordingly, the way to learn from history begins by understanding the differences between the past *discontents* and *obstacles to change* and those of the present day. In the case of international education, clearly past obstacles as geographic isolation (or even wars between nation-states) no longer seem to be the dominant obstacles to (or set the conditions for) international education in the present moment. For Yack, then, productive approaches to conceiving new possibilities for international education, in this case GCE, would involve examining present-day conditions to illuminate the new obstacles facing the formerly conceived dreams or hopes of international education. An implication of Yack's intervention is that the categories of the hopes and dreams themselves need historicization. For example, if the dream of international education is centered around the hopes that a certain kind of education, not narrowly aligned with the national interest, can develop and support students to act to make a better, less violent world, then a whole set of categories need to be scrutinized (rather than be treated as historically stable): the 'national interest,' 'the student,' 'acting,' 'better world,' 'violence' and so on. Differentiating the contemporary 'problem space' from a past one becomes a way of illuminating how these meanings have been reinflected across periods.

At stake in this examination, it should be noted, is to move beyond or between (nostalgically) holding onto past strategies for social change that have become ineffectual or counterproductive under present conditions and accepting the present (and future) as fixed and without 'hope,' circumscribed by the hyperindividualist, competitive, militaristic, ecologically catastrophic, neoliberal capitalist version of progress. Scott articulates the challenge as follows:

> But if what is at stake in critically thinking through this postcolonial present is not simply the naming of yet another horizon, and the fixing of the teleological plot that takes us there from here, still, what is at stake is something like a refusal to be seduced and immobilized by the facile normalization of the present. (2)

For Scott, the past emancipatory narratives for 'total revolution' and the teleology of progress under the anticolonial trope of romance are no longer credible. But we cannot simply submit to the 'loss of hope' in tragic times, nor believe that the contingencies of the neoliberal and militaristic present represent the only alternatives.

In the body of this chapter, I respond to Scott's challenge to historicize the 'problem space' and animating questions or desires of international education across two distinct historical conjunctures where international education had and has a heightened prominence: the period of the 1960s and early 1970s (Heater 1980; Hughes 1985; Mundy 1999) and the post–Cold War global times of today (1990–2010—but particularly the last decade). I hold onto the term *international education* not to represent, again, a more literal notion of flows and functionalities channeled through national governments, but as a signifier of a set of liberalhumanist visions of education and its place in the larger world. To take up Scott's challenge, I will offer up a coarse description of the 'dreams' of international education in the earlier period and how these dreams are expressed in relation to certain conceived obstacles or challenges of the times. Next I describe some of the dramatic changes characteristic of the contemporary moment. I will then gloss over some similarities and differences in representations of 'education for international understanding' of the earlier period with GCE of the contemporary period as illustrative of how meanings and uses of international education have, at least superficially, shifted. Following the comparison, I will probe more deeply into the specific desire for 'action' of the global citizen in a 'making-a-difference' ethos characteristic of present times. In closing I will discuss key difficulties for GCE to intervene in a productive way and tentatively suggest how educators might want to respond.

To support the core argument I make in this chapter on the difference between past and present historical conjunctures, I draw, in part, upon my research on the historically shifting expressions of the 'global dreams' of the International Baccalaureate Organization (IBO) (Tarc 2009). I also symptomatically read a number of expressions that illustrate current conceptions of, and wishes for, the 'active' global citizen and for 'making a difference' under a (neo)liberal imaginary. To ground my conception on prescribed practices for GCE, I draw on Oxfam (2006), entitled *Education for Global Citizenship: A Guide for Schools,* as a prominent and substantive exemplar of GCE.

I argue in this chapter that international education has growing salience under heightened globalization. However, a caveat is in order because it is also true that in many domains, particularly those outside of liberal or neoliberal spaces, there are movements towards the parochial or the 'local' against more global or worldly engagements. Globalization produces contradictory pressures that manifest in both unifying and fracturing movements. Since the 1980s economic globalization has pressed (particularly) Western governments to privilege schooling citizens who can help the nation be globally competitive over schooling citizens who are loyal 'flag-wavers' (Green 1997). Obviously, this is not necessarily the case with other governments. Moreover, as Appadurai (2006) notes, as state governments' economic sovereignty is challenged and weakened there is a reactionary tendency for states to attempt to reinstill a sense of national ethnos, sometimes by targeting minorities (43). Additionally, increased transnational cultural flows that trouble the stability of identity markers of majority and minority often further intensify anxiety and xenophobia (83). In terms of schooling, the parochializing of the curriculum in the recent Texas school-reform controversy (Mckinley 2010) is an excellent counterexample to my focus in this chapter, where I am referring to the more neoliberal and liberal publics of national and trans-national spaces.

THE TWENTIETH-CENTURY 'DREAMS'
OF INTERNATIONAL EDUCATION

In recent centuries, internationalism and outward-looking foreign policies (of imperial powers) have waxed and waned often in relation to territorial expansion, economic development, conflict and war. Consider the wider world conditions during the last peak of international education in the 1960s and early 1970s. In the aftermath of the Second World War, the U.S. has emerged as the unquestioned center of the capitalist world with a strong ally in a reconstructed Western Europe. It is a time of rising hope, progress, democratization and anti-imperialism. The United Nations is fully opera-tional in the multinational scene; decolonization and new nation building is emergent in parts of the 'developing' world; and embedded liberalism is flourishing in the Western 'developed' countries. Under embedded liberal-ism, with its Keynesian policies, the state government is 'large' and active, responsible to manage the markets, create jobs and fund the social pro-grams for its citizens. Through struggle and protest, great gains of social progress are made in civil societies of the West. These gains are also made possible by the high economic growth that allows a compromise between capital and labor (Brown, Halsey, Lauder and Wells 1997).

However, the Cold War with occasional 'hot flashes' continues to struc-ture and shape relations between capitalist, communist and nonaligned nations. The threat of an all-out nuclear war is heavy in the worldwide social imaginary. While there is an increase in internationalist activities during this period, these initiatives are often embedded in the interests of Cold War interests and politics (Sidhu 2006). Nevertheless, in the 1960s, exemplified symbolically by the United Nations, the internationalist (West-phalian) order is at a peak, as is interest in and funding for international education. Liberal agencies such as the Ford Foundation are providing grants to support various internationalist initiatives, such as the creation of the experiment of the International Baccalaureate diploma. President Lyndon Johnson's 'international education act' is initiated in 1966; 1970 is the United Nations' 'Year of International Education' (Tarc 2009, 21–22). In this period, the more outward-looking visions of schooling circulat-ing in progressive circles across the twentieth century were finally gaining prominence and finding expression in an array of new initiatives in interna-tional and alternative education. But what were these visions or underlying dreams of international education and what set of longings or discontents fueled their expression?

To draw out an answer, I draw on research tracing the meanings of the 'international' of international education (Tarc 2007). First, there is the literal meaning of international—as working across or between countries. This more empirical meaning then tends to center conceptions of international education on the mobility of students, on international standards and bi- or international agreements, partnerships and certification frameworks. However, 'international,' where modifying education, also invokes a set of liberal-humanist and progressive visions of schooling and society (Tarc 2009). International education thus has carried this double signification, or tension, between the pragmatic—international functionality—and the motivating visions or dream of a liberal-humanist education oriented to making a 'better' world. These idealist humanist visions are most relevant to the analysis presented in this chapter. Although idealist visions of 'international education' might be relatively stable for many decades, their expressions shift on much shorter time scales. Moreover, while I emphasize that the 'international education' has become an expedient under heightened performativity, internationalism has never been 'pure' or independent of pragmatic concerns (Iriye 1997; Peterson 1987; Jones 2000; Sidhu 2006).

In coarse terms, the twentieth-century "dreams" of international education center on a liberal-humanist vision that human connections forged across borders can make a more egalitarian, less-violent world. In the pursuit of knowledge and culture, a common humanity can be found and progress across and in spite of national and cultural differences. A Wilsonian political internationalism that motivates the experiment of the 'League of Nations' in the 1920s finally takes a more solid footing in the creation and operation of the United Nations in the 1950s (Jones and Coleman 2005). Although some versions of international education have advocated for students to learn explicitly about the United Nations, multilateralism and geopolitics, the key advocates of international education have tended to advance a cultural internationalism (Iriye 1997). Irrespective of the dominance of national politics or geopolitical order, cultural internationalists valued the cultural, artistic, economic and scientific modes of contact and exchange that bring people of the world closer together. They were internationally mobile, working and living in different countries, speaking two or more languages, influential inside and outside their respective institutions, and idealistic about the role international education could play in making a better, more peaceful world (Tarc 2007).

The massification and democratization of schooling that coalesces in the 1950s and 1960s (theoretically) enlarges the pool of users of international education and also, in some sense, magnifies the expectations of schooling to advance the dreams of making a better world. In this historical moment, international education is useful not just to royalty, diplomats and future leaders but to the schooled 'masses.' The (colonial) logic espoused (Peterson 1972) is that where national citizens are more knowledgeable and empathetic to others, they may be less likely to rise up and take arms against their follow humans. Schooling also became a site of hope in the developing world, both in the imaginary of decolonization and new nation building and in the programs of international development to aid the 'developing' nations (Weiler 1978).

In pedagogical terms, international education was often expressed in relation to a set of discontents: slow-to-change national systems of schooling, ethnocentric curricula (for example, the glorification of national battles and heroes in history texts), conservative encyclopedic methods of teaching, and national compartmentalization of education (Tarc 2007). In the case of the key developers of IB, they were less representatives of their respective national systems than progressive reformists advancing a humanist notion of children and pedagogy (Mayer 1968). In the spirit of progressivism, Peterson (1972) envisioned the best education as developing the whole person: intellectual, physical and moral/aesthetic. To go further back in time, the International School of Geneva, created in the 1920s for the sons and daughters of the League of Nations and the International Labour Organization, drew heavily on child-centered pedagogy (Mayer 1968). The progressive modes of teaching remain closely tied to most varieties of international education throughout the twentieth century (Skidelsky 1969; Heater 1980) and up to today (Oxfam 2006).

Nevertheless, international education had very marginal status, remaining on the fringe of nationalist programs and discourses of schooling in the twentieth century (Heater 1980). Politically it was contentious and practically it affected few students. Even where there were initiatives supported by governments, international education was susceptible to attacks of being 'indoctrination,' of being 'unpatriotic,' or of 'not have standards' (Heater). These criticisms continue to surface in pockets in the present (Bunnell 2009), but now it is these criticisms that are on the fringe as internationalization has become a strategic aim of multiple state providers of schooling. Indeed, the present opportunities for international education are now abundant under performativity and heightened global interconnectedness.

THE CONTEMPORARY MOMENT: 'NEOLIBERAL IMAGINARY' AND 'PERFORMATIVITY'

The world in which GCE finds expression is dramatically distinct. In loose terms we can talk about the rise of the economic and of the penetration of market and neoliberal logics across multiple domains and social spaces. If the orthodoxy of Keynesian liberalism begins to falter under the economic crisis in the early 1970s, it loses much more legitimacy in the years to follow through the political discourses of Reagan in the U.S., Thatcher in Britain, and Deng Xiaoping in China (Harvey 2005). The most striking turning point for the rise of the economic, however, is the collapse of the Soviet Union, which set the stage for capitalism to go fully global. In some sense the 'thought experiments' posed by the economic internationalists of how economic interdependence on a world scale would solve the problem of conflict and war (Silberner 1946) had the chance to be tested. In hindsight, these hopes seem naïve given the ongoing intensity, and spread into civilian spaces, of state and terrorist-group violence (Appadurai 2006). Nevertheless, immigration, the compression of space-time and 'the Internet' have created more and novel opportunities for intercultural contact and collaboration. Yet, these come with challenging complexities and profound obstacles. Before considering these opportunities and complications, I want to be a little more precise on how I understand the dominant social imaginary (Taylor 2002), most conventionally referred to as 'neoliberal,' that has heightened the expediency of international education and the commodification of education more generally (Borg and Mayo 2006; Rizvi 2007).

My use of the term *performativity* as a dominant organizing logic draws on Lyotard (1984, 47–53), among others (Henry, Lingard, Rizvi and Taylor 2001; Ball 2004). Performativity represents the heightened demand for measurable quantities and processes in an era marked by the 'incredulity of metanarratives' (Lyotard 1984). Where there is no longer a unifying story in which members of a pluralistic societies can believe, the loss of trust generated in authority (whether the church, state or truth) presses for performativity, "where knowledge ceases to be an end in itself" (50) and the use value of knowledge dominates over the search for truth or normative ends. Lyotard's account is quite prescient of the sweeping reforms witnessed in education in the past twenty-five years that have largely fallen under the label *neoliberal*. I think that performativity might be a more precise term to use to describe the continued pervasiveness of accountability goals and regimes despite the growing critiques of neoliberal policies, not to mention the recent, seemingly catastrophic, blow of the economic meltdown precipitated by deregulation and 'free-market' mechanisms. Of course one can make the case that free-market policies were in fact really never engaged. But regardless, the point I am making here is that a crack in the legitimacy of neoliberal political economic orthodoxy has done little to impede the dominance of performativity in structuring programs and processes in domains such as education. Neoliberalism, or the penetration of the market logics, may have more to do with the conditions of postmodernity that have laid bare efficiency, productivity and transparency of the social system.

In other words, neoliberalism did not become dominant because an overwhelming number of individuals began to believe in small, noninterfering governments and in the sanctity of market mechanisms. Rather, accountability and transparency have become dominant criteria in a competitive context where individuals, and particularly parents, want tangible results in the absence of trust and the increasing presence of material and psychological insecurities. Even the latest sensationalist depictions of various CEOs and high-placed officials running up expenses on taxpayers' contributions illustrates the kind of disconnect between 'trickle-down' economics and the dominance of accountability and transparency. Clearly, top-down agendas of political parties and media groups have helped solidify the 'neoliberal imaginary,' so to speak. But these wider conditions of uncertainty and exposure to risk have in a sense left market processes and logics as the kind of lowest common denominator remaining for individuals relating across difference in pluralistic societies. In addition to the influences of top-down ideology, then, there are more existential kinds of attractions to buy into neoliberal educational reform with its offerings of standards, accountability and choice. And these ground-level attractions, I think, inform why groups who may well have the most to lose from neoliberal reform sometimes end up being neoliberalism's strongest advocates.

To account for the distinction between neoliberalism as a theory of political economy or even as an ideology and how individuals take up economic rationality 'for themselves,' it is useful to draw on the concept of an imaginary. The term *neoliberal social imaginary* or *neoliberal imaginary* is attuned to both a top-down media-spun neoliberalism and (a related but distinct) more individualized and affective bottom-up dimension. Charles Taylor (2002) defines a social imaginary as

> the ways in which people imagine their social existence, how they fit together with others, how things go on between them and their fellows, the expectations that are normally met, and the deeper normative notions and images that underlie these expectations. (106)

So a neoliberal imaginary would refer to the centrality of counting (financial), exchange, value and efficiency in how individuals understand and assume how professional and personal relations with others work and ought to work in local contexts.

EDUCATING FOR INTERNATIONAL UNDERSTANDING VERSUS GLOBAL CITIZENSHIP

In some sense, the term *global citizenship* itself already inflects the altered conditions of the twenty-first century. If political citizenship has remained more static in a still mostly Westphalian order, the economic and cultural dimensions of affiliations and acting take place both above and below the level of state governments. This shift is not to suggest that the nation-state is not actively involved in some of these processes. As Sassen (2006) has argued in meticulous detail, the state is a key player in processes of denationalization. Although states still want and need the 'loyal citizen,' the specifics of what this means have become very complex. More importantly to this chapter's argument, the active 'global citizen' is no longer negatively defined in relation to the 'national citizen.' Indeed, rights of national political citizenship provide the conditions for acting as the 'global citizen.' From the state's agenda, clearly 'global citizens' can help the state gain positional advantage in the global marketplace. Moreover, as will be discussed later, the demand that the 'global citizen' help those in need fits quite well in a context of reduced public funding on social programs, services and safety nets.

In the 1950s and 1960s, even the more benign 'international understanding' was a politically contentious term in the domain of national schooling. For example, in the case of the International Baccalaureate experiment of the 1960s, the term was strategically downplayed whenever officials of national schooling were addressed. Moreover, Alec Peterson, IB's key spokesperson, consistently spoke of the primacy of national understanding for students, who at a later stage would learn about peoples from other places. Indeed, it is not until the early 1990s that new terms such as *world citizen* enter IBO's official policy discourse. *International understanding* was a popular term in the post–WWII decades in educational discourses by multilateral organizations such as UNESCO. Heater (1980) summarizes its classical, somewhat narrowly focused usage by UNESCO and others as a "concern to improve knowledge of and empathy for other countries and their ways of life" (29). His study, which centers on the meanings and approaches of education for 'international understanding' in Britain until 1979, correlates well with the periodization offered in this chapter's analysis.

Heater presents five distinct emphases of "education for international understanding" in the wider field. The first and most basic is "knowledge about and comprehension of other societies" with the caveat that "knowledge about" sometimes produces "sympathy for" (28–29). The second centers on international relations and institutions such as the United Nations, again with emphasis in the cognitive domain. Heater assigns "education for world citizenship," common in the 1930s to 1950s, as the third category. Education for world citizenship includes values and attitude formation. Further, this approach attempts to teach a sense of loyalty that stretches beyond the nation-state. A major difficulty of this approach has been in defining specifically upon *what* this loyalty hinges. Heater notes that this approach has come under strong criticism as ideological, with insufficient rigor, and as unpatriotic (29). A fourth category has to do with the teaching for the "universality of human values" that transcends cultural difference by emphasizing "the highest common factors of human life . . . a willingness will be instilled in people to live in harmonious brotherhood with one another." "Education for peace" is the final category. This approach stresses not that one should "love the enemy" but that one should refrain from fighting him to avoid the destruction of (nuclear) war (30). Heater also makes mention of "global education," a terminology more popular in the U.S. Global education is framed on the "cobweb" model of international relations and emphasizes interdependence and "systemness." Outside the groupings of education for "international understanding," Heater turns to a discussion on the "more recent and radical developments" under the rubric of "peace education" developed in the 1970s. The radical turn draws on Marxist theory with its anchoring concepts of "structural violence," oppression and "social justice" (31–32).

If one includes all the elements of Heater's typology, there would be much overlap between the former education for international education and today's education for global citizenship. Oxfam (2006) represents global citizenship education as encompassing the three 'elements' of (1) knowledge and understanding, (2) skills and (3) values and attitudes (4). This breakdown has long been used in international education. Convergence can be seen in many of the individual criteria under each of these 'elements.' For example, 'critical thinking,' 'argumentation,' 'cooperation and conflict resolution' are desired skills for global citizenship; 'diversity,' 'peace and conflict' and 'social justice' are listed as topics for knowledge and understanding; and, 'self-esteem,' 'empathy' and 'respect for diversity' are desired attitudes. Most of the individual pieces that make up GCE according to Oxfam (2006), and indeed according to other representations of GCE practices, could be mapped onto the earlier education for international understanding.

Additionally if we consider Oxfam's description of the 'global citizen,' only two of the seven criteria could be considered novel to GCE. The document has the following text window:

Oxfam sees the Global Citizen as someone who:

- is aware of the wider world and a sense of their own role as a world citizen
- respects and values diversity
- has an understanding of how the world works
- *is outraged by social injustice*
- participates in the community at a range of levels, *from the local to the global*
- is willing to act to make the world a more equitable and sustainable place
- takes responsibility for their actions (my emphases, 3)

Apart from participating at the levels of the 'local to the global,' the novel component here is really only the criterion of being 'outraged by social injustice.' In part, this inclusion comes out of Oxfam's historical roots in international development and its critique of structural inequity. But it is also symptomatic of the awareness of the intensifying uses of international education for individual and national advantage. Oxfam wants to stress that global citizenship ought to be centered by a commitment to social justice in light of the growing uses of international education for individual, institutional and corporate advantage. Also, in a later section, Oxfam explicitly emphasizes that GCE is 'not about raising money for charity' (3). Again, I read their emphasis as a reaction to how charity and fundraising have become dominant modes of acting for the 'global citizen' (in the making).

The single significant novel aspect of GCE that I read from Oxfam's representation, then, is the heightened and more nuanced attention to transnational interdependencies—what we might call the heightened awareness of 'action-at-a distance' or of 'global-local' relations. Oxfam emphasizes these global-local relations across a number of points in the document. Here are but three examples: "The lives of children and young people are increasingly shaped by what happens in other parts of the world" (1); "Today more than ever before, the global is part of our everyday local lives. We are linked to others on every continent" (2); "[GCE is] revealing the global as a part of everyday local life, whether in a small village or a large city" (3).

The International Baccalaureate Organization, to consider a second prominent advocate of GCE, centers its representation of the twenty-first-century student-subject of international education on developing learner dispositions. The IBO shares many of Oxfam's pedagogical aims, albeit in a less political way. The IB discourse does not draw on the language of social justice or center its vision on the inequity of world resources and the widening gap between rich and poor. Nevertheless, at the level of desired learning outcomes there is again much overlap. For IBO, the espoused mission of their programs is "to develop internationally minded people who, in recognizing their common humanity and shared guardianship of the planet, help to create a better and more peaceful world." The learner profile document elaborates upon the desired dispositions for the IB student: "IB learners strive to be: inquirers, . . . knowledgeable, . . . thinkers, . . . communicators, . . . principled, . . . open-minded, . . . caring, . . . risk-takers, . . . balanced, . . . reflective. . . ." In course terms, the main difference is that the IBO offers a more liberally framed education as opposed to Oxfam's more critical orientation. Both hold onto the importance of learning knowledge, skills and attitudes and both espouse the importance of action. They also both hold onto the liberal ideal of each student striving to reach their potential and of participatory and inquiry models of learning. The difficult tension in Oxfam's approach is produced in advocating for an outrage against social justice whilst claiming that the issues are complex and students ought to think for themselves. The IBO approach is perhaps more coherent but less attuned to the stark asymmetries and conflicts in which education is imagined to intervene.

In summary there remains little distinction between descriptions and prescriptions of GCE and the earlier variant education for 'international understanding.' Perhaps this is suggestive that, in Scott's (2004) terms, we are still attempting to answer similar questions under the same institutional constraints (read schooling) as before and have yet to uncover the new questions that might animate the dream of international education in the present. Nevertheless, I have included this section to provide a sense of how international or global citizenship education is idealized as a set of practices of schooling. Certainly some topics or themes have been reframed by the changed conditions of the present; however, basic educational aims, outcomes and learning methods are largely the same.

One significant change is the heightened attention to interdependencies between locals. As well there is a greater emphasis on the 'active' of active citizenship in the present. Action was also emphasized in earlier times. For example, the founder of Atlantic World College, Kurt Hahn, particularly emphasized the importance of action, bravery and service. Peterson, the first director general of IB, was inspired by Hahn and also valued action as a necessary complement to thought and to the development of values; with action Peterson emphasized the importance of service to others and the development of compassion for others (IBO 2004). Nevertheless, it seems that in the present, *acting* by multiple agents (individuals, NGOs and corporations) has a heightened presence. Yet, 'acting' largely has become incorporated within the neoliberal imaginary (despite, I would argue, Oxfam's critical attention to 'social justice'—indeed 'social justice' is also in need of historicization). The next section elaborates upon the new modes of acting in global times.

'ACTING' IN A MAKING-A-DIFFERENCE ETHOS

> In the last days in preparing this speech, I received an e-mail from my daughter who is now in Eastern Africa's Kenya (where the first ancestors of humankind came), informing me of her blog. After graduation from Harvard University, she now works at an internationally renowned investment bank. In her blog, I learn about her voluntary work—"At long last, I am no longer a cog in the capitalist machine and can *'make a difference'*. Even though I wasn't working at Doctors without Borders (my life long dream job) I was finally working at a non-profit. . . . I would be a part of something bigger than myself, I would be helping develop sustainable economies and markets, and I would be doing something noble and 'worthwhile'. I'm glad that young people of today have begun to act. [my emphasis, closing remarks by keynote, Professor Paul Yip Kwok-wah, at Education for Global Citizenship Conference 2006, Shanghai, China]

These words of the keynote's daughter, signifying hopeful action on the part of the next generation, capture very well the zeitgeist of 'making a difference' in the global scene. I think they are emblematic of how acting as the 'global citizen,' at home or away, is embedded in privilege and confounded by its dependence in exploitive capitalist structures to produce or sustain the capacity and resources to 'help others.' Making profit in global capitalism is both the source of the problem and the solution. Being a *well-paid* 'cog in the capitalist machine' provides the proximity and the resources for the benevolent work of 'making a difference' in a 'depressed' region. In this case the global citizen, having found the 'non-profit' NGO, can 'be noble' and help those most vulnerable to participate in 'sustainable economies and markets.' The keynote address fails to consider how the conditions of poverty or need might be interdependent with (certain benefits accrued by) the 'internationally renowned investment bank' to enable the 'global citizen' to choose to 'make a difference,' not to mention how the NGO itself is dependent upon the 'capitalist machine.'

The quote highlights the enabling, yet constrained, positioning of performing as the global citizen under an asymmetrically orchestrated global capitalism. In a sense the global citizen metaphorically stands on, and adds weight to, a large wooden *platform* that is on top of and crushing 'the poor.' Here the 'platform' represents both one's inherent material embeddedness in capitalism's operations and effects, and the 'stage' where one performs global citizenship, constructing self and other in a (post)colonial field of power-knowledge (Foucault, 1980). Unlike the less engaged, the 'global citizen' is not simply oblivious or carefree to the plight of others; rather, she is reaching down to the 'global poor' to, in some way, lighten the pressure of the platform upon the individuals with whom she is 'helping'/relating. Some forms of her helping may inadvertently increase her weight on the board; others may not. Some forms of her helping also become advantages that she can apply to gain a more preferable position on the platform, thereby increasing her own material resources, which can be applied back to helping others below or not. Becoming a 'leader' she can also mobilize others around her to start reaching down to help below, but most often the helping is in the form of charity where individuals provide money to help those already reaching down increase their impact. In this context, the ethico-pedagogical act of, and effects of, reaching down to engage the other (what we might call the 'education' of international education) often becomes secondary to fund-raising and financial administration. Again, all of these more financially centered activities might also inadvertently increase the overall weight of the board oppressing the poor. To be fair, with these financially centered activities come educational opportunities, but they are often more indirect or vicarious. Most charities aim to both raise funds and educate their audience on the context of their interventions. Donors, however, can remain far removed from where the funds are set to work, even in light of 'transparent' accounting practices. Further, the aim of fund-raising, as in giving a simple message about what can be done to solve the problem, is likely in conflict with developing a deep understanding of the 'problem' and the intended resolutions.

In the background, so to speak, governments do less and less to lift up on the platform. Celebrity philanthropists work to mobilize individuals for increased giving. In certain fora they have gained greater voice than informed social scientists or politicians on the problems of poverty and development (Moyo 2009). Informed by the latest market research, transnational corporations are heavily vested in 'ethical branding'; indeed, corporations are drawing on consultants who can help corporations shape their brand to connect with the younger generation's desire to 'make a difference.' Even antibranding activists are courted by corporations that want, in guerrilla fashion, to draw on the 'antibrand' to win the loyalty of consumers (Harkin 2001). Some corporations are sitting very heavy on the board but offering incentives to 'ethical buyers' by way of giving back small percentages of profits to those in need, as, for example, the 'Buy Red' campaign. Some corporations shape the meaning and responses to disease through their 'philanthropic' donations. Buying 'pink' can fund breast-cancer treatment but privileges treatment and cure over prevention; corporations can participate in cause philanthropy to shift attention away from their complicities in producing environmental carcinogens (King 2006). Increasingly, responsibility lies with the individual who, through smart schooling, smart purchasing, and smart giving, can 'make a difference,' particularly where extreme poverty sets the conditions by which a small amount of charity can make a significant difference in an individual's life. Given a well-developed aid infrastructure and the large disparity of wealth between the middle classes and the multitude living on a couple dollars a day or less, Northerners can act as economic agents largely independent of the political. In short, the hyperindividualist 'making-a-difference' ethos shrinks the horizon of social action to individualized acts of consumption and the contingencies of charity and benevolence.

CONCLUDING DISCUSSION

The purpose of understanding these complicated conditions, however, is not in turn to criticize the work of individuals engaging in any number of practices of helping others, many of which do improve the individual circumstances of deserving human beings in profound ways. The purpose, to return to Scott (2004), is to recognize and examine these neoliberal enabling conditions as a profound contemporary *obstacle* thwarting the idealist dreams of international education. Now there are multiple calls for 'criticality' and for 'social justice' in railing against this obstacle as if it were simply a matter of emphatic polemics and implementation. Indeed, the language of 'outrage to social injustice' will not help us here. In the first place, there would be no outside of outrage as there is no sanctum from injustice. 'Outrage' by middle-class Westerners (newly) encountering poverty in the South may fuel the most uncritical activism. To be fair, I think it's the very recognition of the expediency of international education that informs the more emphatic call for justice and action. Oxfam is trying to press, ineffectually in this case I think, for GCE to be something more than résumé building or even learning critically about the world at large without an attendant will to act. Again, the difficulty in calling for 'action' is its present co-option by neoliberal logics. I think we need a better understanding of 'acting'; certainly we can't take at face value that acting represents some inherent good. Neither, though, do we want to cynically equate and thereby mimimize the potential singularity of actions.

But how do we then think 'social justice,' where neoliberalism itself claims the radical, as opposed to nostalgic, ground (Rust 2000)? A case in point is economist Dambisa Moyo's (2009) call to stop the West's governmental aid to Africa, given its failure across decades to improve economic and social conditions. Her proposals to switch to microcredit schemes to build human and social capital could easily be a report authored by the neoliberal World Bank; and yet it effectively *is* a radical intervention. That her neoliberally informed argument *is* radical is symptomatic of the times and looms large as the obstacle facing 'acting' as the global citizen in the neoliberal imaginary. What can GCE do if the way to be active is circumscribed by individualistic economic rationality? How can we learn from crossing boundaries of difference when difference is tokenized/minimized and incorporated into consumer choices in the capitalist machine? How might we better understand and act upon the difficult relation between understanding and action?

Amidst the multiple agendas of schooling and the still undertheorized dynamics of power inherent to compulsory schooling, conceptual understanding and critical thinking remain difficult challenges for pedagogies of many forms, not just international education. For this reason I want to avoid simply calling again for deeper or more critical pedagogies. Of course in practice there are different qualities and levels of GCE that have varying levels of effectiveness. In past work (Tarc 2009) I illustrated how under a 'making-a-difference' ethos the former knowledge—understanding—sympathetic action chain was shortchanging the stage of 'understanding.' In the rush to make a difference, to go beyond understanding to action, one brings one's pennies to help build schools in the Global South, rather than studying the historical relations that produce a 'them' in need of aid from 'us.'

I want to also be careful with this critique, however. First, I am not criticizing acts of helping or of charity but of how these actions get interpreted as necessarily educative, productive or as representing social transformation. Second, a hypercritical stance is difficult in the space of schooling. On the one hand, the teacher needs to hold onto a sense of agency for citizens-in-the-making—the possibility that students can make a difference and that what they think matters—but, on the other hand, the teacher is weighed down with the awareness that this feeling of 'empowerment' or 'agency' might have little to do with *learning*—engaging alterity in any significant way. Students may learn that understanding is not that essential, that being a global citizen means helping others or 'doing good,' which can potentially reconstruct the colonial relation between the empowered giver and the deficient receiver.

To return to the web of complicities discussed under the metaphor of the 'platform,' perhaps the content of study for GCE should include the examination of complex matrices that map the dimension of one's actions (helping/working across difference) in relation to the dimension of one's complicities to an exploitive capitalism that does damage to others. GCE could work to mark out the less damaging, more productive modes of acting and perhaps also expand the horizons of the imagination. Educators might investigate, with their students, the conditions under which the dreams of international education are short-circuited under present-day processes and imaginaries heightened under performativity and globalization. They could investigate the ongoing effects of their 'actions' emanating from a GCE approach as an emergent curriculum, rather than conceiving of their actions as (celebratory) end points. Perhaps the imperative for GCE is best framed as a demand to examine a set of cosmopolitan humanist desires to make a better world and how they come up against the emergent economic, social, pedagogical and ethical constraints, contradictions and contingencies of present-day contexts.

To return to Scott (2004) in closing, this chapter set forth a challenge to bring thinking to the complicated crisis of international education in the contemporary moment. It has taken some detours, to be sure, and has left important regions unthought. My hope is that I have at least illustrated a productive *approach* for critically examining limits and possibilities for GCE in the contemporary moment. Ultimately a project of (cosmopolitan) progressivism and social justice through education requires ongoing examination of shifting histories, contexts and outcomes towards imagining more desirable and possible futures.

REFERENCES

Andreotti, V., Jeferess, D., Pashby, K., Rowe, C., Tarc, P. and Taylor, L. (2010) 'Difference and Conflict in Global Citizenship in Higher Education in Canada', *International Journal of Development Education and Global Learning*, 2(3): 5–24.

Appadurai, A. (1996) *Modernity at Large: Cultural Dimensions of Globalization*, Minneapolis: University of Minnesota Press.

———. (2006) *Fear of Small Numbers: An Essay on the Geography of Anger*, Durham, NC: Duke University Press.

Appiah, K. A. (2006) *Cosmopolitanism: Ethics in a World of Strangers*. New York: W.W. Norton and Company.

Ball, S. (2004) Performativities and Fabrications in the Education Economy: Towards the Performativity Society, in S. Ball (ed.), *The RoutledgeFalmer Reader in Sociology of Education*, London: RoutledgeFalmer, 143–155.

Benhabib, S. (2008) *Another Cosmopolitanism*. New York: Oxford University Press.

Borg, C. and Mayo, P. (2006) *Learning and Social Difference: Challenges for Public Education and critical Pedagogy*, Boulder, CO: Paradigm Publishers.

Brown, P., Halsey, A. H., Lauder, H. and Wells, A. S. (1997) The Transformation of Education and Society: An Introduction. In A. H. Halsey, H. Lauder,

P. Brown and A. S. Wells (eds.), *Education: Culture, Economy, and Society*, Oxford: Oxford University Press, 1–44.

Bunnell, T. (2009) The International Baccalaureate in the USA and the Emerging 'Culture War.' *Discourse: Studies in the Cultural Politics of Education*, 30(1): 61–72.

Cheah, P. and Robbins, B. (1998) *Cosmopolitics: Thinking and Feeling beyond the Nation*. Minneapolis: University of Minnesota Press.

Davies, L. (2006) Global Citizenship: Abstraction or Framework for Action? *Educational Review*, 58(1): 5–25.

Dower, N. (2003) *An Introduction to Global Citizenship*. Edinburgh: Edinburgh University Press.

Foucault, M. (1980) *Power/Knowledge: Selected Interviews and Other Writings, 1972–1977* (C. Gordon, Trans.), Toronto: Random House of Canada.

Green, A. (1997) *Education, Globalization, and the Nation State*. New York: St. Martin's Press.

Harkin, James (2001) The New Statesman Essay—The Logos Fight Back, http://www.newstatesman.com/200106180018 (accessed October 31, 2010).

Harvey, D. (2005) *A Brief History of Neoliberalism*. New York: Oxford University Press.

Heater, D. B. (1980) *World Studies: Education for International Understanding in Britain*. London: Harrap.

Held, D., and McGrew, A. G. (eds.) (2003) *The Global Transformations Reader: An Introduction to the Globalization Debate* (2nd ed.), Cambridge: Polity Press.

Henry, M., Lingard, B., Rizvi, F. and Taylor, S. (2001) *The OECD, Globalisation, and Education Policy*, Amsterdam: IAU Press, Pergamon.

Hughes, T. L. (1985) The Twilight of Internationalism, *Foreign Policy*, 61(Winter): 25–48.

International Baccalaureate Organization (2004) 'Peterson Lectures: Alec Peterson Biography'. Available at ibo.org/council/peterson/documents/Peterson_biography_eFINAL.pdf (accessed May 12, 2007).

Iriye, A. (1997) *Cultural Internationalism and World Order*. Baltimore: Johns Hopkins University Press.

Jones, P. W. (2000) 'Globalization and Internationalism: Democratic Prospects for World Education', in N. P. Stromquist and K. Monkman (eds.), *Globalization and Education: Integration and Contestation across Cultures*, Lanham, MD: Rowman and Littlefield, 27–42.

Jones, P. W. and Coleman, D. (2005) *The United Nations and Education: Multilateralism, Development, and Globalisation*, London: RoutledgeFalmer.

King, S. (2006). *Pink ribbons, inc.: Breast cancer and the politics of philanthropy.* Minneapolis, MN: University of Minnesota Press.

Kwok-wah, P. Y. (2006) 'We Humankind, Our Earth: Education for Global Citizenship in the Globalization Era. Available at http://www.intedalliance.org/page.cfm?p=21 (accessed November 1, 2010).

Lyotard, J. F. (1984) *The Postmodern Condition: A Report on Knowledge*, Minneapolis: University of Minnesota Press.

Mayer, M. (1968) *Diploma: International Schools and University Entrance*, New York: Twentieth Century Fund.

Mckinley, J. C., Jr. (2010, March 12) 'Texas Conservatives Win Curriculum Change', *The New York Times*, http://www.nytimes.com/2010/03/13/education/13texas.html?_r=1 (accessed November 1, 2010).

Moyo, D. (2009). *Dead Aid: Why Aid Is Not Working and Why There Is a Better Way for Africa*, New York: Farrar, Straus and Giroux.

Mundy, K. (1999) 'Educational Multilateralism in a Changing World Order: UNESCO and the Limits of the Possible', *International Journal of Educational Development*, 19(1): 27–52.

Nava, M. (2007) *Visceral Cosmopolitanism: Gender, Culture and the Normalization of Difference*, New York: Berg.

Oxfam (2006) Education for Global Citizenship: A Guide for Schools, London: Oxfam. Available online at http://www.oxfam.org.uk/education/gc/ (accessed August 15, 2010).

Peters, M., Blee, H. and Britton, A. (eds.) (2008) *Global Citizenship Education: Philosophy, Theory and Pedagogy*, Rotterdam: Sense Publishers.

Peterson, A. D. C. (1972) *The International Baccalaureate: An Experiment in International Education*, London: G.G. Harrap.

——. (1987) *Schools across frontiers: The Story of the International Baccalaureate and the United World Colleges*, La Salle, IL: Open Court.

Pike, G. (2008) 'Citizenship Education in a Global Context', *Brock Education: A Journal of General Inquiry*, Special Issue—Citizenship Education in the Era of Globalization: Canadian Perspectives, 17(1): 38–49.

Pinar, W. F. (2009) *The Worldliness of a Cosmopolitan Education. Passionate Lives in Public Service*, New York: Routledge.

Rizvi, F. (2007) 'Internationalization of Curriculum: A Critical Perspective', in M. Hayden, J. Levy and J. J. Thompson (eds.), *The Sage Handbook of Research in International Education*, London: Sage, 390–403.

Rust, V. D. (2000). Educational reform: Who are the radicals? In N. P. Stromquist & K. Monkman (eds.), *Globalization and education: Integration and contestation across cultures*, Lanham, MD: Rowman & Littlefield, 63–76.

Sassen, S. (2006) *Territory, Authority, Rights: From Medieval to Global Assemblages*, Princeton, NJ: Princeton University Press.

Scott, D. (2004) *Conscripts of Modernity: The Tragedy of Colonial Enlightenment*, Durham, NC: Duke University Press.

Sidhu, R. K. (2006) *Universities and Globalization: To Market, to Market*, Mahwah, NJ: Lawrence Erlbaum Associates.

Silberner, E. (1946) *The Problem of War in Nineteenth Century Economic Thought*, Princeton, NJ: Princeton University Press.

Skidelsky, R. (1969) *English Progressive Schools*, Harmondsworth, UK: Penguin.

Tarc, P. (2007) 'What Is the "International" of the International Baccalaureate? Towards a Periodization of IB in the World', unpublished doctoral dissertation, York University, Toronto.

——. (2009) *Global Dreams, Enduring Tensions: International Baccalaureate in a Changing World*, New York: Peter Lang.

Taylor, C. (2002) 'Modern Social Imaginaries', *Public Culture*, 14(1): 91–124.

Todd, S. (2009) *Toward an Imperfect Education: Facing Humanity, Rethinking Cosmopolitanism*, Boulder, CO: Paradigm Publishers.

Weiler, H. N. (1978) 'Education and Development: From the Age of Innocence to the Age of Skepticism', *Comparative Education*, 14(3): 179–198.

Wood, P. (2008) The Impossibility of Global Citizenship, *Brock Education: A Journal of General Inquiry*, Special Issue—Citizenship Education in the Era of Globalization: Canadian Perspectives, 17(1): 22–37.

Yack, B. (1992) *The Longing for Total Revolution: Philosophic Sources of Social Discontent from Rousseau to Marx and Nietzsche*, Berkeley: University of California Press.

7 'I'm Here to Help'

Development Workers, the Politics of Benevolence and Critical Literacy

Nancy Cook

In her article 'Global Citizenship and Study Abroad: It's All about U.S.,' Talya Zemach-Bersin (2007) confronts American university administrators who uncritically encourage their undergraduate students to study abroad. In promoting the internationalization of higher education, these administrators—supported by federal initiatives and funds—hope to recuperate America's reputation around the globe, which has waned in the wake of the U.S. government's responses to the World Trade Center attacks of September 11, 2001. In particular, they anticipate that sending American students to live and study in other countries will encourage cross-cultural understanding and 'global citizenship,' alleviate ignorance, and compensate for failed U.S. foreign policy. But this enthusiasm for taking learning on the road, Zemach-Bersin (2007, 17) argues,

> overlooks the many ways in which the discourse of study abroad surreptitiously reproduces the logic of colonialism, legitimizes American imperialist desires, and allows for the interests of U.S. foreign policy to be articulated through the specious rhetoric of global universality. Though presented with an appealing veneer of multicultural understanding and progressive global responsibility, the current discourse of study abroad is nationalistic, imperialistic, and political in nature.

If American university administrators and the federal government fail to acknowledge the 'unintended consequences' of studying abroad and becoming a 'global citizen,' then most of the participating students (the majority of whom are women) likely are not aware of their inculcation in contemporary forms of imperialism as they "harvest the resource of international knowledge" (Zemach-Bersin 2007, 22) and bring it home to advance and strengthen American economic, cultural, and political interests.

Barbara Heron (2004, 2005a, 2005b) is also concerned about how social-work students who go abroad to fulfill their program practicum requirement are implicated in contemporary transcultural power relations that linger in nonlinear ways from the colonial era. In her more recent work *Desire for Development: Whiteness, Gender, and the Helping Imperative*

(2007), Heron turns her attention from students to Canadian women who have traveled to Africa to do development work. Heron argues that these women's desire to do the good work of development is largely motivated by the personal longing to construct a helping self, an identity as a global 'good guy' who makes a positive difference in the lives of needy others by implementing Western-derived reforms. She draws many of the same conclusions as Zemach-Bersin (2007, 24), particularly that development workers, like students who study abroad, join the ranks of "missionaries, colonizers, anthropologists, and humanitarian aid workers who have served as 'goodwill ambassadors,' promoting the soft power interests of the metropole."

I am also interested to analyze the effects Western development workers have on global power relations as they live and work abroad, often in once-colonized locales (Cook 2005, 2006, 2007). The political aim of my research, as in this chapter, is to encourage development workers to undertake the difficult work of reflecting on how they forge a life abroad, how they understand their development work, and how they represent the supposed 'recipients' of development in order to understand the unintended consequences those decisions and representations have for both the people among whom they live and global relations of power. But the new American rhetoric about the 'global citizen,' which Zemach-Bersin describes and universities, governments, and development agencies claim to be fostering, obscures these power relations. While the 'global citizen' is increasingly invoked, "rarely is a concrete definition presented or explored. Typically the term is employed as an empty signifier, without even a contextual definition" (Zemach-Bersin 2007, 19). I want to use this chapter to fill that signifier, to develop the concept of 'global citizen,' but not as someone who unwittingly uses it and its related practices to maintain Western hegemony. Rather, I want to understand and claim a 'global citizen' as someone who reflects on their complicity in global power relations, considers their responsibilities to those who are disadvantaged by current global arrangements, and who actively resists perpetuating them so that Othered groups can actively exist in a more just social reality. Advocating for Western development workers to become this sort of global citizen requires encouraging them to reflect on their work goals and motives, as well as their everyday practices abroad.

How do we begin to do this self-reflexive work? Vanessa Andreotti (2006a, 2006b; Andreotti and Warwick 2007), who has been working with Voluntary Services Abroad to help development volunteers consider these issues before they go overseas, argues that self-reflection often productively begins when volunteers are asked to shift their development focus from 'making a difference to them' to 'mutual learning,' which involves volunteers learning to listen, to learn from others, to learn about difference, and to learn how to alter harmful practices and representations. As Andreotti (2006b) argues, this kind of 'critical literacy,' as an educational practice, helps Western development workers "analyze the relationships amongst language, power, social practices, identities and inequalities, to imagine 'otherwise,' to engage ethically with difference, and to understand the potential implications of their thoughts and actions" at both the local and global scale.

Considering these concerns about initiating processes of self-reflexivity and critical literacy in development workers to engender socially just global citizens and less oppressive development practices, my aim in this chapter is to provide an analysis of the lives of a group of white Western women development volunteers I studied while they were living in the Muslim community of Gilgit, northern Pakistan, in 1999 and 2000. In describing their work motives, everyday practices, and representations of the people they were 'helping,' I show how they act to increase their own autonomy through global travel and benevolent development work while simultaneously thwarting the autonomy of Gilgitis. These negative and often unintended outcomes are rooted in imperial power relations that linger from the colonial past. My hope is that development volunteers can use this analysis as a tool to help them reflect on their own goals, motives, and daily lives abroad so they can begin to act and imagine otherwise.

MAKING A DIFFERENCE TO THEM

The 'helping imperative' that Heron discusses pervades the testimonials development volunteers post on the Internet when they return home from a stint abroad. Here are a couple of examples from the Cross-Cultural Solutions (2007) Web site:

> Sometimes I did wonder how my being there was helping, but when I saw eyes light up and people rush to greet me at the center, or welcome me into their homes with open arms, I knew that just my presence let them know that people care, and for that they were so grateful.

> It finally hit me full force one day when working with a student . . . I realized then that I was making a difference and a contribution just by being who I was. I never lost patience with that student, or any other. No matter how many times he called me over, I would stand by him. In that or any other moment, when faced with someone's need to feel connected, all I had to offer was myself.

This desire to improve the lives of others is also an important factor that encouraged my research participants to travel abroad, the 'official' reason most of them gave for why they took development placements in Gilgit.[1] Most women told me they felt lucky to have had a good education, comparatively satisfying and well-paid work and materially abundant lives. They want to share the fruits of their good fortune with less privileged people by putting their expertise to work in a developing country. Elena,[2] a single twenty-nine-year-old British teacher trainer, told me that

> I've been really lucky, because I've done anything I wanted to do . . . I wanted to go to university . . . and become a teacher, and I was able to do that. And then, I always wanted to live and work abroad some-where, but not earn like loads of money . . . I feel, honestly, that we're still much better off than a lot of people here, but a local wage is what I wanted. So I'd describe myself as being very lucky. And I want to give something back.

Joan, who is a fifty-year-old British school principal, has also wanted to help for a long time: "I think there were lots of reasons why I got to the point of deciding to come. I'd always had it in my mind that I would like to come and work in a developing country—that's not Pakistan, just a devel-oping country—at some point in my career, to help." Margaret has come to Pakistan as a volunteer development worker to repay her debt to people in other developing countries who have been overwhelmingly generous: "I've done a lot of traveling [in developing countries], and I'd reached the stage where I said 'I've got so much out of my experiences, how can I give back?' And this seemed to be a way."

The women I interviewed and observed in my study are not unlike many of the volunteers who discuss their development motives on the Web. They are a group of thirty British, Canadian, Dutch, American, and Australian volunteers working for international development agencies in Gilgit, many on two-year contracts negotiated through Volunteer Services Overseas (VSO). They are health workers, teachers, librarians, English-language coaches, and teacher trainers who instruct local educators on new methods of teaching the curriculum in English. None of these volunteers have educa-tional degrees in international development studies or consider themselves 'professional' development workers with international experience and in-depth knowledge of the context in which they work. Rather, they are lay teachers and health-care workers who understand themselves as 'volunteer-ing' two years of their lives to help others by unproblematically transferring their skills and expertise into a different social context. Most are paid a local wage in local currency, and are prepared for their tenure abroad only through a short VSO training session (with VSO library access) in London and another in-country session once they arrive in Pakistan to learn the basics of Urdu and Islam. Critical perspectives on development are not dis-cussed in either preparatory regime. Surprisingly, even the NGOs for which women work do not 'train' or educate them about the local social setting, work context, or goals and philosophies that drive overarching development agendas. NGOs limit their role to assigning foreign volunteers particular responsibilities and jobs in the field and assisting them as they learn to negotiate the practicalities of everyday life in Gilgit. Consequently, these volunteers may have different perceptions of their work and a different sense of themselves and their limitations than other types of development workers. Their understanding of 'development' is framed not as much by the official institutions of international development such as universities, nationally-funded development agencies, and grassroots NGOs but more by a nonorganizationally rooted helping imperative.

Interestingly, a desire to help is not the only thing that motivates volunteers to do development work abroad. Here are a few more testimonials from the Cross-Cultural Solutions (2007) Web site that draw our attention to what I call the 'self-development' motives for volunteering:

> This was a life changing experience! It has opened my eyes up to the reality of a new culture and it has given me the courage to face challenges alone.

> This is an amazing experience! Every aspect of it, the volunteer work, the cultural immersion, the traveling, extracurricular activities, and the personal sense of satisfaction that it all brings is overwhelming.

> I learned a lot about myself and how to survive even when I don't speak the language. It taught me a lot about myself and how self-sufficient I really am.

My research participants are equally straightforward about these less altruistic benefits of doing development work abroad. Evelyn, a forty-three-year-old Canadian teaching consultant, concludes that "nobody has 100 percent pure motives . . . I'm at the point where I can't define who's here because they really want to help people, or, as in my case, part of the reason for me taking the job was that I needed the *money* . . . I want to do good work, but I can only take that so far." In explaining to me why she decided to do development work after just getting her feet wet in a teaching career, Susan says, "It sounds a bit *crass*. I wanted to do something, I wanted to feel worthwhile . . . If I'm honest, I'd say the main reason I'm here is for selfish reasons. The job opportunity is *great*. We get a lot of professional freedom here, which you don't get in Britain." Dolly also "needed to do something that's *worthwhile*. That sounds really *pious*, doesn't it . . . That's for me, never mind anyone that's on the receiving end. That's trying to be honest about it. It actually fulfills something in me. I only feel half a person if that's not happening." Jean suggests that the benevolent aspect of her work is even downplayed in favor of personal development by the volunteer agency that sent her:

> Australian Volunteers International has this other philosophy that, because you're bringing home the cultural experience, it's fine if you live

in a community in a fairly harmless way. It doesn't really matter if my skills are transferred. That's the way it's working out in my placement ... I'm having a good cultural experience ... Ideally AVI would like both to happen, the cultural exchange and the skills transfer, but, in most cases, just the one happens.

These 'selfish' motives intermingle with the helping imperative in each of my research participants' stories of development travel. However, they tend to put far more emphasis on what 'pushed' them, rather than what drew them to development work in Gilgit. René, Evelyn, and Amanda were unable to find well-paid jobs at home. In Evelyn's words, they came "chasing money." But this job offered Evelyn more than an income: "I'm a bigger fish in this small pond than I was at home. I found that my career was nose-diving in Canada ... Discretionary money and consultancies were drying up. It was impossible [to find that work] anymore. So *here*, I revived my career." Other women were fleeing an empty nest. Troubling family relations, including divorces, elderly parent nursing responsibilities, and bereavements, compelled several others to leave home. But no matter the source of the push, almost all of the women in my study claimed some kind of 'emancipation aspiration' in their departure narrative, which they hope to fulfill through development work and the experience of global travel. Janet, for instance, concludes that her experiences in Gilgit have improved her preparedness for old age: "If I've had an experience of having just *physically* survived here, it brings me into a slightly more confident old age in Britain ... I had hoped that as an outcome that I would be a *stronger* and less *fearful* old lady, going into old age knowing that you can cope with things and not be fearful." Gaining confidence through her work abroad has helped Dolly escape an increasingly dull life at home: "I don't think I can settle back in the UK. It's just not enough ... I think I need the variety ... I don't know what's missing there. I've outgrown those experiences ... I wouldn't be satisfied to go back to that. But I'd quite like to go and see what's around a few more corners, now that I've got more experience of traveling and more confidence about traveling with VSO." Traveling abroad to do development work seems not to be solely a selfless venture of helping for Western women in Gilgit as the politics of benevolence would have it, but also, as it was in the colonial era, a means for metropolitan women dissatisfied with their lives at home to constitute themselves as full, independent, and authoritative individuals and thereby achieve some sense of personal autonomy (Knapman 1986; Ware 1992; Sharpe 1993; George 1994; Kaplan 1997; Ghose 1998).

Scholars have claimed that the function of travel for Europeans in the colonial era was to realize a fuller sense of self (Buzard 1993). I argue that this is still the case, especially for women, who historically have had a marginal relationship to travel. The traditional requirements of femininity involve sticking close to home, making travel a largely masculine activity. By choosing to leave home, my research participants disrupt these requirements and thereby enhance their self-understanding as independent individuals. Their strategies of escape through travel enact personal autonomy by allowing women to transgress gender norms at home; to shape a self-confident, somewhat elitist feminine identity; and to gain some sense of control over their lives. The feelings of independence and confidence Western women achieve from traveling helps them to realize other, more autonomous selves. If volunteering to do development work is inspired by motives of self-development as well as the helping imperative, then in helping others volunteers can simultaneously help themselves. Sounds like a win-win situation. But is this the case? In many instances it isn't because, as I will show, helping Self often involves implicitly and unintentionally denigrating Others.

THE 'RECIPIENTS' OF DEVELOPMENT

During formal interviews, the women in my study, without prompting, spent considerable time describing local women, the people they had come to help, despite also confessing that they were not intimately familiar with Gilgiti women's everyday lives. And those descriptions were fairly uniform. Most of my research participants understand these Muslim women as a homogenous, undifferentiated group with identical interests, experiences, and goals that is oppressed by the dictates of Islam and patriarchal husbands and that has little ability or aptitude to challenge their oppression. Amanda, a thirty-seven-year-old Dutch teacher, provides a good example: "Here, the women are always suffering. They give too many children birth. And they let men handle them like weak people. That's their lot. They can't be seen or heard. That's a big problem here for me, the plight of Pakistani women." Gilgiti women's apparent lack of agency to fight their 'lot' is almost as bluntly represented by twenty-six-year-old Andy, who was "brought up in the UK to know that I did have a say, and that I could say 'No!' to [men]. And I think women here *don't* have that. When my girlfriends were visiting, we were talking about women here who don't even know they have the right to say 'No.' Is it abuse or is it rape? Probably not, it's just *life* here." Why do my research participants have such ideas, especially when they have no close friendships with local women and therefore do not know the intimate circumstances of their lives? We need to look to history for an answer to that question.

From its very inception, Islam has been represented in the West as one of the most powerful threats to metropolitan civilizations (Said 1978, 1981; Kepel 1992; Al-Azmeh 1993; Bulbeck 1998). It is stereotypically imagined by white Westerners as composed of consenting masses of maniacal men, who keep their veiled women shut up at home, postured in prayer before a howling mullah. Anxiety about Islam has heightened with the increased migration of Muslims to Europe, North America, and Australia, the Iranian Revolution (1979), the Salman Rushdie affair (1989), the World Trade Center attacks, and most recently with Western military incursions into Iraq and Afghanistan. News reports, media and state representations of veiled women, political cartoons, and everyday interactions with Muslim women in the West encourage my research participants to 'know' an irrational, oppressive Islam and of Muslim women who passively accept their subordination under Islam. These 'facts' prompt them to feel sorry for victimized Muslim women, to understand them as essentially different from and subordinate to 'liberated' Western women who are free to travel, do development work, and make their own choices. They also make patriarchal practices in Europe and North America disappear.

This tendency to homogenize women from the so-called third world and represent them as oppressed and different from white Western women is common when referring to non-Muslim groups too. Chandra Mohanty (1984) argues that this construct of the 'Third World Woman' as a singular and monolithic subject is a racist and imperialist move, meaning that it is based on white-centered experience, knowledge, and judgments that gloss over the differences between third world women and ignore that the experience of oppression is diverse, contingent on time, place, and culture, and just as much a part of social organization in Europe and North America as it is in poorer regions of the world. For example, in their ethnocentric 'helping agendas,' development agencies and volunteers, like many researchers, judge third world economic, religious, and familial structures by Western standards. Rather than trying to understand the ways in which women are situated within and negotiate these social structures, Westerners insert a preconstituted 'Third World Woman' into them, in the process defining her as religious, housebound, illiterate, and completely subject to the whims of her husband, extended family, and state and religious leaders. These depictions of passive and oppressed third world women are paternalistic; they imply that these women cannot emancipate or develop themselves, but rather must rely on benevolent Westerners to supply ideas and implement programs that both organize social chaos and initiate progressive social change. Furthermore, representations of the 'Third World Other' enable white Westerners to understand themselves, in contrast, as liberated and independent people who control their own lives and have valuable knowledge and expertise to share. What is implied here is that third world women are stuck in history; they have not yet 'evolved' as far as the West has and, therefore, need help to 'modernize.' These ideas, and their related practices, are racist and imperialistic.

Relational representations of 'liberated' Self and 'oppressed' Other emerge clearly in interviews with my research participants. When I asked the women in my study to describe themselves for me, they almost always characterized themselves as 'free' Western women who contrast favorably with Gilgiti women. René is adamant that

The *best* thing about Americans is their tremendous freedom. It stops my heart when I think about the freedom of America . . . Independence is a very Western thing and dependence is a very Eastern thing. For an American, to be very independent can be good, as far as expanding their minds. And creativity is a very positive thing that comes from in-dependence . . . Whereas dependence, with this extended family or cul-tural expectations, that can be very confining and keep a person from developing themselves and their skills, and having the joy of learning things . . . Dependence can be very oppressive and confining.

Marion thinks that "what [Gilgiti women] envy about us is our indepen-dence, our ability to live alone and to make our own decisions, to make our own money. I point out to them that there can be *too much* inde-pendence, and that people can become very lonely and very isolated, but they, of course, like everybody else, can only see good in what they don't have yet." My research participants often see their independent selves as sources of inspiration and redemption for Muslim Gilgiti women. Andy believes "You can't solve the world's problems. You can't fight all the bat-tles. And I prefer, in a way, to work at empowering local women to do it themselves. But I sometimes make a point of walking through the bazaar wearing a t-shirt and pants, because I think if I don't, no local woman will ever be able to." Using the ethnocentric logic I describe above, Andy assumes that Gilgit women want to dress as Western women do, but are prohibited. She also invokes the imperialistic and racist 'helping imper-ative' by positing herself as a model of emancipation and an urgently required agent of modernization.

Christine, like Andy, defines herself as favorably situated in relation to Muslim women. For instance, she complains that "There's this assump-tion here that, as a woman, you will just fall in with [men's] ideas. I mean, they're used to me now. They know that *I* won't." But at another moment, Christine seems ambivalent about how much freedom local women have or can achieve: "Some [local Sunni women teachers] can't leave for jobs outside the valley, because, of course, they're not allowed to travel and the men just can't be bothered to escort them everyday. So, blow me, instead of sitting by the fire and moaning, they've opened their own little school. It's just brilliant, just wonderful." In one instance Elena seems similarly uncon-vinced that all local women face a lifetime of oppression. She is impressed with her work coordinator, who has ignored family pressure to take a sec-ond wife so he can sire a son: "They're *so* much in love, he and his wife. It's a *wonder* to see. They've got, I suppose, as equal a relationship as you can get here." But a few minutes later she laments that

Women here, ahhh [sighs], they never get to go anywhere, and they're stuck in their homes all day, every day. That honestly breaks my heart, it does. I just think 'God, I don't know what I'd do.' You can't think that all these women are born like this, wanting to stay home and be humble and shy and quiet. There must be people like us [Western women] around who are extroverted. It's just pushed down. It's terrible . . . The way women live here is sad. Just to have *babies* and be servants to their husbands.

Although she trains local women teachers, and thus realizes that they experience possibilities as well as constraints, Elena ignores that agency by perpetuating the view that Muslim women, *en masse*, are confined to the male-dominated space of the home.

Although my research participants sometimes have conflicting ideas about the status of Gilgiti women, they most often see these Muslim women as radically different from white Western women. By viewing local women through an imperial lens as 'oppressed,' they can perceive themselves as 'free' and autonomous. But in these representations, Muslim women remain faceless and silent. They are absent objects, muted figures, foreclosed Others with no independent condition of existence (Spivak 1985, 1988). The heterogeneity of Gilgiti women's lives is colonized so that their voices are rendered inaudible, their material realities and daily struggles are overlooked, and their cultural productions disregarded. Their subsequent lack of subjecthood robs them of agency, making them seem reliant on outside development initiatives. Transcultural relations between groups of women in Gilgit, then, are situated within a colonial legacy of power relations that strengthen Western women's self-images and social efficacy at the expense of local women's autonomy, understood as their capacity to achieve an independent subjecthood in transcultural interactions, as opposed to the object status that has been already constituted for them through imperial representations. If we grant that these are unintended consequences of my research participants' desire to help, coupled with their quest for self-development, then contemporary development practice is risky business for its 'recipients.'

DEVELOPMENT PRACTICE

Harmful ideas about the recipients of development structure most volunteers' understandings of their development work and their everyday development practices. Most women in my study understand their development work as helping work (or benevolence), as well as a sign both of their freedom to travel as independent women and of their cultural superiority. Consequently, the racism implicit in Self/Other representations is sustained as my research participants strive to differentiate themselves from Gilgiti women through the world of work. But once this racism becomes enmeshed in material practices of development that are meant to 'improve' Gilgiti people and sociocultural systems, some of my research participants also enact imperial power relations. As I mention earlier, most women in my study are working overseas in educational development. Teaching abroad is part of a strategy of self-development as it allows Western women to increase their knowledge, specialization, and experience, which can translate into professional advancement, work autonomy, and pay increases once they return to the West. Although they are involved in the nurturing, feminized field of education, my research participants gain cultural authority by being Western educated, thinking of themselves—in contrast to Gilgiti women—as independent and smart enough to do the work, and representing that work as an essential cultural 'improvement' project. The sense of achievement they experience through their development work helps them develop a sense of themselves as confident, capable, and worthwhile people in various spheres of life. The second set of Cross-Cultural Solutions testimonials I quote above provides further evidence of this claim.

But development work fulfills more than volunteers' aspirations for personal growth. It also allows them to effect modernization and local social change. For Louise, "Work's the most meaningful thing in life here. I do observations of teachers, and to look back at them, it's lovely to see that they've actually changed because of something I've done." Janet is also satisfied to shape a legacy as a cultural benefactor: "This whole crowd of people I *know* have benefited from the service I have helped to provide. And there's this [local] colleague who's *grown* in stature and assurance and competence. That's not a bad legacy." Christine more explicitly focuses on the 'improving' aspect of her work: "I pointed out [to the teachers I train] that I was here to do a *job*, and the way we worked in the West was that you took your job *seriously*. I was here to do something, not just to drink tea with them and have a laugh all the time. Obviously I tried to make training as light-hearted as I can, but, at the end of the day, they're to do a job and I'm here to train them to do it better." By stressing her superior leadership, Christine contrasts herself—an independent, competent British woman with a good education and important work responsibilities—to local teachers who are represented as professionally uncommitted, rather than as individuals who work according to a different set of values and a different understanding of an appropriate home/work balance.

Development work poses several difficult challenges for my research participants. They have to cope with being alone on training courses in neighboring villages, where they are unsupported and alienated for several weeks at a time. They do not speak local languages. NGOs usually provide educators with very little information about their work context and even less guidance regarding local learning, teaching, and management styles. Women also work long hours, six days a week, to meet the high expectations NGOs set for dramatic development results. Despite these challenges, the volunteers in my study aim to address as many facets of local education as possible, bringing them in line with Western standards and methodologies. Conforming to an ethnocentric logic, they try to 'improve' local teaching and learning styles, teachers' fluency in English, math, and science, the dominant work ethic, classroom discipline, school management and schedules, hygiene standards at schools and in local homes, and the status of local women through educational initiatives to meet a 'higher quality' Western standard. To their credit, they also strive to promote educational content that is cosmopolitan in perspective but still meets the needs of people whose culture, geographical location, and unwritten first languages are not addressed in government-issue textbooks.

Most of my research participants believe these changes are valuable and welcomed by local people. When they learn otherwise, the sense of autonomy they gain through development work may be unsettled. Jane, a forty-year-old teacher, reflects that "You have these ideas back in the UK that you're going to be able to do something and really make a difference to people's lives. And yes, there has been a lot of that, but we hadn't realized that there'd be opposition from *within* communities. Who would guess . . . people are not sure they really want our education and have misgivings about what it might do to the structure of society?" Ignoring the limited scope of many educational curricula in the West, Lyn also believes her teaching initiatives can improve local education and local culture by extension: "One of the *biggest* problems is this incredibly *narrow* education they have. Ask somebody where Canada is and they won't have a clue. They have no concept of anything. And the biggest shock to me was that they don't *want* to know . . . So better education comes first, and I think through education that would flow to the culture more generally. We *have* to free up the girls." Using the same ethnocentric logic that assumes locals do and know nothing, Rose, a fifty-four-year-old Dutch teacher trainer, finds the local work ethic "*unbelievable* . . . It's nice [for teachers] to have this salary, but no one worries about work . . . About maths they know nothing. They even can't teach in Urdu . . . I can only show them how to do everything, giving demonstrations. Yeah, and basic things . . . like washing their hands and bringing a notebook . . . These teachers don't know how to do this . . . I hope my example will work."

By drawing on this sense of themselves as improving philanthropists, which incorporates racist and imperialistic impulses, my research participants forge liberated and authoritative, yet nurturing, self-understandings as they do their development work. Development work thus constitutes and confirms their identities as autonomous, benevolent, and superior metropolitan women. And the notion that local women are not allowed to do this work, or do it poorly, substantiates this construction of Self. For example, Joan told me, "There are only two or three professional women that I know here who have jobs that bring in money. And they say to their families, 'I have a full-time job, I'm having children. I'm prepared to peel potatoes, make the *chapatti*, but I will *not* maintain animals or go to the fields.' They're creating a different work role for themselves . . . but these are *very* small beginnings." The women in my study, as I have briefly shown, often depict Gilgiti women as economically dependent house servants with few life opportunities. Therefore, they believe Gilgiti women rarely obtain the education necessary to teach, the opportunity to land a job, and the time to do the work well, often despite what they see every day to the contrary during teacher training sessions.

At the end of this analysis, what inferences can be drawn from my research with these development volunteers in this setting that are relevant to my project of creating global citizens with critical literacy? First, my research participants forge a sense of personal autonomy and professional empowerment through their social philanthropy. These salient aspects of self-development often override altruistic helping impulses. Second, 'benevolent' development work often incorporates racist representations and practices that define differences between Gilgiti women who are ostensibly homebound, needy, and dull-witted and metropolitan women who are free to work abroad as capable benefactors. Third, 'improving' initiatives frequently enact imperial practices and identities as Western volunteers represent Gilgitis, in deeply patronizing ways, as unable to improve themselves. By denigrating most aspects of local education systems, they justify Western interventions, especially into the lives of local women, as part of a contemporary 'civilizing' mission. These dominant understandings have a long, but fractured, legacy in South Asia (Spivak 1985; Ramusack 1990; Jolly 1993), as do practices of social, cultural, and intellectual reform through white women's burden of education and health care (Ware 1992; Jolly 1993; Ghose 1998). While these well-established practices and perceptions have always been contested by particular Westerners and thus have shifted over time, they have been further unsettled by antiracist agendas within contemporary feminist and multicultural movements that caution teachers against prejudiced, ethnocentric worldviews and activities, especially in the classroom. However, some women in my study recuperate imperial practices of conversion when they try to mould Gilgiti lives to fit a Western prototype and to impose metropolitan, yet ostensibly universally applicable, models, principles, behaviors, knowledge, and values through education—especially in the English language (Jayaweera 1990; Ramusack 1990; Jayawardena 1995).

FROM 'HELPING' TO CRITICAL LITERACY

In this chapter I draw on the insights of feminist and postcolonial theory (Young 2001; Loomba 2005; Andreotti 2006a) to analyze my research participants' development motives, practices, and representations of the people they want to 'help' in Gilgit. My aim was to show that the 'helping imperative' that purportedly motivates their volunteering is a trickster; it slips and slides alongside desires for self-development, among racist ideas and imperialist practices that perpetuate the marginality of 'Third World

Others' in the twenty-first century. These contemporary processes are linked to ventures in the colonial past, but not as part of the pragmatic and diverse sets of practices used to establish and manage colonies abroad that we now call colonialism (Young 2001). Rather, they are elements of a lingering imperialism, a system of global social, economic, and cultural domination that operates from the metropolitan center over ostensibly inferior subaltern populations without the agenda of political rule. Overt missionary conversion in the colonial era, for example, has a legacy in contemporary international development because similar ideas and representations organize their practices. While they are different global mechanisms with particular trajectories, they are characterized by overlapping histories of global domination.

In development work, global citizenship is enacted in a way that sees the needs that others have as being predetermined, and this results in the unintended and harmful outcomes outlined in my analysis. Critical reflection on these processes, histories, and outcomes is necessary for imagining and acting otherwise. How do Others lead their daily lives and under what circumstances? What do they need? What do Western volunteers have to offer? How do relations of power organize current ideas and practices of development? How can those ideas and practices be changed to realize less oppressive development agendas and a more just social reality? As I suggest in the introduction, perhaps reconsidering the primary focus of development is a useful initial reimagining site.

Following Andreotti's (2006a, 2006b; Andreotti and Warwick 2007) advice, volunteers may be better served by shifting their focus to 'mutual learning' in an effort to reflect on the important questions I list above. Mutual learning as a way to develop critical literacy involves relinquishing the development driver seat. From the passenger sidelines we can listen (rather than preach) to others, learn from them what their lives are like and what they need, what has not worked in the past and why, who are the best people to initiate change. Critical literacy encourages a respect for difference, as opposed to ethnocentric judgments and 'civilizing' agendas. It requires taking a generalized learner stance toward others that assumes they are competent and knowledgeable about their own lives and social circumstances. In this way, 'Third World Others' are transformed from the objects of development into people with full subjecthood from whom valuable lessons can be learned. Becoming global citizens with critical literacy is a humbling experience. And considering the colonial past that haunts us today, that humility is long overdue.

NOTES

1. Gilgit is the largest town in the Gilgit-Baltistan, a federally administered province of Pakistan. It is located in the far north, near the Wakhan Corridor of Afghanistan and the Chinese border, and lies in a steep valley at

1,400 meters at the confluence of the Hindukush, Karakoram, and Himalaya mountain ranges.
2. Pseudonyms chosen by individual research participants are used throughout the chapter.

REFERENCES

Al-Azmeh, A. (1993) *Islams and Modernities*, London: Verso.
Andreotti, V. (2006a) 'Theory without Practice Is Idle, Practice without Theory Is Blind: The Potential Contributions of Postcolonial Theory to Development Education', *Development Education Journal*, 12(3): 7–10.
———. (2006b) 'Soft Versus Critical Global Citizenship Education', *Development Education: Policy and Practice* 3(Autumn): 83–98.
Andreotti, V. and Warwick, P. (2007) 'Engaging Students with Controversial Issues through a Dialogue Based Approach', Published online by CitizED, http://www.citized.info/?r_menu=res&strand=3 (accessed November 10, 2009).
Bulbeck, C. (1998) *Re-Orienting Western Feminisms: Women's Diversity in a Postcolonial World*, Cambridge: Cambridge University Press.
Buzard, J. (1993) *The Beaten Track: European Tourism, Literature and the Ways to 'Culture,' 1800–1918*, Oxford: Clarendon Press.
Cook, N. (2005) 'What to Wear, What to Wear?: Western Women and Imperialism in Gilgit, Pakistan', *Qualitative Sociology*, 28(4): 349–367.
———. (2006) 'Bazaar Stories of Gender, Sexuality and Imperial Space in Gilgit, Northern Pakistan', *ACME: An International E-Journal for Critical Geographies* 5(2): 230–257.
———. (2007) *Gender, Identity and Imperialism: Women Development Workers in Pakistan*, New York: Palgrave Macmillan.
Cross-Cultural Solutions. (2007) 'Volunteer Voices', from http://www.crossculturalsolutions.org (accessed January 10, 2008).
George, R. (1994) 'Homes in the Empire, Empires in the Home', *Cultural Critique*,(Winter): 95–127.
Ghose, I. (1998) *Women Travelers in Colonial India: The Power of the Female Gaze*, Delhi: Oxford University Press.
Heron, B. (2004) 'Gender and Exceptionality in North-South Research: Reflecting on Relations', *Journal of Gender Studies*, 13(2): 117–127.
———. (2005a) 'Changes and Challenges: Preparing Social Work Students for Practicums in Today's Sub-Saharan African Context', *Journal of International Social Work*, 48(6): 782–793.
———. (2005b) 'Self-Reflection in Critical Social Work Practice: Subjectivity and the Possibilities of Resistance', *Journal of Reflective Practice*, 6(3): 341–351.
———. (2007) *Desire for Development: Whiteness, Gender and the Helping Imperative*, Waterloo, ON, Canada: Wilfrid Laurier University Press.
Jayawardena, K. (1995) *The White Women's Other Burden: Western Women and South Asia During British Rule*, London: Routledge.
Jayaweera, S. (1990) 'European Women Educators under the British Colonial Administration in Sri Lanka', *Women's Studies International Forum*, 13(4): 323–331.
Jolly, M. (1993) The Maternal Body and Empire. In S. Gunew and A. Yeatman (eds.), *Feminism and the Politics of Difference*, Halifax: Fernwood Publishing, 103–127.
Kaplan, E. (1997) *Looking for the Other: Feminism, Film, and the Imperial Gaze*, London: Routledge.

Kepel, G. (1992) 'ReIslamisation Movements in Contemporary History', *Contention* 2(1): 151–159.

Knapman, C. (1986) *White Women in Fiji, 1835–1930*, London: Allen and Unwin.

Loomba, A. (2005) *Colonialism/Postcolonialism*, New York: Routledge.

Mohanty, C. (1984) 'Under Western Eyes: Feminist Scholarship and Colonial Discourses', *Boundary*, 2 12(3)/13(1): 333–353.

Ramusack, B. (1990) 'Cultural Missionaries, Maternal Imperialists, Feminist Allies: British Women Activists in India, 1865–1945', *Women's Studies International Forum*, 13(4): 309–321.

Said, E. (1978) *Orientalism: Western Representations of the Orient*, New York: Vintage Books.

———. (1981) *Covering Islam: How the Media and the Experts Determine How We See the Rest of the World*, New York: Pantheon Books.

Sharpe, J. (1993) *Allegories of Empire: The Figure of Woman in the Colonial Text*, Minneapolis: University of Minnesota Press.

Spivak, G. (1985) 'Three Women's Texts and a Critique of Imperialism', *Critical Inquiry*, 12(1): 243–261.

———. (1988) 'Can the Subaltern Speak?', in C. Nelson and L. Grossberg (eds.), *Marxism and the Interpretation of Culture*, London: Macmillan, 217–313.

Ware, V. (1992) *Beyond the Pale: White Women, Racism, and History*, Verso: London.

Young, R. (2001) *Postcolonialism: An Historical Introduction*, Oxford: Blackwell Publishing.

Zemach-Bersin, T. (2007) 'Global Citizenship and Study Abroad: It's All about U.S.', *Critical Literacy: Theories and Practices*, 1(2): 16–28.

8   Making Poverty History in the Society of the Spectacle
Civil Society and Educated Politics

Nick Stevenson

The link between education and global citizenship has recently been a matter of explicit focus for the campaign group Oxfam. Educators in this respect are urged to teach young people about global poverty, fair trade, the need to respect diversity and of course to become more ecologically responsible. The campaign for a more globally orientated citizenry has arguably been one of the more positive developments within education more recently. Further, as we shall see later, the 'Make Poverty History' campaign has also played a crucial role in helping educate a wider public about the persistence of chronic poverty in a world where more than a billion people live on less than a dollar a day. While I don't want to be overly critical of these developments given that many of them are new and evidently challenge a number of more cynical responses that either seek to deny our responsibility or simply encourage us to look the other way, they do pose a number of more critical questions. In some of my own pedagogic relations with young people I have often been shocked by some of the attitudes towards global poverty. Many young people I meet here at a British University seem to think extreme poverty is simply a way of controlling population levels. When I have expressed my profound indignation with this view, a number of other far more complex investments come to the surface that expresses a more disillusioned orientation towards the possibility of a politics of transformation. In this context, then, some of the more 'positive' aspects of the idea of global citizenship or campaigns against global poverty are hard to criticize as at least they are facing up to some key global issues. However, as we shall see, I argue that a more substantial emphasis upon questions of political economy, economic and cultural justice and democracy are required if alternatives to neoliberalism more generally are to be discovered within mediated public spaces and education more generally.

A culture of cynicism is not best addressed through an easily consumable politics that does not offer contested democratically organized public spaces that offer alternative explanations and more dialogic forms of engagement. Here I wish to recapture the idea of emancipatory politics after it has been deconstructed by postmodernism by suggesting that the struggle for justice and democracy is in fact far from finished. In this respect, I will critically reinvestigate the work of Franz Fanon and Paulo Freire and argue that, despite some of the problems they encounter, both offer a vision of an emancipatory global politics that has rejected domination while embracing more humanized social relations. Further, I will briefly look at the contribution of Guy Debord in respect of the society of the spectacle and reread his contribution as a warning as to the consequences of what happens to the civic domain once commodified images start to replace more contested forms of politics. Here I am guided by the argument that any emancipatory politics requires not only a contested public realm but also new narratives which can suggest different identities and subject positions which would encourage citizens to reflexively rethink their own current identities and perspectives. These features are not only essential to the future of any substantial critical theory but are important ingredients in any future ethical life or idea of the good society.

REREADING FRANZ FANON AND PAULO FREIRE

Fanon then needs to be understood in the context of a national liberation struggle against colonial French occupation. The colonial context gives rise to a segregated world where the natives are opposed to the colonists as if they are 'two different species' (Fanon 2001, 30). The brutal and violent rule by the French, argues Fanon, gave rise to a certain kind of oppositional politics. This is not 'a rational confrontation of points of view' but is instead the confrontation of absolutes (Fanon 2001, 32). Colonial rule reveals the struggle for supremacy on the part of white Europeans over cultures they have deemed to be inferior. For Fanon the native's response is divided between a mocking laughter at the idea of Western values and violence. Colonial cultures, then, are not places of reason and discussion but of violence. Indeed, colonialism is a sphere where reason seemingly has no place and is overdetermined by a context that can only be transformed where violence is 'confronted with greater violence' (Fanon 2001, 48). For Fanon it was the violence of colonialism that actually allowed for the well-being of Europeans whose economic prosperity is built upon the exploitation of the peoples of the underdeveloped world.

Despite the violence of this confrontation, the struggle for independence from colonial rule can easily turn into a curse. Fanon feared that the winning of national 'independence' would prove to be a Pyrrhic victory for colonized peoples fearing the withdrawal of economic resources. Indeed, he even goes as far as to say that the contestation within colonial cultures may well prove to be historically of less significance than the global need to redistribute wealth (Fanon 2001, 77–78). In this respect, the defeat of European occupation is unlikely to be enough to repay the debt to the people that they colonized. At this point, Fanon explicitly acknowledges the connections between European fascism and colonialism. Fanon argues that

European capitalists have behaved like 'war criminals' utilizing deportations, massacres and forced labor in order to increase its wealth (Fanon 2001, 80). Given Fanon's own personal history fighting both with and against the French, the link between European totalitarianism and colonialism would have been apparent. Nazism in this context is understood as the attempt to colonize Europe from the 'inside.' National socialism was literally an attempt to reduce Europe to the status of a colony. Previously colonized third world societies then have a legitimate demand for reparations from their capitalist occupiers. Indeed, Fanon's novel solution was that if the Cold War could be ended, then large-scale investments and technical aid could be given the globe's less developed regions. This would require a mutual transformation of the relationship between Europe and the third world from one of violence and oppression to one that aimed to 'rehabilitate mankind' (Fanon 2001, 84).

Given Fanon's concern to locate the struggle for independence in more global coordinates, he viewed the idea of 'national' struggle with a degree of ambivalence. The idea of a specifically 'national' root to liberation for colonized peoples was both a necessary transition and a potential trap. In particular, Fanon was concerned that the relative political inexperience of the colonized middle class coupled with the flight of capital could only lead into a 'deplorable stagnation' (Fanon 2001, 121). For Fanon, questions of political economy were indeed central to the liberation struggle, given the need to forge new trading relations and break relations of dependency with Europeans. Indeed, Fanon had a deeper concern that without the politics of socialist transformation it was likely that the rising national bourgeoisie would merely 'replace the foreigner' (Fanon 2001, 127). By that, Fanon meant that rather than securing justice the resulting independence struggle could end by reinscribing similarly racist and tribal attitudes that had been developed during colonial domination. The national bourgeoisie fail to provide a politics of transformation in that they end up mimicking the prejudices and feelings of superiority of the colonists. The problem that Fanon is wrestling with is how can newly independent states emerging from colonialism escape from a form of neocolonialism likely to be imposed upon them by capitalist relations of development. Fanon then is not antinational but seeks to connect anti-imperialism to internationalism based upon social forms of development.

Notably, however, the Fanon that has recently been so intensively discussed in postcolonial debates is not the theorist of national liberation struggle but of the colonialist condition (Lazarus 1999). Indeed, in a broadly poststructuralist rereading of Fanon, Homi Bhabha (1994) and Stuart Hall (1996) focus on Fanon's (1972) earlier text *Black Skin, White Masks*. Here the argument is that whereas Marxists have tended to privilege Fanon the political activist, later generations have been more concerned with the cultural politics of racism, colonialism and psychoanalysis. Here Fanon (1972) is primarily concerned with the ways in which a colonialist culture is able to fix certain stereotypes about black Africans and white Europeans. In this relationship, the black African becomes the 'Other' of European civilization. This not only elevates European cultures but leaves the colonized with a crippling sense of their own inferiority. As Fanon (1972, 79) writes:

> I discovered my blackness, my ethnic characteristics; and I was battered down by tom-toms, cannibalism, intellectual deficiency, fetishism, racial defects, slave ships, and above all else, above all: 'Sho' good eatin'.'

Indeed, it is not just that the Other is stereotyped, but as Stuart Hall (1996, 17) has argued, the subject 'has no other self than—this *self—as—*Othered.' The colonial subject is not only economically exploited, but is saddled with a deep sense of inferiority. Colonial racism produces two camps of the white and the black where colonial subjects can only relate to themselves through a demeaning culture. This evidently raises an important set of questions avoided by an exclusive focus upon political economy. Centrally the concern here becomes how does it become possible to reconstitute our identities in a cultural context inscribed by relations of domination. Even in the colonial context, racism is not just something that the Other does to us, but depends upon the agencies and struggles of the colonized.

Homi Bhabha (1994) has taken these arguments further by arguing that Fanon is not so much insisting that the colonized be granted liberal rights, but more he is investigating the way that the colonial subject becomes determined through cultural practices that trade upon image and fantasy. Questions of madness, self-hatred and violence become cultural and psychic features poorly understood through civil discourses of rights. Indeed, by rereading Fanon, Bhabha is able to draw out both colonialist fantasies of megalomania and persecution and the internalized sense of inferiority of the colonized, which seems to suggest either 'turn white' or disappear. However, Bhabha remains troubled by Fanon's violent anticolonial politics. Indeed, Hannah Arendt (1970), who has also sought to connect totalitarianism and colonialism, argues that Fanon's writing glorifies violence. She points out that Fanon does little to mediate the fantasies of blood and lust that reinscribe themselves in conditions of domination. Perhaps more sympathetically, Bhabha (1994, 62) writes:

> Fanon must sometimes be reminded that the disavowal of the Other always exacerbates the edge of identification, reveals the dangerous place where identity and aggressivity are twinned.

Bhabha's more generous criticism opens the possibility of what he sometimes refers to as the hybrid moment of political change. This is a politics that refuses the easy temptation of homogeneity (us versus them) but rather seeks a politics of translation, negotiation and above all difference. This means that, again something partially acknowledged by Fanon, political struggle is both a hegemonic war of position and 'the struggle of identi-fications' that ultimately need to be constructed (Bhabha 1994, 29). The problem being that Fanon's revolutionary politics partially reproduces the hatred of the colonial period through descriptions of colonists as 'flesh-eating animals, jackals and vultures which wallow in the peoples blood' (Fanon 2001, 154). However, before we leave the matter there, we should also remind ourselves of the more positive features of Fanon's humanism. Fanon is under no doubt that the bourgeoisie's proclamation of universal values is nothing more than a cover for racism that seeks to impose its rela-tions of dominance on all humanity. However, once humanity becomes free of colonialism and relations of dominance, then a genuinely intercultural dialogue becomes possible (Bernasoni 1996). Despite the well-founded fears of Fanon's ideas concerning the necessity of violence in the colonial context, it is the dream of a radically reconstructed humanity that ulti-mately underpins his politics of liberation.

This feature of Fanon's work is often passed over by his liberal and post-structuralist critics, but has most recently been revisited by Paul Gilroy. Gilroy (2000) seeks to return to Fanon to bravely imagine a world that has repudiated talk of race and white supremacy. Gilroy skillfully argues that Fanon's utopian legacy can still be located in contemporary black art forms like popular music that continue to give voice to the desire for transcen-dence and escape from racism. However, if the desire for a future without racism, particularly for black Americans, was linked to the idea of a mythic return to Africa, today it is more likely to take refuge in a purely consumer-ist dream. If the popular black American music of the sixties and seventies articulated a yearning for a better tomorrow, it has now given way to post-modern consumerism. An alternative black public sphere of hybrid musical culture has been colonized by a mostly visual culture that emphasizes the power and vitality of the black body. If Fanon's dream of 'starting a new history of Man' found aesthetic expression in the utopian yearnings of pop-ular music, it now urgently needs to be given a more gritty political expres-sion (Fanon 2001, 254). These are crucial configurations. Arguably what is being opened up here is the view that questions of political economy and those of culture need to find new ways of interrelating with one another to help make another world possible. Following Lisa Duggan (2003) we should resist the either/or split that suggests we decide between political economy or cultural politics. Rather than viewing cultural politics as the 'Other' of serious analysis we should remember discourses of economics are also imbricated with relations of race, class, gender and sexuality.

Arguably, a similar intellectual trajectory can also be followed in respect of the radical educationalist and anti-imperialist Paulo Freire, whose early writing was greatly influenced by Fanon. Similar to Fanon, Freire's own complex intellectual history (being influenced by intellectual cur-rents from both inside and outside the West) and the ways in which he has crossed a number of cultural borders invite a careful rereading of his life and intellectual production. Freire's (1970) classic text *Pedagogy of the Oppressed* remains key in this context given that it brought his work to an international audience, and sought to articulate an anti-imperialist cultural struggle. Henry Giroux (1992, 184) has carefully argued that in interpreting this text we are engaging in a process of critical border crossing which should alert the reader to the fact that Freire is not a 'recipe for all times and places.' Freire argues that educated forms of development offer the possibility of either humanization or dehumanization, and that in turn these possibilities remain tied to the prospect of a revolutionary movement seeking to end class and racial oppression. Human beings who are oppressed and enslaved are compelled to live a life of unrealized human potential. A politics of liberation is required so that both the oppressors and the oppressed are able to live more responsible, autonomous and fulfilled lives. However, Freire is deeply critical of Marxist-Leninist ideas concerning the leading role of the party in the formation of revolutionary consciousness. A critical pedagogy needs to both oppose the strategy of the oppressors, who are largely motivated by money and profit, and seek to address the dispossessed not as the objects of revolutionary strategy but as subjects who have internalized their own sense of inferiority mirrored back to them by the oppressors. The act of liberation for Freire cannot be achieved by relating to those participating in the act of revolt as objects, but must be engaged with as potentially critical and reflective human beings. The recovery of the humanity of the oppressed can only be achieved by challenging the oppressive relationships that can be found at the heart of traditional forms of education. As Freire (1970, 48) argues, "Liberation, a human phenomenon, cannot be achieved by semi humans." More specifically, a democratically inspired pedagogy should break with the 'banking concept' of education. Freire (1970, 53) argues:

> Education thus becomes an act of depositing, in which students are the depositories and the teacher is the depositor. Instead of communicating, the teacher issues communiqués and makes deposits which the students patiently receive, memorize, and repeat.

For Freire the legacies of colonialism and capitalism have helped reproduce hierarchical civil and cultural relations that actively disallow authentic learning. If knowledge is something which is merely transferred, this disallows the possibility of students participating in their own learning. It is then only through the reconstitution of the teacher/student relationship in both more democratic and dialogic settings that reintroduces the possibility of critical thinking. Here Freire advocates a form of problem posing education where the student and the teacher seek to learn from one another. This should not be an abstract process, but on the contrary involves acts of concrete and critical thinking. At this point Freire has learned a great deal from Fanon on the idea of the existential human subject who is always incomplete, but when drawn into dialogue becomes aware of their location as a historical subject with certain creative capacities. For Freire there is no learning or humanization without the act of mutual dialogue. Yet for dialogue to be transformative it needs to be carried out in relations of love, mutual respect and trust. If the capacity to dialogue offers an alternative to the 'banking concept' of education, it does so because it no longer reduces oppressed human beings to the status of a thing or object. What Freire meant by this process is the development of the capacity on the part of the human subject to reflect upon and criticize as well as act upon the world creatively. Here the human subject becomes humanized as he or she begins to realize their 'independent' capacity for action and thought. The dialogue then is a necessary condition of revolutionary action that does not end in reproducing another set of oppressive relations. For Freire (1974, 121), 'there is no oppressive reality which is not at the same time antidialogical.'

Hence Freire's arguments about the divisions between the colonized and their colonial rulers, the possibility of a revolutionary transformation, the existential capacities of the human being and the internalization of a negative view of self as Other all find an echo within Fanon. Franz Fanon (1972), like Freire, worked both inside and outside of Western intellectual traditions and contexts, and has sought to press home the economic and cultural violence of colonialism, especially in the context of France's occupation of Algeria. If Fanon was principally concerned with the ways in which colonialist culture sought to fix certain stereotypes about black Africans and Europeans, then Freire is equally indignant about colonist attempts to reinscribe hierarchies that are supported rather than resisted by the education system. The banking system of education is where a colonist sense of superiority and a capitalist need for hierarchy find a meeting point. Further, both Fanon and Freire emphasize the importance of a liberation struggle that connects cultural spheres, self-images, nations and wider relations of economic dependency and domination. For Freire and Fanon, these wider relations of global domination find their expression in the human subject but also in familial, cultural and educational relations. These features, I would argue, are crucial for a critical rereading of Freire's early writing as they connect questions of education to wider concerns about the possibilities of anticolonial struggle and the desire for liberation.

However, this intellectual legacy is not without its own internal problems and contradictions when viewed from the point of view of the present. The question then becomes how relevant is Freire to an understanding of more contemporary postcolonial societies and post-Marxist frames of reference? Here a number of difficulties seemingly become apparent. bell hooks (1994, 49) argues that Freire's early writing 'constructs a phallocentric paradigm of liberation.' hooks is concerned not only with Freire's (and of courses Fanon's) use of sexist language but his lack of concern for relations of gender more generally. Similarly to other Marxist intellectuals,

Freire has little to say about questions of gender, and is mainly concerned with economic relations and how they become translated into cultural relations. Other feminist critics, such as Kathleen Weiler (1994), have argued that Freire's opposition between the oppressed and the oppressors fails to take account of questions of cultural difference. There is then a notable lack of complexity in the essentialized language that would find it difficult to take account of more complex cultural relations. Further, the student and the radical tutor are assumed to be 'on the same side,' yet there is little exploration of the inevitable power relations involved in this relationship. The teacher, after all, is granted a certain amount of authority (and responsibility) given the ways in which institutions create hierarchies in education and learning. There is also the assumption that once the student becomes humanized through dialogic processes of exchange, 'he' will then want to join a revolutionary movement. Jeanne Brady (1994) argues that Freire's writing contains a reluctance to address the complex, contradictory and multiple meanings of human subjectivity involved in a dialogic process. Instead, Freire's Marxism presupposes a modernist project that legitimizes the passage of consciousness through predefined stages. As Jennifer Gore (1993) points out, the concern here is that the 'liberatory' teacher simply acts to empower students in the interests of a universal humanity. Yet the idea of the 'liberatory' teacher not only ignores more complex realities, but also can easily end up reinforcing a form of dogmatism where peasants are educated to produce revolutionary consciousness. These objections, of course, come close to positioning Freire with the kind of Marxism he was actually keen to criticize. However, the charge from much of the feminist criticism, even when it has been sympathetic to Freire, has been concerned about his inability to reflect upon the ways that his own background and intellectual influences have failed to problematize an unreflective modernist masculinism.

However, Freire, unlike Fanon, was to live long enough to critically revise some of his arguments in the light of ongoing criticism. If his early work is mostly preoccupied with revolutionary struggle, his later writing is explicitly concerned with the ethics of education in the context of injustice. Paulo Freire (2001), despite this notable transformation, never relented in his criticism of global capitalism and the way it sought to preserve certain pedagogic approaches rather than others. However, Freire changes tack, preferring to defend the importance of a universal ethics that affirms the need to grant dignity and respect to every human being on the planet. For Freire, it is the pragmatism of neoliberalism that prefers training to education, adaption to thinking and cynicism rather than hope, which means that it is inhospitable to education. Indeed, it is neoliberalism's own indifference to globally structured inequalities that leads Freire to argue that teaching and educating can never be a neutral act. Freire, in this respect, still seeks to write critically from the point of view of what Fanon (1972) called *the wretched of the earth*. What is noticeable is that Freire's (2001, 23) hostility is towards a political doctrine (rather than, say, a class enemy) and that this allows him to speak from the point of view of what he calls a 'universal human ethic.' This is an ethic of all humanity that seeks to protest against racism, sexism and class discriminations of all kinds. For Freire, education is built upon the dignity of others, which means it cannot be indifferent to mass starvation, hunger and unemployment on a global scale.

Neoliberalism, then, stands condemned for its pragmatic acceptance of reality and its failure to speak of 'humanity's ontological vocation' (Freire 2001, 25). By this Freire means our ability to simultaneously recognize ourselves as incomplete or unfinished beings that are capable of learning and transforming the world by dreaming of alternatives while taking responsibility for the world which we help create. Critical pedagogy necessarily resists neoliberal attempts to convert education into forms of technical training, and instead emphasizes critical thinking, dialogic forms of engagement and the autonomy of the learner. As human beings, through an ongoing process of critical reflection, come to experience themselves as historically and culturally formed creatures capable of learning and transformation, then simultaneously subjects, they begin to dream of new possible futures for human society. If human beings are necessarily incomplete and capable of processes of transformation, then the same can be said of the social order. To educate is to both develop a pedagogic practice that respects the dignity of the other and also engages in an act of hope by opening the possibility of change. Authentic education is about the mutual process of becoming. Teaching, then, is an implicitly ethical act that is involved in opening up closed questions, listening to others, being responsive, while avoiding a fatalistic acceptance of the status quo. To follow this vision, Freire argues that educators are involved in a deeply political act that joins together the possibility of a more just future without betraying the idealism that is necessary to the purpose of education in a democratic social order. However, like Fanon, Freire remains skeptical of a liberal-rights-based universalism that aims to mask more violent and authoritarian relationships. In this respect, Freire (2007) makes a distinction between the right to an education (which may coexist with ideas of cultural inferiority) and a liberating dialogic education where learning is centered within democratically conceived human relationships.

GUY DEBORD AND THE RETURN OF THE SPECTACLE

Remarkably similar to Fanon and Freire in this context are the contributions of Guy Debord, given his concern with the antidialogic nature of the spectacle. However, Debord was more concerned by the ways in which capitalist modernity had involved itself within internal forms of colonization. Recently there has been a reemergence of interest in the idea of the society of the spectacle in order to help understand the ways in which capitalism has transformed the public realm. Douglas Kellner (2003) argues that media spectacles have become a key organizing principle of the dominant capitalist society. Following the earlier work of Debord (1994), Kellner argues that the society of the spectacle reproduces itself through the promotion of reified images of sensation and scandal. In Debord's original formation, just as workers are separated from the products of their labor through capitalist social relations, so images take on an autonomous appearance that have little connection with everyday life. The masses consume dramatic images of human misery and suffering that increasingly take on the appearance of unreality. In this respect, the spectacle is not the effect of technology but is the product of a centralized capitalist society that institutes an 'essentially one-way flow of information' (Debord 1994, 19). Further, such a system of capitalist domination is built upon alienation as people learn to recognize their needs and desires through the images and commodities offered by the dominant system. Needs and desires, then, are not arrived at autonomously but through a society of affluence where people are driven to consume images and commodities built upon 'the ceaseless manufacture of pseudo-needs' (Debord 1994, 33). The society of the spectacle has its roots in the economy and represents the further penetration of capitalism into the psyche of modern citizens. Notably, however, some forms of critical theory and Marxism have been complicit with the dominance of the spectacle through the imposition of similarly authoritarian modes of struggle and rule. For Debord, if the alienation effect of the spectacle is to be defeated, then the subjugated would need to revolt against their imposed passivity and a 'purely contemplative role' (Debord 1994, 87). Alienation can only be countered by entering into forms of political and social struggle that have rejected alienated forms of life. This, then, demands a 'theory of praxis entering into two-way communication with practical struggles' (Debord 1994, 89).

The other way in which the spectacle dominates the lives of modern citizens is through the elimination of historical knowledge. If the rise of capitalism eclipsed the dominance of cyclical time of the medieval world, then it did so by instituting irreversible time. For Debord, this involves ideas of progress that came along with capitalist modernity and calculable time necessary for the disciplining of labor and the production of commodities, but also spectacular time. Spectacular time prevents the development of historical knowledge as it organizes information as dramatic events through the media that are quickly displaced and forgotten. Such features for Debord (1994, 154) can only be resisted once 'dialogue has taken up arms to impose its own conditions upon the world.'

Debord was perhaps amongst the first to grasp the emerging connections between capitalism, technology and media that became increasingly concentrated upon the spectacular. The reconfiguration of capitalism in the age of information has massively expanded the reach of transnational corporations into the fabric of everyday life. The development of superinformation highways through the digital convergence of the computer, telephone and the television set provide new, profitable markets for the future.

For Kellner, updating Debord's original reflections, in the society of the spectacle, fashion, models, celebrities and icons become increasingly important. Culture is increasingly dominated by the power of certain images and brands. Societies' central feature is not greater cosmopolitan awareness but the dominance of a new form of technocapitalism whereby capital accumulation, the knowledge revolution and new technology have combined to produce a new kind of society. The culture of the spectacle then instigates a new form of domination of mass distraction, profit and the continuing expansion of social and cultural domains that fall under its sway from politics to sport and from music to the news media. The society of the spectacle in Debord's original formulation continues to pose the question of what a more authentic and less manipulated life might be like. Debord remains important, given the need to search for alternatives to the mediocrity, absence of democratic control and boredom that can dominate everyday life. Material abundance in this sense cannot compensate for a life that lacks either passion or autonomy (Plant 1992). Indeed, we might consider that what happens to contested forms of civic engagement if they are converted into a commodified image that despite the appearance of new media largely disallows more dialogic relationships.

MAKING POVERTY HISTORY

The idea that Western societies need to reinvent their relations with the global South has been the explicit focus of the campaign to 'Make Poverty History.' Arguably this has provided an opportunity to rethink cultural as well as structural relations with former colonies and with the global South more generally. Yet what becomes crucial in this respect is an understanding of the context within which the predominantly Western campaign sought to promote trade justice, cancel debt and promote more and better aid. Indeed, there has been a considerable amount of debate recently as to whether the globe is currently going through a period that can be accurately described as a new imperialism, empire or neoliberal globalization. For example, David Harvey (2003) has argued that over the course of the twentieth century the United States has become an imperial power. This power has largely economic roots, and since the oil crisis of 1973 it has aggressively sought to promote a global strategy of accumulation by dispossession. Through the World Bank, the IMF and the World Trade Organization, the United States has sought to privatize public resources, commodify labor power and suppress alternative forms of production and consumption. Alternatively, Hardt and Negri (2000) have argued against the idea of a dominant American lead imperialism and propose a notion of empire that breaks with ideas of imperialism. The logic of empire is different from that of imperialism because it does not depend upon the expansion of state power but is a borderless world that fosters consumer subjectivities and the rule of postmodern global capitalism. However, despite the different sides to this debate there does appear to be considerable agreement in respect of the dominance of neoliberal economics. Jan Nederveen Pieterse (2004) has argued that there are indeed contrasts between neoliberal globalization and the recent imperial turn evident in United States foreign policy. The interconnection of neoliberal measures of privatization and tax cuts with the expansion of military budgets is less the blind expression of the economy than it is a matter of politics. In this respect, the Bush administration's forceful promotion of neoliberal economics and militarism has strong political and cultural similarities with Reaganism in the 1980s. Hence the Make Poverty History campaign takes its inspiration from The Millennium Development goals (www.un.org/millennium/declaration/ares552e.pdf), which promised to halve global poverty by 2015. In the context of neoliberal globalization, then, we might be tempted to view these goals as a smoke screen; however, we could equally view them as offering a form of immanent critique giving protestors a set of standards from which progress or otherwise could be judged. This indeed was the view of the broad-based campaign.

Despite the popular impact of the campaign to 'Make Poverty History,' it is notable that it has thus far failed to politicize the dominance of neoliberal policies on development and question a number of assumptions that can be connected to the culture of colonialism. The 'Make Poverty History' grouping is best thought of as a broad coalition that includes Oxfam, Friends of the Earth, the World Development Movement as well as political parties like New Labour and well-known celebrities like Bob Geldof and U2's lead singer Bono. During the summer of 2005 the coalition in the lead-up to the G8 meeting in Gleneagles ran a number of high-profile cultural events in order to raise awareness on questions of global poverty. This included Bob Geldof's appearance at the music festival Glastonbery and the Live 8 music festival (held in Tokyo, Berlin, London, Paris, Moscow, Ontario, Rome and Philadelphia). In the run-up to these events, Oxfam sought to promote the idea of global solidarity through a white wristband that read 'Make Poverty History.' The campaign actively encouraged ordinary people to buy the bands and either text, e-mail or write to the government ahead of the G8 meeting urging action on global poverty. In Britain the television networks were full of documentaries and more popular forms of television on the plight of Africa. These features were particularly evident on the BBC, where especially commissioned programs carried the strap line 'Africa Lives on the BBC.' Despite notable exceptions, many of these programs were both populist, easily consumable and continued to trade upon well-known stereotypes. For example, Bob Geldof presented a series of programs on the African continent ('Geldof on Africa') where he was viewed pictured in a white suit serving up tales of native superstition, political corruption and African irrationality. In the lead-up to the Live 8 concerts, Geldof received a considerable amount of media criticism for failing to include any African artists in the original lineup, which had included mostly Western popular music artists such as Paul McCartney, Coldplay, U2 and Pink Floyd. Geldof had countered such criticism by arguing he was simply seeking to attract as many people as possible to the event. Yet the fact that Live 8 and the 'Make Poverty History' campaign more generally lacked any critical cultural politics is best represented by Madonna's performance at Live 8. Before Madonna came on to the stage, Geldof came on and introduced an eighteen-year-old woman from Ethiopia (Birham Woldhu) whom, he claimed, 'we' had saved with the money raised from the original Live Aid concerts. Madonna and Geldof were then pictured hugging the woman 'we' had 'saved' before she was ushered off the stage. Here my point is that the invisibility of African performers and the stereotypes of helpless Africans both depoliticized the event and turned the focus away from the plight of Africa into an explicit focus on the generosity of white Europeans. If 'they' are poor and needy, this is 'our' chance to play the role of generous providers. Despite well-publicized claims that the day was about justice for Africa—the dominant discourse was one of Western charity. The lead-up to G8 then became 'our moment, the time for us to make history'. The images and identities that were reproduced through popular media cultures were less about an antagonistic politics and more about a normalizing culture of the spectacle. The mass television event of 2005 was indeed an educative opportunity to open up a number of critical viewpoints about global economics, development and the historical relations that continue to inform the present; however, in all these respects it failed.

In certain quarters many political commentators felt that the campaign suffered from being overly directed by New Labour. The construction of a 'Third Way' alliance of the progressive center severely restricted the capacity of a number of social movements to press for a more radical political and cultural agenda. As Chantal Mouffe (2005) has argued, democratic politics is actually dependent upon passionate expression within an agonistic public sphere. The displacement of radical politics actively disallowed the emergence of a more openly contested public sphere where different interests and positions could have been articulated and negotiated. Cultural forms of democracy and citizenship requires a more adversarial form of politics that could not find expression in the 'united' front presented by the 'Make Poverty History' campaign.

Further, the celebrity-endorsed spectacle utilized a number of dangerous and misleading expectations and assumptions. A film that was continually replayed during the lead-up to the G8 included a number of A list celebrities such as Richard Grant, Emma Thompson and George Clooney clicking their fingers to emphasize the fact that every three seconds a child dies of poverty. This in itself could have been a powerful message, and yet it was hard to escape the impression that all the member countries of the G8 needed to do to make poverty disappear was to click their fingers. Indeed, Richard Curtis's film *The Girl in the Café*, which began the BBC's coverage, pressed a similar impression. The film's narrative featured an 'ordinary' woman who became caught up at the high table of global politics only to insist to the globe's leaders that they take their responsibilities seriously. In the absence of any politics, these images suggested that defeating global poverty is a matter of personal commitment, lifestyle choice and consuming the right products.

Should we press these features too far, it is also worth remembering that it was estimated that two billion viewers watched Live 8 and that over 250,000 demonstrators gathered in Edinburgh to protest against global poverty. These cultural and political events were not surprisingly contested by many on the political right for not emplacing Africa's own political corruption. This was an easy political point to make in a campaign where Africans were either rendered invisible or stereotyped. More positively, however, we could argue that we are witnessing the beginnings of a global social movement concerned about the global polarization of wealth. Indeed, 'Make Poverty History' is a broad coalition that includes a number of disparate voices and perspectives that has converted questions of global poverty into an ongoing public campaign and discussion. Despite some of the images traded upon by the 'Make Poverty History' campaign, they have played a crucial role in raising public awareness of the indebted and impoverished nature of African societies. Yet in hindsight it is currently noteable that the so called global social movement to end poverty has largely disappeared from view. This is because the 'movement' was largely (although not completely) a construction of fleeting media messages. However, part of the problem is the concentration on the themes of poverty rather than inequality and neoliberalism. Especially since the 1980s there has been a rapid increase in inequality both within and between global societies (Pieterse 2004). Yet a more complex and contested politics struggled to make itself heard beneath a media-generated spectacle that seemingly canceled the possibility of a more dialogic politics.

Viewed in the context of a genuinely educative politics, then, the public campaign to end global poverty was less about learning about the histories of colonialism and violence than about forgetting to learn. Further, we might also add the broad-based campaign was successful in mobilizing large numbers of people but that ultimately this was done by upholding a consumerist idea of politics rather than more forms of dialogic engagement. Inevitably within complex mass-mediated societies it is not possible for everyone's voice to be heard; however, the mediation of the events of 2005 gave the impression of an overly homogenous Western public which focused upon our generosity and their neediness. There were warnings that the campaign had failed to achieve much in terms of the transformation of either economic or cultural relations not long after the media had focused its attention elsewhere. Noreen Hertz (2005) complained that only eighteen countries had had their debt canceled, leaving a further sixty-two countries that were unlikely to receive assistance unless they accepted the World Bank and the IMF taking control of their economic policies. Hertz argued that if the world's richest economies had committed themselves to halve global poverty by 2015, at the current rate this was likely to take over one hundred years. Here Hertz argues the campaign needs to renew itself by more substantially focusing on questions of justice, while linking these questions to those of democratic empowerment in respect of the rights of trade unions as well as access to health care and education. The campaign against poverty then points to the dangers evident in overly commodified and co-opted forms of civic agency.

GLOBAL POVERTY, EDUCATION AND THE GOOD SOCIETY

In this final section I want to make the perhaps surprising claim that Fanon, Freire and Debord were all theorists of the good society. By this I mean that they were all critical of a rights-based liberalism that simply sought to protect human autonomy through an abstract universalism. They were, as I have indicated, all philosophers of liberation who wanted a world where human beings were not only engaged in the counter-hegemonic struggle for a better world but thought this inevitably would involve the construction of a deep democracy that fundamentally reimagined relationships between the self and the wider community more generally. However, for some of the reasons I have indicated, there is no straightforward return to the perspectives presented here as Fanon, Freire and Debord who were all writing at a time that was deeply by the politics of national liberation. A new politics is required then in societies that are both increasingly mediated and interconnected.

However, our own time currently shows (at least here in Britain) no such desire to engage in the kinds of political and cultural forms of experiments of the 1960s. Yet the critical interventions of Fanon, Freire and Debord all ask us to think about the ways in which we imagine politics crosses over political and cultural boundaries. For example, much of the recent debate in respect of a global civil society and the possibility of introducing new global rules to produce a more humane order has largely ignored the role of culture in this process. A new global civil society is expected to emerge out of the actions of civic actors who progressively seek to tame the power of even the most powerful states (Kaldor 2003). Similarly, new perspectives in media and communication have investigated different ways in which our globalized world has become interconnected, thereby allowing the stranger into our midst (Silverstone 2007). These are all important cultural and theoretical interventions that pointed beyond the confines of a despairing and hopeless politics. Yet what is missing is the emphasis that Fanon, Freire and Debord placed upon the need for us to become more democratically constituted subjects. As Henry Giroux (1992, 60–61) has argued, postmodernism has revealed the extent to which the presumed unified and rational subject of earlier waves of critical and cultural theory is 'multiple, layered, and nonunitary.' However, Giroux goes on that we need to remember that previous generations of critical theory may have displaced the languages of contingency and difference they remained committed to a language of critical pedagogy that sought to press the need for both agency and more dialogically engaged and democratic public spaces. These aspects need to be reconnected to a critique that seeks to play an active role in criticizing the ways in which public identities become constituted in active civic campaigns.

However, I don't think the argument in respect of democracy goes far enough. Instead, we need to recapture ideas of the 'good society.' Rather than asking what is right or how might we build a society that does not lapse into barbarism, the Aristotelian tradition has sought to consider how we might construct a society based upon human happiness. Human happiness could not be achieved through the pursuit of wealth, but rather we begin by asking in what kind of society we would both thrive and be virtuous (McIntyre 1988). In more modern times, such reflections should make us reflect upon the limitations of a dominant model of citizenship based upon consumerism, waste, and growing levels of inequality. Indeed, a more global interconnected age asks us to think about this question at a number of levels, which include local, national and global institutions. Here there is an urgent and critical need to challenge the model of the good life promoted by neoliberalism and reimagine the idea of a globally oriented good society. A society based upon high rates of consumption, atomism, inequality and waste is not only unfit for export to other parts of the world but is unlikely to foster thriving citizens who are concerned about the well-being of others either at home or more distant in time and space. If few citizens seem to be ready to take on the identity of being 'global' citizens, this is perhaps not surprising given the lack of cultural specificity evident within this definition. More fruitful, I think, is Paulo Freire's (1997) view of global citizenship that emerges through a sense of connection to particular locations and places that gains a sense of hope from a sense of politics that aims at transformation. To speak of hope in our current context would mean that citizens discover fulfillment in forms of life other than that of hyperconsumption and minimal forms of citizenship. Such a politics would need to recover the possibility of contested forms of dialogic engagement in place of an education system increasingly geared towards training for standardized tests and a media system whose dominant logic is that of the spectacle. This is of course unlikely to be a form of politics without considerable ambiguity, and acts with no or little guarantee of success. Such an ambitious public political project that arguably returns to some of the more utopian aspects of Fanon's arguments in respect of reimagined relationships that had finally rejected domination could only be built through the emergence of new kinds of public space. As Henry Giroux (2008, 136) states, a politics of the public would potentially allow for new vocabularies and new identities to emerge allowing the possibility of citizens to take on or at least explore new identities and identifications.

REFERENCES

Arendt, H. (1970) *On Violence*, New York: Harvest.

Bernasoni, R. (1996) 'Casting the Slough: Fanon's New Humanism for a New Humanity', in L. R. Gordon, T. Sharpley-Whiting and R. T. White (eds.), *Fanon: A Critical Reader*, Oxford: Blackwell, 113–121.

Bhabha, H. (1994) *The location of culture*, London, Routledge.

Brady, J. (1994) 'Critical Literacy, feminism and a politics of representation', in McLaren, P. and Lanshear, C. (eds.) *Politics of Liberation: Paths from Freire*, London: Routledge, 142–153.

Debord, G. (1994). *The Society of the Spectacle*, New York: Zone Books.

———. (1998). *Comments on the Society of the Spectacle*. New York: Verso.

Duggan, L. (2003) *The Twilight of Equality? Neoliberalism, Cultural Politics, and the Attack on Democracy*, Boston: Beacon Press.

Fanon, F. (1972) *Black Skin, White Masks*, London: Paladin.

Fanon, F. (2001) *The Wretched of the Earth*, London: Penguin.

Freire, P. (1997) *Pedagogy of the Heart*, New York: Continuum.

———. (2007) *Daring to Dream: Toward a Pedagogy of the Unfinished*, Boulder, CO: Paradigm Publishers.

Gilroy, P. (2000) *Between Camps: Nations, Cultures and the Allure of Race*, London: Routledge.

Giroux, H. (1992) *Border Crossings: Cultural Workers and the Politics of Education*, London: Routledge.

———. (2008) *Against the Terror of Neoliberalism: Politics beyond the Age of Greed*, Boulder, CO: Paradigm Publishers.

Gore, J.M. (1993) *The Struggle for Pedagogies: Critical and Feminist Discourses as Regimes of Truth*, London: Sage.

Hall, S. (1996) 'The After-life of Franz Fanon: Why Fanon? Why Now? Why Black Skin White Masks?', in A. Read (ed.), *The Fact of Blackness*, London: Institute of Contemporary Arts, 12–37.

Harvey, D. (2003) *The New Imperialism*, Oxford: Oxford University Press.

Hardt, M. and Negri, A. (2000) *Empire*, Cambridge, MA: Harvard University Press.

Hertz, N. (2005) 'We Achieved Next to Nothing', *New Statesman*, December 12, 2005, www.newstatesman.com (accessed October 25, 2008).

Kaldor, M. (2003) *Global Civil Society: An Answer to War*, Cambridge: Polity Press.

Kellner, D. (2003). *Media Culture: Cultural studies, identityand politics between the modern and the postmodern*, New York: Routledge

Lazarus, N. (1999) 'Disavowing Decolonization: Fanon, Nationalism, the Question of Representation in Postcolonial Theory', in A. C. Alessandrini (ed.), *Franz Fanon: Critical Perspectives*, London: Routledge, 161–194.

McIntyre, A. (1998) *A Short History of Ethics*, London: Routledge.

Mouffe, C. (2005) *On the Political*, London: Routledge.

Pieterse, J. N. (2004) *Globalization or Empire*, London: Routledge.

Plant, S .(1992) *The most radical gesture: the Situationist international in the post-modern age*, London: Routledge.

Silverstone, R. (2007) *Media and Morality: On the Rise of the Mediapolis*, Cambridge: Polity Press.

Weiler, K. (1994) 'Freire and feminism', in McLaren, P. and Lankshear, C. (eds.) *Politics of Liberation: Paths from Freire*, London: Routledge, 12–40.

9 Recolonized Citizenships, Rhetorical Postcolonialities

Sub-Saharan Africa and the Prospects for Decolonized Ontologies and Subjectivities

Ali A. Abdi and Lynette Shultz

The conceptual popularity of global citizenship education has been impressive in the past ten or so years. There have been, of course, some pre-twenty-first-century, extensive discussions of citizenship, especially in Western academic contexts and with a specialized notation on the philosophical and social locations of the issues including the works of John Dewey (1926) and others, preceded, of course, by the important foundational works from John Locke, J. J. Rousseau and J. S. Mill. In the so-called developing world (an expression we will continue using, albeit with some reservations), we can note the saliency of temporally intervening works produced by, inter alia, Julius Nyerere (1968) and Paulo Freire (1998, 2000 [1970],) which have had important theoretical and practical implications for the lives of progress aspirants across many zones of the world. One can also speak about most of the scholarship that heralded the anticolonial liberation movements in former African colonies (e.g., Achebe 1958; Fanon 1967, 1968; Biko 2002 [1979]; Cabral 2007 [1979]) as specific disquisitions that affirmed the primordial citizenship intersections that have been lost through global imperialism and its proxies all over the world.

One main opponent of viable citizenship was the program of colonialism, which we must continue talking about and extensively analyzing mainly because of its continuing, longue durée effects on the majority of the world's people, who via such ontologically horizontal experience are placed on different platforms of citizenship contexts that are either enfranchising, disenfranchising or are locating people in a middle borderland that promises something viable but does constitute enough agency for the full claim of the cherished prize. With the expansive absence of the pragmatics of citizenship from a massive block of people, therefore, one should be cautious about the newly stylistic proliferation of the theoretical domains of the case. As we have seen in so many academic conferences, classrooms and published projects, it seems that suddenly so many of us, including the writers of this chapter, have become de facto experts, indeed, competent constructors of everything citizenship spaces represent, including the global, the local and the occasionally misnamed glocal. Technically speaking, the exponential growth in the scholastically qualified competence of the case is at best questionable and, at worst, untenable. The reasons for this less than encouraging assertion is not too complicated to see.

Citizenship is a very complex concept; when it is achieved, it is should be multidimensional, historically and culturally ingrained and dynamic, sociopolitically and economically attached or detached, and carries with it or is devoid of material redemption. Despite this complexity, citizenship is not very difficult to ascertain, appreciate or explain. It is, by and large, an immediate phenomenon in the lives of people; as such, outside the realm of the university research or teaching, one may not need to academicize it or subject it to neat theoro-metrics that, on counting things, either qualify it or disqualify it. Without all the talk and related linearities, average persons anywhere in the world can, in a straightforward manner, tell you whether they are citizens or not. That is, whether they access the benefits of citizenship as rights and responsibilities vis-à-vis public institutions, private enterprises and in relation to other individuals or groups. At a primary level, lack of relevant education and adequate health care is lack of citizenship; so is unemployment, weak political agency, absence of habeas corpus, and the rescinding of freedoms of expression and movement are undoubtedly draconian schemes of de-citizenization. Reading citizenship from such precarious location, it is not really difficult to figure it out. In our own research, we have experienced this not long ago in sub-Saharan Africa (Shultz, Abdi and Nungu 2010), where ordinary people who were not at all trained in citizenship research showed their brilliance and ability to analyze the idea and its practices with a level of sophistication that enlivens both its discursive and concrete placements and outcomes.

So what is all the noise about Western academic platforms, governments and other institutions suddenly rushing to teach the world, especially the developing world, how to define and practice citizenship? Stated otherwise, why so much of global citizenship scholarship at this juncture of human history? We submit this is an important, timely and praxically just question that needs to be raised and inclusively and selectively answered. In our research and teaching contexts and in relation to our preference for decolonized cognitive spaces of life, we will, in this chapter, try to assume a multicritical perspective that responds (not necessarily fully answers) to some issues that are related to the false promise, indeed, absence, of citizenship realities in the many spaces of the so-called postcolonial with specific focus on sub-Saharan Africa. We contend that this problematic situation of what we are calling recolonized spaces of citizenship is a result of the unrealized promises of decolonized citizenship that were to happen after countries in these areas of the world achieved 'independence' from colonial rule around mid-twentieth century. To avoid any descriptive or analytical alibis, we admit that we have already some bias against the currently fashionable Western exportations of global citizenship to peoples with different histories, cultures, expressive contexts, unique cosmoreligious attachments and undoubtedly actual unique needs in their survivabilities and lack thereof.

In speaking about citizenship possibilities as well as its current dramatic weaknesses in places such as Africa, we shall continue analyzing the case through Western-imposed facts of two extensive and historically enduring global phenomena that have increased in both magnitude and impact in the past five hundred years, which in the course of human history is so much less than the real history of the willfully de-historicized and subjugated populations of the world: the one we already mentioned above or colonialism, and the one which has lately become the most ubiquitous presence in people's lives, globalization. The reason this is important is that current formulations of global citizenship actually contain a thick air and texture of superiority that affirms a pre-facto triumph of the West over the rest. As Sophie Bessis (2003) noted, Europe's celebrated victory at the mental and, by extension, life style and concretizable levels of life was important in cementing the rest of us, not only submitting to the psycho-cultural formations of the story, but as well, to its unknown outcomes and commands. In that meaning, we live in un mondo where the conceptualizations, theorizations as well as the practices of everything (indeed, everything) has a unidirectional flow where in Karl Marx's de novo appreciable maxim, only the dominant group has and must have the right ideas. We believe it is with this multilocationally internalized ontologies and its epistemological constructions that the practice of global citizenship represents a potential recolonization of non-Western space where, without much discussion and enquiry, this new 'postcolonial' remedy, which is also a fragment of the overall inertia of globalization, is being sent with the label 'use as prescribed' to those whose lives are certified as deficient in the 'democratic' liberalizations and monetarizations of the globe.

THE UNI-POLARIZATION AND UNI-CONCEPTUALIZATIONS OF THE WORLD

With the fall of the Russian empire (mistakenly known as the Soviet Union), and the end of the select temporal end of the bipolar world, the hubristic reconstructions of global political system, and what was termed the 'new world order' were to move forward unhindered by the tired ideas and philosophies of the winning European (Euro-American) faction. Here, the recasting of the lives of those who resided in extra-European territories were seemingly presumed to be a natural course of history, and all that was needed was to dispense the instructions for new formations of citizenships that were to be followed with no expectations or dissent. After all, in the absence of the previously opposing and capable political bloc, the options for opposing the Western ways of life were nil, or in terms of people's needs, in negative territory—that is, with so many countries in Africa, Asia and Latin America now at the mercy of Western European and American banking and loan hegemonies, only those who toe the prescribed policy and economic lines were to be accorded assumed national or territorial citizenship prospects. This was the dominant world story in early 1990s, and to formalize it beyond the policy papers and for wider public reader- ship, Francis Fukuyama's much talked-about book *The End of History and the Last Man* (1992) heralded the undisputed global triumphalism of the liberal democracy exactly as it was being practiced in Western, hypercapi- talist societies. Indeed, the prognosis here was so bold that you were either in the promised land of liberal democracy citizenship or rapidly on your way to partake in the celebrations and practices of this now expanding global system.

Our reasons for attaching democracy to citizenship is mainly because we intend to read the notions and practices of the former as emanating from the wider space of the latter. That is, while democracy is technically a political project and, by its extension, an economic system, citizenship is not only social, political and economic; it is also, and as much, educational, historical and cultural. The understandings and constructions of citizenship should therefore locate the quality as well as the outcomes of democracy, which, based on the way we are deploying it here, is suddenly assuming an air of normalcy that should not be accorded so easily. As we do not wish to engage a detailed critique of democracy in this chapter, let us very briefly and rightly localize it for what it is. The perforce universalization of liberal democracy (you take it or leave it at a great risk), which basically aims for the saliency of individual rights and reduces public political systems as mainly servicing such rights, should not dissuade us from appreciating all forms of democracy. No matter who is credited with its literal inventions, this system of governance existed in many parts of the world long before the much-talked-about Athenian democracy, which really was a system of extreme patriarchy that elevated the situation of propertied men over other men, and did not even consider the rights of women, children and those enslaved Greeks (by other Greeks, of course). The evolution of that oppres- sive system, which was misnamed 'democratic,' is actually what produced the type of dominant liberal democracy that is shaping our lives today.

As a component of the discussions on the possible multiplicities of global citizenships, we argue for primordial naturalness of democratic systems of life. Indeed, we believe that democratic ways of governance, especially at the policy level where resources and conditions were to be shared, should be as old as the first formations of human groups, and as such, we suggest that the invention of democracy and the citizenship circles that inform it should be seen (ad infinitum) as a function of our collective social intelli- gence, without which many communities would not have survived, let alone thrive, for millennia. This notion is important in that, among other things, it challenges the false triumphalism of the current dominant political order that has also achieved something interesting, indeed perverse: All contexts of citizenship are now seemingly subsumed into the dome of liberal democracy, so much so that it is not the system serving the interests of citizens but citizens responding to the demands and commands of the system. It is also the case that liberal democracy and its citizenship subsets are, for most countries in Africa, remnants of the European political hegemony that not only served the interests of colonialism but, as well, supported the schemes of the postcolonial native elites who selectively used it to entrench their power vis-à-vis the controlled masses. Indeed, in some parts of Africa, the practice of indigenous governance systems that were based on chief-mediated consultations with the people were in place forever. In Somalia, for example, historically entrenched programs of what Lewis (1961) called pastoral democracy were functional and selectively effective in mediating the affairs of the community. To appreciate the overarching reality of patri-archy, though, even here, the arrangements were gender-biased, with only adult men (propertied or not propertied) as the ones who were included in the deliberations and conclusions. But the main difference here was the focus on the interests of the community versus those of the individual, and we submit that to achieve an inclusive project of citizenship, what we may term *communal deliberative democracies* should fit more the lives of such societies. Even when analyzed with countercapitalism lenses, this could be true for those in today's numerically shrinking but politico-economically rising global power elite (Wedel 2009). Indeed, with the rise of the triumphalist, Eurocentric political order, we see the expansive recolonization of not only political spaces of life but, as well, the overall citizenship contexts of living, and the relationship between the two, in the immediate situations of citizens, is breathtaking. From here, let us talk, via eclectic foci, on the interactive circles of politics, economic and probabilities of well-being, about the case of sub-Saharan Africa.

With uni-polarism, one of the supposedly most 'democratized' spaces of the world should have been sub-Saharan Africa. From 1990, almost every country in the subcontinent heeded the major call from the West and announced the formation of democratic regimes that should uphold the rights as well as the responsibilities of democratic citizens. As we studied some of these trends in the decades following such announcements (Abdi, Ellis and Shizha 2005; Abdi, Shizha and Ellis 2010), we realized that among the missed crucial links of the project was lack of any viable discussions about the meanings and outcomes of liberal democracy for societies that have never used it, and were historico-culturally detached from such systems of public management. As John Dewey (1926) noted, people cannot adopt and practice new political systems such as democracy unless they understand them and can explain them to themselves, which should at least carry the imperative of the systems' proponents highlighting their meaning and functionalities for the new lands. That was not the case; Africans were literally commanded to adopt these structures, and the results have been so far problematic that at one primary level of life, unemployment rates have increased by more than 50 percent (Abdi, 2008). That has expectedly led to an increasing mass disengagement from the political arena, which itself is highly problematic, for without correcting these countries' political points and intersections of life, the social development context will not be ameliorated. So how should it be done?

The answer can be both easy and very difficult. The answer can be both easy and very difficult. To begin, we could talk about decolonizing citizenship spaces which could lead to the analysis of historical, social and cultural locations of political and economic systems, and from there, establish deepened engagements that might be considered mainly indigenous but also constructively attached to other systems in the world. The purpose here is always to effectively benefit the people seeking to meet their basic needs. The difficult thing, of course, is that these spaces are subject to the ideological commands of the West, and the 1990 directive to adopt democracy is still unidirectionally binding, and with the loan/monetary conditionalities affirming its continuities, the options for the so-called dependent countries are very limited and most certainly undemocratic. Needless to add that the current arrangements are not just upholding the nominal governance impositions of the West but, as well, those of the local elite who have reconstitutionalized themselves as the new democratic leadership. As Hoogvelt (2002) noted, the elite of developing countries share less and less with the people they govern, and so much more with people in the developed world. She speaks about the quasi-permanence as well as the thickness of the concentric circles that divide the world into haves and have-nots, with the upper classes of Africa, for example, having so much in common, in educational, economic and consumption qualities, with the middle class and upper classes of the West. This seems to have also created another problem; with Western policymakers dealing with the ruling class of the East, and in reality having no means to reach the masses, a 'democratically' binding pact has been seemingly established between the global enfranchised groups. The pact, if and when found on any paper it was written, could read as the following: "While we in the West will publicly demand a full adherence to the basic principles of liberal democracy, we understand your people may not understand any of it; so basically make as many public pronouncements as you can, and never miss the elections cycles that should present some democracy for your people." Yes, this would sound simplistic to the positivist mind, but it will actually be the real story relayed verbatim from citizens across those places on the receiving end of the Western project. And it clearly assures us the continuing fourth-worldization of hundreds of millions who, via their exposure to these nominal democracies, will also experience diminished citizenship possibilities that actually strengthen the hand of their government vis-à-vis their rights and expectations.

As Ihonvbere (1996), in his widely read essay 'On the Threshold of Another False Start,' so effectively noted, the so-called processes of democratization that theoretically and, indeed, rhetorically swept the sub-Saharan landscape in early 1990s were nothing more than the rearrangements of the old order where, at the end of the day, hardly much has changed for the average African, and in many instances, as we pointed out above, the immediate livelihood context actually got worse. Such schemes, regardless of who designs or implements them, represent a new recolonization of both citizenship and possible democratic spaces. Indeed, while structural adjustment programs (SAPs) performed this task on behalf of globalization and its main drivers, the rhetoric of false democratization was in the service of unipolar triumphalism, and the collective of these agents assured us a contemporary postcolonial (still nominal) African space that advances the rights and the needs of the powerful, while habitually de-citizenizing the many aspirants of the story and its potentialities. And it is more than that: With the globally diffused perspective that it is liberal democracy or nothing, the initiatives to establish alternative governance and economic development prospects have been so weakened that many times even the time-tested communal ways of public life management are increasingly being rescinded.

The assumed omnipotence of the liberal democracy project should actually remind us of its well-known sibling, development, and how it was driven as the only solution for all issues that concerned people's complex life situations in the past sixty years. As Rahnema (1997) noted, the deriding of every other system as a problem that needed to be thrown away, and the elevation of Western schemes of development as the sine qua non of everything that could be good about life, effected the opposite of its rhetoric: the pauperization of more people than ever, and the subjective loss of confidence that assured the strengthening of the current world order where first world citizens continually prosper at the expense of the rest. Needless to add that the connection between the two should actually be bigger than it might seem. While liberal democracy and development are important pillars of globalization, they are also metamorphosing ideological constructions that refuse to incorporate the ideas as well as the experiences of non-European populations into either their sphere of analysis and/or as components of the policies and their attendant programs. Also not admitted are life governance or resources policy possibilities that may be of European origin but do not flow in line or submit to the neoliberal paradigm, which through the tool of liberal democracy actually monetizes the world via the rigid principles of the grossly misnamed laissez-faire economics.

The picture, as well as the practice of misnaming in this central aspect of global control systems, is interesting. While the contextually repainted line of surrendering to market supremacy might have effectively flowed from Adam Smith's work, and immediately after, through David Ricardo, later proposed by Friedrich Hayek, and more recently by the late Milton Friedman, the 'let-it-do-as-it-wishes' theory of economics is actually more controlled than ever and, as such, systematically rations both the theoretical and practical dispensations of development and attachable possibilities of ecological well-being. In Friedman's ideology, for example, the system of monetarism he so personally and institutionally advanced serves more competently, indeed, more deliberately, those who have a tangible stake in the ownership of money. Here, the relationship between this dominant form of economic imperatives and the probabilities of achieving viable space of social well-being should be clear. If you are already individually or communally pauperized, and you cannot access money, mainly at the behest of this ideology's globally sanctioned instructions, then you will either go down (in more ways than one), or you heed the conditions imposed upon you by the prevalent order. Here, in advancing what we can now call the imposed and, by extension, the false promises of democracy, which led to the weakening of basic citizenship rights, it was not only specific persons or groups that were exposed to the case; it was also non-Western governments that were not only instructed to do the bidding for the monetarist or neoliberal projects of everything. Pragmatically, though, these governments in Africa and elsewhere were actually given the wrong blueprint to apply it to their people's contexts, and regardless of the problematic consequences that were reaped and are being reaped by the victims of story, the commandments are still in vigor.

So where is the 'let-it-do-as-it-wishes' radical market philosophy that might have allowed developing countries some venues of escape from the money management and money-use lifestyles of the West, which are, by the way, more cultural than meets the Western(ized) eye? As should be known to many of us, life systems are reminders and remnants of historical and cultural constructions that define the way we view and interact with the world, and that includes how we value money, how we strictly adhere to general economic transactions and, yes, how we relate our actions to our understanding of success in both domestic and extradomestic terms and locations. So the idea of free market functions and relationships as the economic wall of citizenship has been recolonized to the extent where it becomes anything but free will and space to exercise or adhere to the practice of the laissez-faire ideology. And we are not even at this point questioning the relevance of this for the Africans and other previously colonized populations, which should be obvious, but even with all other things having been considered, the levels of economic de-democratization and de-citizenization are so thick that one need not do too much work to see them in the actions of governments and in the lives of citizens who are showing the scars of the ideological plunder.

A case in point is the outcome of SAPs, which, as noted above, were the main project of externally imposed social-development schemes that were designed for the 'underdeveloped.' As Schatz (2002) noted, the World Bank actually knew, from as early as 1996, that this program has failed to achieve its pronounced objectives, and has actually created more livelihood problems that were directly affecting the lives of people. The case was not difficult to understand. Even relying upon pure socioeconomic numbers, which many times do not capture the true magnitude of the failure, the available facts showed a situation where in sub-Saharan Africa, for example, after almost twenty years from the first systematizations of SAPs (around 1980), that is, in 2000, about 70 percent of countries in the area found themselves in less viable development situations than they were at the beginning of the experiment (UNDP 2003). So what did the World Bank do? As should be expected from any sober institutional setting, did it rescind SAPs as models of social well-being, or at least extensively modify them, so they yield something more meaningful for the concerned publics? No, and, at least officially, not much has changed. African governments and others in similar locations in the prevalent global order are still to conform to the de-rational and undoubtedly de-reasonable dispensations and ordinances of the case where, despite all the pain they have created in the lives of hundreds of millions of Africans, and globally the violation of the citizenship of billions, the counterdevelopment (indeed, antidevelopment) instructions of decreasing public expenditure on social development programs and the creation of more private enterprises (including in the areas of education and health care) are still being pushed by Western governments and their institutions, including nongovernmental organizations (NGOs), with some of these having become the foot soldiers of the de novo underdeveloping schemes.

Indeed, long before any of us started writing about the 'on-the-ground untenability' of SAPs' prescriptions, common people in the streets were clear on the difficulty of understanding the relevance of private schools as public policy programs in places where, beyond the tiny elite circles, anyone would afford school to pay for these schools, or how nations that are so disadvantaged (in educational, health and economic terms) should deprive such institutions the right funding when they should be the primary developers of educated, healthy people who can become the vanguard of economic well-being. Good ideas and pragmatic thinking of course, but common people or academics like ourselves did not control the dominant dispensations of the story, and had no access to the policy forums in Washington, London or Paris, where the aims as well as the expected outcomes of the situation were conceived, designed and implemented. So to address the concern of citizens and formal observers of the situation, Western institutions need not explain too much. In succinct terms, all the issues discussed above, whether they be about general citizenship understandings and practices, the post–Cold War inventions of democratization or the main fragments of those including SAPs and their economic and development liabilities, represent the ideas and current practices of the dominant group, which in Marxian terms, ipso facto, become the right ideas. Needless to add that what is also evident is the rigidity of the ideological platform that is apparently willing to sacrifice so many lives to the altar, for lack of a more civilized term, of monetarism. Interestingly, this was happening in contexts that were, relatively speaking, demonetized by the false promise of the laissez-faire religion in the first place,

PROSPECTS FOR DECOLONIZATION

In discussing the possibilities for decolonization, we could start, not necessarily with immediately rescinding the policy items that are dictated from the West (such quick action will be very difficult to achieve, anyway), but with ways of rereading and reanalyzing the psycho-cultural relationships that we have inherited from colonialism. In such relationships, one group (Africans and others in related trajectories of historia) was mentally deconstructed as not only not capable of managing its affairs but, as well, naturally needing the guidance and the support of the European and Euro-American metropolises. As Chinua Achebe (1990, 2000) said, even in the so-called postcolonial space, everything, including the creation of ideas about life, experiences and ways of doing life in Africa, has to be first verified by the first citizens of the world; and, apparently, it is only after obtaining the right approval or the desired appreciation from there that the new natives might move ahead with their intentions. That represents, of course, a stark case of what Marie Battiste (2000) called cognitive imperialisms where citizenship rights, the meanings of democratic governance and the practice of social justice should not come for the long-ago de-citizenized but for those who wield global economic and political power. The point of using the term *de-citizenized* here and above is always deliberate in the sense that what we term today postcolonial in most African countries does not represent full projects of citizenship but, as implicated above, an essentiality of citizenship-subjecthood mixture that actually tilts more towards the negative side of the graph.

To establish decolonized spaces of citizenship, therefore, the project should start with a deliberate undertaking that facilitates the possible production of liberated subjectivities that should not only think for themselves but, as well, can achieve a cognitive sovereignty that heralds inclusive social development prospects which affirm the rights of all citizens not only in relation to their governments but also vis-à-vis Western institutions such as international financial agencies (IFIs), United Nations agencies and NGOs, which have been hitherto imposing their will on people. Mental or cognitive decolonization is actually more complicated and more difficult to achieve than direct physical decolonization. As we have learned from many brilliant students of the psychological and social foundations of colonialism (see, inter alia, Achebe 1958, 2000; Fanon 1967, 1968; Cesaire 1972; wa Thiongo 1986, 2009; Memmi 1991), mental colonization involves, among other things, the ontological, existential and epistemological de-patterning of the colonized's life. As such, it endures for a very long time, it becomes and intergenerational inheritance and even induces (in the being of colonized) a desire for the oppressor's presence and ways of life. To deal with something as extensive as this in today's critical reconstructions of citizenship and viable human well-being, therefore, one needs to acquire the capacity to reimagine a place called Africa that at one point freely defined its citizenship contexts, created and occasionally revamped its governance structures and, indeed, practiced extensive systems of social development that attended to the well-being of its people. This place also had learning platforms that responded to the community's need not only for realignment of its life contexts but, as well, to its futuristic imaginations and aspirations in readying people for the continual and practical forward movement in cultural, political, environmental and economic matters. The project of reconstruction should, therefore, have heavy doses of memory reconstitution that should be expansively and freely available to the perforce deconscientized masses who are yearning for some meaningful agency and for pronto-recriticalizations that can recenter the actualities of their lives.

With pre-colonial life realities and relationships derided by Europeans as backward, primitive and unworthy, memories were gradually lost (Mandela, 1994; wa Thiongo, 2009), leaving communities of people who live as shadows of their former selves (Biko, 2002 [1979]), and who therefore urgently need to regain liberated subjectivities that accord them the confidence as well as the right to define their own primary needs of citizenship and to develop attached governance and development systems that enhance rather than alienate lives, past and present. The liberated subjectivities should replace the damaged selves that are not as agency-endowed as they should have been, which when coupled with the deformed identities imposed by colonialism, and continued under the predatory practices of false laissez-faire economics, diminished citizenship dispensations and in earnest, underdeveloping projects disguised as development, all under the command of global capitalism, should be facing the very difficult task of re-creating a new world that is not necessarily purely of the old, but should not be and cannot be devoid of the old. In emphasizing the importance of authentic identities for viable social development in current postcolonial spaces, the Canadian philosopher Charles Taylor (1995) spoke about the damage that misrecognition, in the form of externally imposed identities that do not come from the subject of identity (Africans in this whose identities were deformed, replaced by new imposed and demeaning ones), inflicts on people, leading to clusters of negative self-esteem formations that problematically interact with self-efficacy possibilities (i.e., one's capacity to define tasks and successfully achieve them), thus endangering the overall perspective of inclusive social development. Here again, the important connectedness between colonial deformations of citizenship and development, postcolonial failures to recast these and the continuing colonization of African public spaces should discerned more comprehensively than the perpetrators of the act want us to believe. To deal with today's citizenship, governance and development problems, the realization of a strong decolonization of the mind must be appreciated by African public institutions and the general public on the continent, and these must be supported by African diasporic communities, who may be selectively well positioned to access the ideas as well as the ideologies behind the willful constructions of the monocentric paradigm that tries to homogenize disparate life systems that cannot homogenized, and in the process destroys the meanings and, by extension, the existentialities of the disempowered selves and their locales.

So the task is not easy, but doable; it is needed. For the project of decolonization to happen, insists Ngugi wa Thiongo (2009), a new project of reconstituting the lost memory and new ways of heralding a genuine African*ist* renaissance (not like those rhetorically and otherwise sponsored by the sources of the problems) must be rebuilt. He writes that "remembering Africa is the only way of ensuring Africa's own full rebirth . . . The success of Africa's renaissance depends on its commitment and ability to remember itself, guided by the great remembering vision of Pan-Africanism" (100). The arrow to Pan-Africanism (whether in original citizenship ideas, policies or programs) is important in that Africans were collectively colonized, collectively given false nominal postcoloniality which affirmed the recolonization of their public and private spaces. In liberating themselves, therefore, one can ascertain the need for a collective African effort to rescind the problems we have explained in this chapter. And to achieve such understanding and appreciation, Africans need to reconstruct their identities, cultures and meanings of development. As things are now, it is not just the problem of lost citizenship and related structures of exclusion; it is also the memory location where the past and the present are not representative of the real cases of life that have taken place or are taking place. To reclaim lost ontologies and deconstructed worldviews, therefore, perhaps we should heed the late Bissau-Guinean freedom fighter and thinker Amilcar Cabral's call for a 'return to the source.' As analytically and practically aligned by Cabral (2007 [1979]), who was writing as he was fighting against Portuguese colonialism, this return to the source involves, as much as anything else, a revaluing and reharnessing of Africa's rich cultural heritage. In Cabral's pragmatism, this return to the source should not necessarily mean that we can establish the primordial order and live it out in current circumstances and relationships. As the world has shifted so extensively in the past five hundred years, and as was indicated above, the ideas, as well as the practices of decolonization, need not be fundamentally antagonistic versus anybody, but would conform to a more open humanist struggle that welcomes the intentions as well as the actions of all those who are willing to contribute to the historical, cultural, political, economic and overall existential freedoms that are being sought in a reestablished and more liberating global order. Indeed, Cabral himself preferred to term what is called democracy in the African context as freedom, so perhaps even there, we should practically rename the current rhetoric of African democracies as African freedoms. Minimally, that will make more sense to the public, who will then be more able to reflect upon and define the type of liberated citizenship they need in more meaningful and culturally more authentic postcolonial spaces.

CONCLUSION

In this chapter, we started with a point on the recent expansions of global citizenship scholarship and writing, and we decided to see these for what they really are: a new line of Western constructions of citizenship that are imagined for the world, and then, without any consultations, exported to all corners of the globe. We, of course, see the danger of these, and we labeled them as counterliberating; we went a little bit further; we are seeing the complexities of these citizenship definitions, constructions and analysis as negatively adding to the already problematic 'democracy' and 'development' situations in sub-Saharan Africa which, after five decades of 'independence,' have not yet achieved the long-awaited subjective-institutional freedoms that were promised for the postcolonial perspective and space. As we continued analyzing the situation, we couldn't minimize, actually did not want to minimize, the collective of uni-polarization, globalization (via laissez-faire economics and its structural adjustment programs attachments), rhetoric of democracy and the new fragments of global citizenship as problematic entities that were, intentionally or otherwise, thickening the recolonization of African public spaces where the loss of public policymaking at the national level, complemented by the oppressive outcomes of ill-understood, indeed, fundamentally nonviable, governance impositions that expanded the socioeconomic and cultural marginalizations of the public. Still, the impact has not been uniform, the African elite is still doing well, and actually willfully engages in measurable conspiratorial schemes that seemingly permanentize the situation, while enhancing the life possibilities of the ruling class. The outcome is, to say the least, very bad, and with the clear weaknesses of the postcolonial prospect, we suggest that we, de novo, consider new ways of mental and material decolonizations that can replant Africa's lost memory and reconstitute more agency for the people who, to be fair, have experienced so much de-ontologizations and disconnections of their cosmologies and subjectivities that their yearning for some justice is actually inscribed on their beings and overall responses to the benighted impositions that wrought so much havoc on their lives.

REFERENCES

Abdi, A. A. (2008). 'Citizenship and Its Discontents: Educating for Political and Economic Development in Sub-Saharan Africa', in M. Peters, A. Britton and H. Blee (eds.), *Global Citizenship Education: Philosophy, Theory and Pedagogy*, Rotterdam, Netherlands: Sense Publishers.

Abdi, Ali A., Ellis, L. and Shizha, E. (2005) 'Democratic Development and the Role of Citizenship Education in Sub-Saharan Africa with a Case Focus of Zambia', *International Education Journal*, 6: 454–466.
Abdi, A. A., Shizha, E. and Ellis, L. (2010) *Citizenship Education and Social Development in Zambia*, Charlotte, NC: Information Age Publishing.
Achebe, C. (1958) *Things Fall Apart*, London: Heinemann.
———. (1990) *Hopes and Impediments*, New York: Doubleday.
———. (2000) *Home and Exile*, New York: Oxford University Press.
Battiste, M. (2000) *Reclaiming Indigenous Voice and Vision*, Vancouver, BC: UBC Press.
Bessis, S. (2003) *Western Supremacy: The Triumph of an Idea?* London: Zed Books.
Biko, S. (2002 [1979]) *I Write What I Like*, Chicago: University of Chicago Press.
Cabral, A. (2007 [1979]) *Unity and Struggle: Speeches and Writing*, Pretoria: UNISA Press.
Cesaire, A. (1972) *Discourse on Colonialism*, New York: Monthly Review Press.
Dewey, J. (1926) *Democracy and Education*, New York: Collier Publishers.
Fanon, F. (1967) *Black Skin, White Masks*, New York: Grove Press.
———. (1968) *The Wretched of the Earth*, New York: Grove.
Freire, P. (1998) *Pedagogy of Freedom: Ethics, Democracy and Civic Courage*, Lanham, MD: Rowman & Littlefield.
———. (2000 [1970]) *Pedagogy of the Oppressed*, New York: Continuum.
Fukuyama, F. (1992) *The End of History and the Last Man*, New York: Free Press.
Hoogvelt, A. (2002) *Globalization and the Postcolonial World: The New Political Economy of Development*, New York: Palgrave.
Ihonvbere, J. (1996) 'On the Threshold of Another False Start?', *Journal of Asian and African Studies*, 31: 125–142.
Lewis, I. M. (1961) *A Pastoral Democracy: A Study of Pastoralism and Politics among the Northern Somali of the Horn of Africa*, London: Oxford University Press.
Mandela, N. (1994) *Long Walk to Freedom: The Autobiography of Nelson Mandela*, Toronto: GREF.
Memmi, A. (1991). *The colonizer and the colonized*, Boston: Beacon Press.
Nyerere, J. (1968) *Freedom and Socialism: Speeches and Writing, 1965–67*, London: Oxford University Press.
Rahnema, M. (1997) 'Introduction', in M. Rahnema and V. Bowtree (eds.), *The Post- Development Reader*, London: Zed Books.
Schatz, S. (2002) 'Structural Adjustment', in G. Bond and N. Gibson (eds.), *Contested Terrains and Constructed Categories: Contemporary Africa in Focus*, Boulder, CO: Westview Press.
Shultz, L., Abdi, Ali A. and Nungu, J. M. (2010) Global Citizenship Education and the Role of Civil Society Organizations: Seminar Series in Lusaka and Nairobi, May 8–13, 2010.
Taylor, C. (1995) *Philosophical Arguments*, Cambridge, MA: Harvard University Press.
UNDP (2003) *Human Development Report*, New York: Oxford University Press.
wa Thiongo, N. (1986) *Decolonising the Mind: The Politics of Language in African Literature*, London: James Curry.
———. (2009) *Re-membering Africa*, Nairobi: East Africa Educational Publishers.
Wedel, J. (2009) *Shadow Elite: How the World's New Power Brokers Undermine Democracy, Government, and the Free Market*, New York: Basic Books.

Youth Study Tour to Africa

Lynette Shultz

Anxious parents sign legal waivers
Releasing their children
On their way to
    See poverty
    See culture
    See life.
They look at their young, wondering at their deficiencies
That no amount of cash or summer camp counseling can hide.
The wounded youth of the rich
Their emancipated swaggers covering emaciated hearts.
Their loneliness resting on teachings that
    The primacy of self
    The commodity of friendship
    The danger of Thou
    Are the path to enrichment.

∞

These young eyes arrive at the village and rest on the exotic
Eager to consume
The vibrant colours and textures of a community
That is resigned to the gaze of these Northerners but
Knows that—while carrying danger—
The gaze is from eyes that are easily distracted
Easily fooled by trinkets,
Their shallowness a way of surviving sixty-billion-dollar ad campaigns
And the latest celebrity-of-the-hour.
The thought that this village should carry the youths' transformation
Another colonial myth.

∞

Departure day arrives
The young are restless
Their glimpse into community profound, Awakening
Ancient knowing of a primal village.
But the scar tissue, where heart and sight were exchanged for the latest
    electronics

Requires years of massaging before it will release
The wisdom of the ages.
The youth make one last orgy of consumption in the local market,
Then strap themselves safely in the seats of an Air Canada wide-
    body jet
Content that nothing has been disturbed.

Part III

Creating Postcolonial Spaces
Global Citizenship
Education 'Otherwise'

10 Beyond Paternalism
Global Education with Preservice Teachers as a Practice of Implication

Lisa Taylor

A global citizenship education of 'bringing the world into our classrooms' forgets that our classrooms are always already in this world, entangled economically, discursively and affectively. Moving global citizenship education beyond consolation and spectacle implies grappling with the discursive and psychic formations driving the spectacularization of suffering and the affective geographies of privilege. In this narrative case study of a preservice course in Social and Global Justice Education offered in a small, fairly homogenous liberal arts university in Canada, I examine the forms of embodied reflexivity that emerge when teacher candidates are asked to grapple with the 'difficult knowledge' (Britzman 1998) of global inequity and specifically. The course engages students in an analysis of the psychic and discursive technologies of (neo)imperialism that structure binary North-South relationships: the cultural practices and semiotic economies constructing citizens of the global North and South, respectively, as sovereign, generous subjects and passive, racialized objects of knowledge. Shifting from 'instrumental' to 'difficult' approaches to learning (Britzman 1998), students are challenged to examine their investment in Eurocentric teleologies of human development, and plan deconstructive curriculum which seeks to learn *from* rather than *about* the Other. I examine examples of this emergent practice of 'learning as implication' from students' reflexive planning of curriculum based on the film *Life and Debt* (Black 2001).

In a recent review of global education in Canadian elementary schools, Mundy and Manion (2008) report that, in practice, global education tends to be pursued piecemeal, divorced from the development of critical thinking, critical literacy and active citizenship, but also as an exercise in learning about distant others, learning to appreciate 'our' comparative good fortune and extracurricular, one-off fundraising events. (Their critique was not of the work of committed, innovative teachers but of the absence of leadership in professional development and curriculum resources by ministries of education.) While global citizenship education (GCE) has emerged out of global education as a project aimed explicitly to foster critical understandings of globalization rather than culturally reductive and exoticized stereotypes, responsibility rather than pity, a growing body of critical scholarship (to which this collection contributes) raises concerns about the persistent colonialist regimes of truth within which even respectful and well-intended North-South relations continue to be constructed in teleological and paternalist terms. Taking up this challenge requires postcolonial critique, but also pedagogical inquiry into the ways psychic dynamics of learning and resistance interlock with colonial epistemological and ontological discourses to reinstate the sovereign Western subject of knowledge and agency.

In this narrative case study of a social justice in education preservice course offered in a small, fairly homogenous liberal arts university in Canada, I examine the forms of embodied reflexivity that emerge when teacher candidates are asked to grapple with the 'difficult knowledge' (Britzman 1998) of global inequity and specifically one's own implication in such inequity. The course engages students in an analysis of the binary psychic and discursive relations of authority structuring (neo)imperialism: the cultural practices and semiotic economies constructing citizens of the global North and South, respectively, as sovereign, generous subjects and racialized objects of knowledge. Shifting from 'instrumental' to 'difficult' approaches to learning (Britzman 1998), students are challenged to examine their implication and investment in Eurocentric colonial imaginaries and exploitative North-South power relations, and plan deconstructive curriculum which seeks to learn *from* rather than *about* the Other.

In the sections below, I situate the study within the broad field of global education; I turn to the work of Todd (2009), Britzman and Pitt (Britzman 1998; Pitt and Britzman 2003), Ellsworth (2005) and Simon (2008, 2009), whose inquiries into the psychic dynamics of 'difficult' learning and specifically "affect's relation to the possibilities of thought" (Simon 2009) afford me a more granular analysis of the tensions striating student responses to global justice education what I propose as a 'pedagogy of implication.'

SITUATING GLOBAL JUSTICE EDUCATION AT THE INTERFACE OF DISCOURSE AND AFFECT

A growing body of scholarship argues that current global citizenship educational theory and practice urgently need to be reexamined through postcolonial and anticolonial critique. Schueller (2009) traces the ways even explicitly anticolonial theoretical and activist projects share with traditions of colonial knowledge production a Eurocentric universalizing framing of the 'global' that reinstates the colonial difference (Mignolo 2000) and reinscribes the "triumph of globality" (Radhakrishnan 2003 in Schueller 2009, 240).[1] Andreotti (2008) discerns Eurocentric, colonial teleologies of 'development' (equating technological and civilizational indicators) in British practices of GCE. Pashby (2009) argues that even critical GCE constructs the subject and object of learning and agency within colonialist imaginaries and ways of knowing. Willinsky (1998, 333, 349) posits an imperialist "educational commodification[:] . . . a will to know that is capable of turning the testimony of others into 'learning experiences' " with curative effects for normalized privileged first world learners: A successful 'learning experience' promises moral sanitization and absolution from the complex, historically implicated locations inhabited by privileged readers.

These critiques place the transformative and in some cases anticolonial agenda of GCE in question, suggesting that the modern/colonial (Mignolo 2000) imaginary to which GCE is an active heir invites students into hierarchical relations of power, authority and agency with fellow citizens of this planet. Global educators have yet to seriously grapple with the ways a Eurocentric colonial imaginary and West-centered global order structure both student desire as well as the terms and limits of "thinkability" (Britzman 1998) when citizens of the North turn their attention to those of the South. Taking this imaginary seriously implies recognizing learning as both a discursive and psychic event (Britzman 1998, 118), situated "where the crisis of representation that is exterior to the self meets the crisis of representation that is interior to the learner" (Pitt and Britzman 2003, 756).

This means bringing a more nuanced analysis of the psychic challenges involved in students' adopting perspectives that radically shift (neo)imperial relations of power/knowledge, that decenter and implicate them in relation to the planetary South.[2] This shifts our examination of GCE from critique to pedagogy: What sorts of demands does learning of one's implication in global injustice pose and what are the affective dynamics of such self-risking learning (Ellsworth 2005)? Todd's (2009) reframing of cosmopolitan education alerts us that first world learners encounter 'global Others' not only through colonial and neoimperial regimes of representation but also through the crisis or 'traumatic wounding' of facing humanity in all its complexity.

Todd argues that the dispositions of cosmopolitanism shared with global education—valorization of diversity and interdependence and active advocacy for universal human rights—cannot be explicitly taught ("humanity" is not some preexistent intrinsic virtue, the opposite of violence) but rather emerge from a relation of intersubjectivity or proximity. From a Levinasian perspective, she insists, this is a relation of violence. Taking a dramatic example from global citizenship education, as I open myself to comprehending the extremes of degradation and exploitation upon which my quality of life parasitically depends within a neoimperial, capitalist global order—a quality of life supported by resources accruing over five centuries of conquest, genocide, slavery, underdevelopment and transnational capitalism—there is a violence implicit in the call of this understanding. This violence is implicit both in my freedom to turn away in indifference and in the overwhelming sense of responsibility I might feel for the Other of my good fortune, the humans and other creatures with whom I share this planet. My ambivalent oscillation between the dual poles of violence—indifference and crushing responsibility—follows a "trajectory, that time and space of ethical responsibility, which signifies a relationship of non-violence without banishing or denying the risk of eruption of violence itself" (Todd 2009, 6).Todd posits that if, in Levinasian terms, "[h]umanity's name *is* the responsibility that is forged out of the trauma and the ever-present threat of violence" that emerges from concrete situations in which we find ourselves (8).

Drawing from Jessica Benjamin and Shoshana Felman, Ellsworth (2005) theorizes this traumatic encounter of human pluralism as a crisis in learning: "Merely by living in this world, we are exposed to . . . the *different* others who . . . in their mere existence as separate human beings reflect our lack of control" (Benjamin 1998, 95, in Ellsworth 2005, 89). Assuming a decentered position within a multicentric rather than Eurocentric worldview, a key aim of GCE, demands forms of agency that are neither heroic nor despairing. But the call to global citizenship is so easily taken up through persistent colonial tropes of *noblesse oblige* and the civilizing mission refashioned as global responsibility and the "desire for development" (Heron 2007). A profound epistemological and ontological crisis ensues when we encounter "others who are not who we thought they were, are not the image we have constructed of them, are not who we want them to be or hate them to be or need them to be so that we can continue to be who we think *we* are" (Ellsworth 2005, 89).

This crisis in global citizenship learning opens a time and space of epistemological and ontological disorientation, one situated between the apprehension of others "whose differences survive our attempts to deny, change, assimilate, demean . . . control," to know, help, rescue or develop them (Ellsworth 2005, 89), and the rushing in of colonial and neoimperial imaginaries to reorder power relations of knowing and being. This space and time of crisis host by what Britzman (1998) and Pitt and Britzman (2003) call "difficult knowledge": knowledge which interrupts and implicates the learning self (Britzman 1998, 117–119); knowledge which "references incommensurability, historical trauma and social breakdowns [in ways that] open teachers and students to their present ethical obligations" (Pitt and Britzman 2003, 756). It is knowledge which demands that learners exceed the bounds of the thinkable upon which their subject position and self-knowledge are predicated (Britzman 1998): "[i]n order to learn something new, as in previously unthought, we must lose that part of ourselves whose identity depends on not thinking that thought . . . that depends on not being the kind of person who entertains such thoughts or understands such thoughts" (Ellsworth 2005, 89). The challenge of anticolonial global justice education lies in pedagogically provoking and sustaining this moment and space of epistemic vertigo, ontological loss and traumatic responsibility from the ego's self-defense, from the refusal of relationality, from the consolation of familiar, hegemonic structures of authority and innocence.

One of GCE's greatest risks, then, consists in becoming a pedagogy of consolation (Britzman 1998) in ways which draw comfort from colonial hierarchies of knowing, being and feeling. Most troubling in the 'spare-a-penny, count-your-blessings' approach described above, for example, is that the crisis in learning initiated when children are exposed to knowledge of global inequity is closed down when pedagogy offers *consolation* rather than critical and ethical tools to respond to this crisis. What is offered is the consolation of reestablishing a subject-object relation of Aristotelian pity ('there but for the grace of God go I'; Boler 1999) that reduces 'their' suffering to spectacle for my consumption; it is the consolation of restoring the self-congratulatory relation of helper-helpless in the act of charity. This relation is cemented in the promise of gratitude from the 'helped' and the acquisition of enhanced 'intercultural' cosmopolitan competencies by the helper.

The specter of such a pedagogy of consolation is articulated by Roger Simon (2008) when he cautions that heartfelt stories of suffering do not necessarily lead to responses of respect, responsibility or a social and political commitment. Simon warns of two ways such stories can be misrecognized: The storyteller may be misrecognized as an essentialized victim of history whose story of suffering is interchangeable with a thousand others, a spectacle with no unique subjectivity; they may also be recognized as an object of pathos through a dissociative splitting off of the emotional engagement from critical analysis of my systemic implication in the conditions of this suffering. In what he calls the "Too Bad, So Sad" syndrome, learners end up "feeling good about feeling bad" (Simon 2008). All of these practices operate to close down the anxious, violent crisis of learning selves exposed to the overwhelming, disorienting call to recognize and revise their habitual and hegemonic relationship to global Others, a closure wrought through the restoration of their moral superiority and authority.

The preservice course under examination in this study focuses on education for social and global justice. It explicitly encourages students through learning materials, activities and a shared conceptual vocabulary to hold open this crisis long enough to resist recourse to ego-defense through colonial traditions of knowledge construction in the move from acknowledging injustice and suffering to knowledge of Others (Simon 2009). The analysis below focuses on the ways students resist crises of implication and difficult knowledge as well as moments in which they sit in the crisis in attempt to respond and self-position in exploratory, ethical ways.

RESEARCH SITE AND METHODOLOGY

As a white Anglophone Canadian-born academic, I recognize the forms of structural privilege that authorize and position me as 'objective' or 'neutral' in the analyses I model and encourage (Schick and St. Denis 2005). It is also important to contextualize this course within the preservice program of the small English-language liberal arts university in Quebec, Canada. The majority of the almost 250 students in this four-year B.Ed. program are white, Canadian-born Anglophones aged 19–24 from ethnically homogeneous rural communities.[3] The sample in this study is thus largely consistent with the predominance of Euro-Canadian middle-class candidates in teacher-education programs across the country (Levine-Rasky 1998). Confirming much antiracism research (Levine-Rasky 1998, 2002; Solomon 2000; Sleeter 2001; Banks 2004), my documentation of this course suggests that Canadian-born, white-identified preservice students tend to bring a poverty of cross-cultural experiences or analysis of structural discrimination and privilege as well as meritocratic ideologies of North American society and the global political economy.

This qualitative study examines samples of student work from six sections of a mandatory undergraduate course on social justice and education in a five-year period from 2004 to 2008. In the assignment that is the focus of this case study, groups of six to nine students are expected to preview and research one of five films viewed in the course (in this case, the documentary on the impact of globalization on postcolonial Jamaica, *Life and Debt* by Stephanie Black), to design questions for and facilitate small-group, postscreening discussions.

This is clarified in an excerpt from the instructions for film discussion facilitation groups below:

1. "After the screening and small group discussions, meet as a group:
   a. Each group member must bring a 2–3 page reflection. Each individual reflection will be graded according to how well you draw from group research, discussions and course concepts in order to analyze the following 2 areas:
      i. The discussion in your small group in response to the questions (Any gaps in prior knowledge? How did students struggle with the difficult knowledge sparked by the film or your questions? How did you guide the discussion?)
      ii. The pedagogical implications of this experience for you as future teachers: What were your goals? What insight does this give you into the challenges of social justice pedagogy? Would you approach these issues differently (at different levels)? Would you incorporate other supports (literature, activities, community involvement)?
   b. Date and sign each other's Discussion Summary Sheet (to verify your individual participation).
   c. Share your Discussion Summary Sheets and compile as a group a 1–2 page addendum to your individual reflections which summarizes these two areas (i. & ii.) from the collective experiences of your group.
   d. Within 2 weeks, hand in a final package which contains:
      i. Your group with member names;
      ii. A table of contents;
      iii. A 2nd copy of the 4–7 page research summary;
      iv. A hard copy of the 1–2 page group summary;
      v. Each group member's 1–2 page signed, dated summary."

Excerpts are cited below from two data sources: discussion questions written by film facilitation groups and individual student facilitators' reflections on the tensions and dynamics in small-group discussions they had led. Limiting my data sources to these two reflects my decision, as an educator-researcher, to create a range of spaces for student individual and group deliberation that are somewhat insulated from instructional surveillance by a professor who does not present herself as 'neutral' vis-à-vis the issues of injustice under discussion. These two data sources form the basis of three data sets: the group-authored discussion questions; individual student facilitators' reflections on their own experiences of difficult learning sparked by the documentary; and individual student facilitators' reflections on the ways they perceived and facilitated their group members' discussion of and responses to difficult knowledge. None of these data sets are treated as objective or transparent, but, rather, suggestive triggers for insight into some of the tensions, traumas and potential spaces of innovation in response to the call of global injustice.

While the data set includes written material from forty-eight partici-pants (in the form of individual reflections or group discussion questions), the analysis below cites the individual work of eight students and the collec-tively produced work of three groups (twenty-five students total). To ensure anonymity, course sections are not revealed and all names are pseudonyms. While these excerpts reflect patterns that emerged across the data set, they have been selected to illustrate possible forms of reflexive deliberation amongst students who are attempting to reassemble and reposition their sense of self in relation to systemic injustice and inequity.

COURSE PEDAGOGY

The course introduces students to conceptual frameworks from integrative antiracism and whiteness studies, feminist, postcolonial and queer theory and cultural studies (Hall 1997) in order to shift liberal multicultural discourses of the plight/problem of the essentialized Other to a critical discussion of the politics of representation: 'Who has the power to define whom, when and how' (McCarthy and Crichlow 1993, xvi). The course, therefore, begins with exercises in analyzing intersecting discourses of racialized, gendered, classed, sexualized, nationalist, ability- and faith-based identity that populate the social imaginary and circulate through our consumption, production and participa-tion in popular and mass culture. In class exercises, the students analyze the ways in which, within cultural processes of representation, dominant identi-ties are constructed through a binary logic that reduces subaltern identities to essentialized foils (Said 1978; Morrison 1992). Analyzing concrete, familiar examples from North American popular and mass media and culture pushes students to examine the ways, as members of this culture, we not only partici-pate in systems of exclusion to which we are opposed (at least theoretically), the ways we are invested in these systems both materially and psychically through not only the resources and privileges that accrue but the binary divisions secured (see Figure 10.1, Course Materials). That is, class exercises guide students in exploring discourses of Eurocentric heteropatriarchal neoimperial capitalism not as abstract theories but rather, as hegemonic identificatory processes in which we each participate, staking our identities as diverse First World subjects through the abjection of "those outside others whom we have used as repositories for what we have repudiated about ourselves" (Ellsworth 2005, 90).

Drawing from the graphic organizer (Figure 10.1) and class lectures, one facilitation group produced the analysis represented in Table 10.1 of the classed and racialized dichotomies constructed within colonial and neoimperial discourses of globalization in preparation for their facilitation of small-group postscreening discussions of the documentary.[4]

Table 10.1   The Social Construction of Difference

Self *We are everything they aren't* *Us*	*Other* *Projection of everything we're not* *Them*
Superior, developed, advanced technology Civilized, Modern, most highly evolved Peaceful, human-rights defenders Law-abiding, safe societies Democratic	Inferior, Under-developed, backward, Uncivilized, primitive, stuck in Stone Age Violent, tribal warfare Criminal, dangerous Dictatorships
Responsible (the G8 runs the world economy) Hardworking, earned our wealth Self-sufficient, Generous Intelligent, Scientific Experts, connected to the 'Information Highway'	Irresponsible 'little' countries with no power in UN Lazy, laid-back, don't help themselves Dependent, Demanding Without any useful knowledge, uneducated, ignorant, isolated (need volunteers to teach how to dig a well)
Peacekeepers, Aid-donors, NGOs "Feel sorry for" Hygienic, clean cities Living ('We are the Future')	Starving victims, victims of war Pitiful Dirty, no sewage systems, diseases, AIDS Dying (Survival of the Fittest)
Normal Unique individuals Subject of the Gaze (media or NGO ads presume the audience is us) Angelina Jolie (protagonist of news reports)	Strange cultures, customs Stereotyped by nationality first (e.g., Bob Marley represents all Jamaicans) Object of the Gaze (exploitative photos of babies, objectified as poor) Scenery, subplot (e.g. servants or 'natives' in tourism ads, villages only important if Jolie visited them)
Consumer in global economy	Producer (farmer, factory worker)
Not responsible for global poverty	Responsible for own poverty

Source: Pamela, Heather, Sophie, Andrée, Marnie, Lisa Classroom Notes 2006.

The Social Construction of Difference

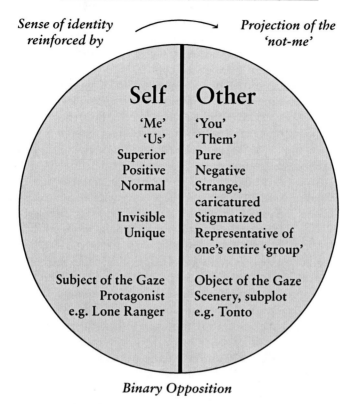

Sense of identity
reinforced by

Projection of the
'not-me'

Self	Other
'Me'	'You'
'Us'	'Them'
Superior	Pure
Positive	Negative
Normal	Strange, caricatured
Invisible	Stigmatized
Unique	Representative of one's entire 'group'
Subject of the Gaze	Object of the Gaze
Protagonist	Scenery, subplot
e.g. Lone Ranger	e.g. Tonto

Binary Opposition

Figure 10.1 Course materials.

Admittedly, this conceptual model risks reproducing the very object of its critique (reproducing, that is, the essentializing binary logic of identification). Pedagogically, it is vital for an instructor to explore this heuristic's limits and contradictions by discussing concrete examples from one's own personal experiences, and insisting on an intersectional analysis of how "Othering" relations of race, gender, sexuality, class, ethnicity, faith, ability, accent and national origin (among others) converge differently on specific bodies depending on the particular context.

These exercises are key to shifting students' attention from a desire for instrumental knowledge (knowledge *about* 'other' cultures, about their 'problems') to a critical excavation of "self-knowledge" (Britzman 2000).[5] They are aimed to interrupt the 'will to know' identified by Willinsky that underpins the institutional drive of educational commodification (especially in teacher education programs) and (neo)imperial discourses of spectacle and epistemic mastery (Willinsky 1998) as well as the ego's defense against

one's implication in difficult knowledge. These are also exercises in critically assessing one's own hierarchical material and symbolic power relations
with one's subjects of study or concern and trying to shift these by turning
the analytic gaze back on oneself. Postcolonial critiques explored above
insist that, like other global theories, GCE risks operating as a colonizing
force as long as "colonial difference" continues to structure our students'
processes of knowing and feeling vis-à-vis global Others (Schueller 2009,
237). Shifting these hierarchical relations is self-risking learning, however;
Schick and St. Denis (2005) call the experience "pulling the rug from under
you while standing on it." It would be naïve to expect students to be willing
or able to take such risks solely on the instructor's invitation or demand;
it would indeed be presumptive, considering our students' differently positioned social and educational histories of privilege and marginalization.

In order to offer students a critical vocabulary with which to observe and
intervene in the subterranean psychic tensions striating the work of self-
implication, redefinition and repositioning in anticolonial, ethical relationships with their fellow planetary citizens, they are introduced early in the
course to the concept of *difficult knowledge* and encouraged to approach
their own experiences of resistance to difficult knowledge *symptomatically*.
This implies approaching epistemological discomfort not as a measure of
the quality of pedagogy or their own learning but as a focus of curiosity and
insight into social-justice education that may inform their own teaching for
difficult knowledge in other settings. In the group task of researching and
facilitating postscreening discussions of the five course films, students are
explicitly encouraged to design questions that might focus their small-group
discussion on one's classmates' experiences of and responses to the difficult
knowledge the documentary sparked for them: knowledge of one's implication in the shocking forms of global injustice explored in the documentary;
and responses to the film's explicit postcolonial 'speaking back' and direct
ethical address, its deconstruction of Eurocentric Northern subject positions
and forms of knowledge that would deny, change, assimilate, demean, control, know, pity, spectacularize, help, rescue or 'develop' their fellow planetary citizens of the South. The individual facilitator reflections cited below
from the second and third data sets are framed as an opportunity to articulate their emerging analysis and insight into the dynamics of resistance that
they experienced as a discussion leader and the ways they facilitated these.

Recognizing the psychic as well as discursive stakes of a postcolonial global
justice pedagogy—a pedagogy that "equates learning with the breaking up of
our identities, the suspension of who we think we are, an opening up to the
outside other" (Ellsworth 2005, 90)—means taking seriously the risks we
ask of our students and designing a pedagogy 'hospitable' to those risks (Ellsworth 2005, 30). Such a pedagogy might act, as Ellsworth (30) suggests, like
Winnicott's (1989) "transitional space": a space that interrupts the rush of
colonial imaginaries and the defense of the self, a "holding environment" or
antechamber that holds ajar the traumatic crisis of difficult knowledge, that

contains and supports our capacities to respond creatively to what is different from ourselves and offers "the flexible stability we need to risk allowing ourselves to be changed by an interaction" (Ellsworth 2005, 32). Several aspects of the postscreening discussion activity are designed to create the conditions of just such a transitional space: the facilitators and discussants share the conceptual vocabulary to examine their experiences of resistance to the difficult knowledge provoked by the documentary; *Life and Debt* is the last of the five films so that all group members have experienced being facilitators and understand the design of the questions; the professor does not listen in on, participate in or evaluate group discussions (thus field notes are excluded from data sets in this study).

To the extent that the small-group discussions of difficult knowledge become a protected, tentative time/space of exploration, there is the potential for them to serve, as Ellsworth proposes, as a "hinge . . . capable of acting as a pedagogical pivot point" between precarious states of experience, between apprehension and comprehension, "from reacting to outside in habitual ways, based only on past experiences, traumas, fears, or senses of who we are or what we want . . . to a state of creatively putting those expectations, traditions and structures to new uses" (2005, 8, 30, 41).

DATA ANALYSIS AND DISCUSSION

Individual student facilitator reflections recount a range of responses to studying the consequences of colonial underdevelopment policies, postcolonial debt schemes, structural adjustment plans, neoliberal decimation of domestic economies and regulatory powers, international trade law and devastating practices of dumping and labor exploitation of multinational corporations. One student wrote:

> I find the most difficult of the difficult learning is when it's about yourself. Learning just how privileged you are in comparison to others is a struggle to sit through, no one had the option of changing a channel like when a World Vision ad comes on TV. That problem is too big, what could I do to help, I can't watch this right now. . . . (Tim 2005)

The demand of the documentary's narrative voice, explicitly addressing an unnamed 'you' who leaves an economically stable North America to relax on pristine beaches oblivious to Jamaica's economic spiral,[6] implicates viewers in a relation of stark economic injustice and exploitation that is particularly destabilizing for viewers whose sense of self has been shaped through classed, racialized, gendered or ethnolinguistic forms of dominance and marginalization within Canadian society. Recognizing one's position of global privilege is especially difficult, writes Tim, for "[s]ome people [who] may not feel particularly privileged in their lives" (Tim 2005).

One group summary reflection recounts the facilitators' surprise at the extent of their classmates' resistance to the difficult knowledge of the documentary:

> [I]n every small group, there was an extreme lack of discussion and willingness to talk about the film. It seems as though everyone suffered from feeling guilty about their lack of prior knowledge about the whole situation and how implicated the first world is in the entire world. There was plenty of avoidance and disassociation amongst our peers, as they neither wanted to admit accountability or involvement in the poverty of an entire nation. Many students felt as though we were not at fault and we cannot change anything, because we are too small a population." (Patricia, Tim, Jane, Dave, Maria, Sally, Roy, Jim, group facilitation package, 2005)

The repeated theme of culpability ('guilt,' 'accountability,' 'fault') suggests that one response to the difficult knowledge of our participation in and benefit from global injustice is to frame the issue in a liberal juridical discourse which positions viewers in self-defense from bellicose attacks. Discourses of guilt and judgment unfortunately close down learning, since resistance, which Britzman (1998, 118) defines as "a precondition for learning from knowledge and the grounds of knowledge itself," is positioned as the termination of a process of learning rather than its inception.

Individual reflections from facilitators in another section suggest a heightened sense of woundedness haunting several small-group discussions. One facilitator writes:

> My group really had difficulty trying to break out of the 'us and them' mindset. They immediately saw themselves (rich white tourists) as the 'us' and the Jamaicans as 'them'. It took some time for me to get them to think about who is telling the story in the film, who is the 'us' of the film [Stephanie Black's narrative voice]. It's very unnerving to be seen as a 'them' and most students resisted it. Eventually they did come to see that the gaze [of the documentary][7] switches back and forth [between Jamaicans and North American tourists]. However, when asked what the film was missing, they wanted to see the tourists' perspective. They felt they were being portrayed one-sidedly and that not all tourists are ignorant . . . the tourist perspective seemed to be the 'way in' for the students, the way they were able to relate to the film. And they felt insulted." (Pamela 2006)

The insult articulated by the group's members may gesture to the discomfort and indignity of objectification within a postcolonial address that 'speaks back' to a monological oppressor, a subject position students might resist as it strips them of their complex sense of self and refuses a stance of knowledge as mastery. It also suggests the injury of the learner self's exposure to the violence implicit to the colonial relation and to a learning encounter that threatens to overwhelm the learner with infinite responsibility for the Other's suffering. Two facilitators described scenes of poverty and exploitation as "heartbreaking": "[t]hese are scenes that break your heart when watching the movie, because as one group member mentioned, what can you do?" (Heather, Sophie 2006). The image of a heart broken suggests a sense of the fracture or disintegration of the sovereign, agentive, stable Western subject of colonial and neoimperial discourse, one that becomes increasingly untenable before the unanswerable call of enormous injustice. In facing the Other who speaks back to Empire, this ethical call and the internal conflict it triggers may be experienced as not only a call but an external aggression. Writes another facilitator, "Throughout most of the discussion, I felt they kept the focus on themselves, and weren't really looking from other perspectives. They kept going back to the issue of tourism, the contrast between the resorts and the villages and 'how much they must hate us' " (Pamela 2006). Of note in this account is the repeated return to the colonial encounter of tourist-native and the returned gaze: the hailing and interpellation (Althusser 1971) into a subject position so nakedly oppressive as to grate our feet as we step into it. Facing and meeting this gaze, as its object, encountering oneself through this gaze, can precipitate a self-division or fracture that is profoundly unsettling in the forms of self-recognition it inaugurates. Writes another facilitator:

> There were students who did feel guilt and expressed so openly. They explained they had been on all inclusive vacations . . . or class trips . . . where they consumed the other, reveled in the ability to buy and indulge in this country. They also explained how they had felt insulted if anyone checked their bags, and couldn't believe that someone would check *our* luggage. They tried to view themselves through the eyes of Jamaicans, and they expressed that 'the natives of a country must really hate us deep down; even though they act friendly . . . I hate us. (emphasis original) (Ruth 2004)

Ellsworth (2005) speculates on the forms of ethical learning that can emerge from the psychic split in the learning self: Describing the pedagogical address of the Ringelblum Milk Can[8] in the Washington Holocaust exhibit, she focuses on the temporality of the "moment that inaugurates the split between the self who is held hostage to the moral imperative of the museum and the self who walks away" (2005, 110). This split inaugurates an interminable haunting, she argues, referencing Muschamp's account of visiting the Dachau concentration camp: "You walk into the daylight, but part of you does not leave. The doorway divides you . . . A moral universe could arise from the imperative to answer the self we left behind" (Muschamp, in Ellsworth 2005, 111). It is the self who "remains behind, wondering how, since no one deserved to die here, we deserve to leave" that haunts the self that leaves, posits Ellsworth (111), the captive self whose ethical questions can never be satisfied.

Ellsworth reminds us that it is possible for the split learning self to work through its sense of insuperable violation and to launch a path through "that time and space of ethical responsibility" (Todd 2009, 6) if our pedagogy can carve out a transitional space that can contain and sustain the learner who finds her/himself haunted by the self fixed and frozen in the native's eye in "an indeterminate and interminable labor of response" (Ellsworth 2005, 112). If, that is, our pedagogy can offer tools to resist the romantic fall into pathos, self-pathos and despair (the need to defend, comfort and restore the wounded, divided learning self) and support a learner's specula-tive deliberation and creative innovation of a transformed positionality and relationality to others and the outside world (Winnicott 1989, in Ellsworth 2005, 30–32), then the interminable labor of response may emerge from this crisis as a practice of humanity and ethics.

Global justice education, then, demands that students learn *from* rather than *about* the relations of injustice, inequity and exploitation in which we participate. Contrasting these two orders of learning posited by Freud, Britzman (1998, 117–119) distinguishes "the acquisition of qualities, attri-butes, and facts" from a detached distance (*learning about*) and the forms of implication and affective investment that characterize a response to difficult knowledge from which insight might emerge. Learning *from* the ethical call of difficult knowledge, according to Ellsworth and Britzman, disrupts, destabilizes and sets the learning self in motion within an inti-mate process of becoming: becoming the kind of person able to entertain or understand such thoughts; a process of becoming-in-relation to Others who are immune to our will to know and who, in refusing "to become like us or to be erased by our fantasies of who they are, embody the potential for our own self change" (Ellsworth 2005, 89). This demand may be expe-rienced as an impossible one, a demand to become someone unattainably different. One group's summary reflection articulated a keen sense of inad-equacy vis-à-vis the selves hailed by the documentary's address:

In order to understand the entire movie and all that it entails, every one of our classmates would have to a) be an impartial candidate b) thoroughly understand the global economy and the interaction of na-tions c) have experienced poverty and helplessness and d) be aware of the effects of colonialism and globalization on developing nations. As a group we did not meet all these requirements but we tried our hardest. (Patricia, Tim, Jane, Dave, Maria, Sally, Roy, Jim 2005)

To become someone who can entertain thoughts of "the effects of colonial-ism and globalization on developing nations" is, as Ellsworth argues, to lose that part of oneself whose sense of being a concerned, well-intended and helpful or charitable global citizen *depends* upon not knowing (being uninformed and therefore innocent of and unimplicated in) the devastat-ing impact one one's participation in global relations of exploitation and exclusion. It is to lose the parts of oneself that take pleasure in the privileges and fruits of this global injustice.

Below, I present three examples of the ways the exercise potentially forged a transitional space of reflection and transformation for the facilitating group. In preparing their research and discussion questions, groups meet repeatedly over several weeks amongst themselves and with the professor. Group members almost always facilitate as a pair of discussion leaders. There may be an informal debrief immediately after the discussion amongst the facilitating group, either with or without the professor. More substantially, individual facilitators are required to write two-page reflections (see excerpt of the assignment instructions above, Methodology section) to be brought to a separate group meeting to share, compare and analyze as a basis for the group summary (individual and group reflections are submitted together to the professor).

The structure of the assignment positions these group members in a complex web of morphing relationships: their relationship to the documentary's director and subjects is one they revisit, individually and in different discussion forums, over the course of preparing, facilitating and reflecting on the postscreening discussion. They may experience a fluctuating shift in their relationship to the professor (becoming more collegial) and their classmates (becoming more pedagogical) as they prepare for, consult on and take on the role of pedagogue vis-à-vis their classmates, often with an increasing personal investment in the issues raised by the documentary as their research progresses. Their relationship to their research-group mates can come to act as a forum and learning community with whom to wade through dilemmas of difficult knowledge and pedagogy, respectively (or both). As they gather to compare discussion facilitation experiences, there is evidence (in group and individual reflections) that they use this space to observe and consider the spectrum of stances, positionalities and relationalities taken up by different students, a spectrum of resistance and creative innovation, entrenchment and movement, refusal and redefinition. More extensive analysis than I can provide here suggests that this complex space of morphing relationships, deliberation and experimentation, individually and in different collectives, can become a variegated, textured space/time "where the skin-to-skin faceoff between self and other has been pried apart so that a reordering of self and other can be set in motion" (Ellsworth 2005, 64).

"It is quite interesting to note the different experience each member of our group lived through facilitating discussion after watching *Life and Debt* with the class . . . one thing's for sure, we never expected it to be so hard to get our peers to think about difficult knowledge! It's so much harder than it looks!" (Pamela, Heather, Sophie, Andrée, Marnie, Lisa, group facilitation package, 2006). This remark from a group summary suggests the rich tableau of relationships experienced by the facilitating group members as well as the importance of nested spaces of deliberation. A majority of individual reflections traced recursive paths between observing their peers' resistance and revisiting their own learning crises. Within these trajectories, many sought insight into the sources of that resistance, insight that might guide them in repositioning themselves, as learners and pedagogues, in ways that were both implicated and hopeful.

It is this dialogue between her own experiences of difficult learning and those of her peers that proves a particularly fertile source of insight for Ruth:

> I found *Life and Debt* to be very challenging film both as a viewer and as a facilitator . . . As a viewer . . . [a]t first, I resisted the difficult knowledge the film imparted, *what did I ever do?* Yet as I researched and worked through various aspects with my group [preparing for facilitation], I realized that even though I have never been to Jamaica, and that I have never been an employee of the IMF, I have to view myself as someone who benefits from the problems of the Jamaican people. What I have and what I do is made possible through what they don't have, and what they cannot do. I have the privilege to travel, to stay in all-inclusive resorts, to buy whatever I want with my Canadian/American dollar. Not just traveling, I can feel rich, educated and important when my life is contrasted to theirs. I can draw pleasure from seeing the 'romantic' Jamaican, listening to their 'fun' and 'relaxing' Jamaican music, eating 'Jamaican' bananas . . . As a facilitator, I realized that many of the feelings I had as a viewer were experienced by the class members in the group I facilitated. One of these is confusion and an inability to really understand the implications of events. The second emotion that was apparent was guilt. When I watched this film, I felt guilty. As much as I wanted to dissociate myself with everything that contributed to their poverty and the conditions they faced, I realized that I am a participant." (Ruth 2004)

Ruth presents a fine-grained analysis of her experience of refusal. In particular, she uses the term *guilt* to describe her viewing refusal to adopt a particular relation to the Jamaican subjects represented: a relation of parasitic, exploitative privilege. This leads her to ask what consequences a similar refusal by her peers might have on their struggles to understand the causes of injustice documented by the filmmaker:

> I felt that some of the students resisted that difficult knowledge to a certain extent. 'Why do they throw out the milk?' some asked. 'Why don't they just give it away for free before it goes bad?' Others asked 'Can't they close their borders, why don't they just refuse products from the US? How did they let it get this bad in the first place?' The reason I feel this demonstrates difficult knowledge is because all of those questions reflect the assumption that the Jamaican people could be better off if they only did something different. It takes the blame off our shoulders; we are no longer responsible for their problems. They are poor because

they have neglected to do something somewhere at some point. These most likely stem from feelings of guilt. In trying to absolve the guilt, we point the finger to someone else, they're to blame . . . The mixed feeling of guilt and resistance to difficult knowledge were perhaps what I view as the greatest challenge as a facilitator. *How do we feel responsible without just feeling guilty?* . . . I worried students would simply view this as a problem that we cannot solve, that we cannot change. They would feel frustrated and helpless in making any changes, much as I did when I first experienced the film. To try to steer away from these feelings, we tried to explain what they could do, and tell them about positive change. (Ruth 2004) (emphasis mine)

Revisiting hher own resistance to viewing herself "as someone who benefits from the problems of the Jamaican people," Ruth made creative use of her insight that her sense of self as "rich, educated . . . important" was defined in relation to opposite qualities projected onto Jamaicans. Spurred by this insight to speculate on the desire underpinning her classmates' leveling of blame for Jamaicans' poverty on their own shoulders, she infers that their certainty of Jamaicans' guilt secured her classmates' position of absolution and innocence. This informs her formulation of the central pedagogical challenge concerning her: "How do we feel responsible without just feeling guilty?" Indeed, how can learners and pedagogues hold open the crisis of implication without the consolation of innocence or despair?

Reconsidering her own reaction to the demands of the documentary's difficult address—"What do you want from me?!"—another student con-cluded, "I needed to do a lot of research in order to take my understanding of the film away from 'it is just a *movie* asking me to rethink my vacation'. I really feel that this film is a lot more than that. I think that this film asks us as viewers to shift our gaze and see things from a different and silenced perspective" (Sharon's reflection journal entry, 2008, emphasis original). This insight is key to her group's planning, she explains: "That's why we showed the Malibu Rum ad: we wanted our class to realize we do partici-pate, so no one could say 'what's that got to do with me?' " That is, her own refusal of the demand for implication in difficult knowledge informed her group's choice of teaching materials and design of discussion questions: the question "Do you see stereotypes in this ad? Who are we becoming as we laugh at these stereotypes of Jamaicans in this ad? Use the Self/Other dia-gram" (Ruth, Anna, Sharon, Hannah, Nadine, Daniela, Susan, Catherine, Marie-France, Sylvie, Frederic, small-group discussion questions, group facilitation package, 2008) asked each of us in the classroom to face the psychic investments we bring as citizens of the North to our participation in colonial forms of knowing and being. These psychic investments in ways of seeing and knowing implicate us in relations of injustice we cannot bear to know: "If we walk away from this film seeing Jamaicans as poor and helpless, what's changed?" (Sharon's reflection journal entry, 2008).

Recognizing one's own investment in an imperial gaze can trigger several revelations as evidenced in these students' reflections. First, it makes explicit the documentary's demand "to shift our gaze" (Sharon 2008). It also makes one's disengagement from and indifference to that very demand *visible* as a form of action and implication. Finally, recognizing one's investments takes hostage that part of oneself able to take pleasure from the fruits of global inequity. Another facilitator in the same group starts with the same question emerging from their viewing experiences:

> 'What's that got to do with me?' The problem is . . . as part of the dominant Gaze, we believe that we do always have the choice to choose our own destiny. We are free to do what we want and this is a very important privilege given to us. Because such privileges happen unconsciously, we do not realize that we have them and we take for granted that everyone else has free choice. Jamaican people did not have such privileges [when they became independent] but *still we want to convince ourselves that the privileges we have can be applied to everybody.* If others are not able to succeed in today's world it is because they do not want to or because they are incompetent and while we think this, *we are blaming them instead of looking at the effects our privileges have on others* . . . This is what I wanted my group to be able to see. (Frederic 2008, emphasis mine)

Frederic concludes that the difficult knowledge of the documentary demands that learners shift the grounds upon which they identify as they seek to understand global poverty. The candid question cited in Sharon's reflection, "Can't they close their borders, why don't they just refuse products from the US? How did they let it get this bad in the first place?" (Sharon's reflection journal entry, 2008), can only be formulated from the position of the universal Western subject of globalization (Schueller 2009), a gaze or stance of knowledge construction predicated on not-knowing or ignoring (Felman 1987; Britzman 1998) "the effects of colonialism and globalization on developing nations" (Patricia, Tim, Jane, Dave, Maria, Sally, Roy, Jim 2005) and, indeed, the reach of international trade agreements.

This passionate ignorance figures centrally in forms of knowledge construction that are prevalent in the ways documentary and testimonial narratives are used in GCE and global-justice education: Students are often encouraged to listen to these narratives in order to humanize, develop sensitivity to and insight into overwhelming relations of global inequity. What happens as students listen, however? More importantly, what are the routes to knowledge when the learner's subject position remains implicitly universal? Listening often proceeds as an "experiment in empathy" in which "the learner attaches to the experience of the other by way of wondering what she or he would have done had such an event occurred in her or his own life" (Britzman 1998, 117–119). Britzman argues that when it is "the learner's undisturbed present and not the way the learner's life has become her present" (117–119) that is projected in this experiment in empathy—when the learner attempts to understand the other within a framework that universalizes the learner's subjectivity, resources and conditions—the learner positions herself as the arbiter of the other's actions within a moral framework that ends up "blaming them instead of looking at the effects our privileges have on others" (Britzman 1998, 117–119). Frederic recognizes above that if his group mates are to achieve insight, it will depend on refusing to universalize Canadian students' positionalities as subjects of a North-centric universalizing gaze—what Schueller (2009, 252) calls "Western parochialism parading as universalism."

Sharon and Frederic make creative use of their own refusal of relationality—"What's that got to do with me?"—to position this dilemma of colonial relations of knowing at the core of their pedagogical project: If GCE can do no better than substitute pathos for abjection within the same hierarchical North-South divide, then what, as Sharon asks, has changed? Indeed, the change GCE might seek would be for privileged learners to become the kind of people who are able to look differently, to enter into relationality with planetary others and position ourselves, not as the totalizing, imperial (though sympathetic) sovereign subject, nor as a measure nor arbiter of others' rights or worthiness, but as one of many groups living in proximate, multilateral interrelation of differentiated but potentially catalytic vulnerability.

Examining and using her own crisis in learning as both a source of insight and a pedagogical resource, one student concluded that a key consideration in teaching for global justice was *time*:

> As much as I'd thought I had prepared myself for resistance from my peers . . . I was in no way ready to face the number of strong, negative reactions . . . the group's *hostility* and *lack of dialogue* . . . I myself went through stages of denial and temptations to put aside this heavy information . . . [when] the group fell silent . . . we used the silence, gave the group a minute to reflect, and then I offered my experience of being *confused, angry*, in denial, *uninformed*. . . . Their hostility reminded me of one of my first comments after watching the film: 'Don't tell me there's more injustice. No. Screw that, isn't there enough already? I knew about Haiti, let's keep it at that. No more.' . . . I had to keep reminding myself that I had had several weeks to come to terms with the film's content, and that I needed to be patient . . . I went through several stages of denial and guilt while working on this project. These included rants to my partner, telephone calls and searches for information from my father, explosions with my peers, and a refreshed look at Canada's economic conditions, actions and consequences of these. I have been able to find ways of researching to better understand. I was able to thrust myself into the project after a good week of denial.

I remember thinking, if it takes me a week to approach this, how long would it take [other adults], set in their ways, who don't even want to admit the existence of [discrimination]? (emphasized words in this typewritten text had been underlined by hand, reflecting the student's layered returns to this reflection) (Patricia 2005)

Patricia's concern for the recursive temporality of difficult learning is reflected in the traversals between different moments of research, facilitation and reflection in her own written text. She concludes that learning depends upon an openness of learners that only open-ended, transitional temporalities can afford:

I know I need to approach my own students with extreme care, in many different angles and ways, and while making the links clear to them— but how long do I give them? What happens when they don't seem to be getting away from the reactions to difficult knowledge? Providing more information will only make them shut down . . . I have to be careful about them shutting down: learning information, the reasons and explanations for things is one thing but you really just have to be *open* to learning about what exactly that entails (Patricia 2005).

Here Patricia draws a distinction between Freud's two orders of learning: "learning information, the reasons and explanations" (learning about) and the challenge of self-implication and insight demanded by difficult knowledge (learning from) that require *time* and *willingness* to bear an open-ended vertigo or crisis, to be transformed, redefined, repositioned within infinite trajectories of responsibility without consolation.

CONCLUSION

While the excerpts examined above are in no way presented as conclusive, generalizable evidence, they do underline the importance of GCE research that sustains a curiosity into the psychic vectors of learning that traverse the nervous liminal space and time of discursive and affective transition. The analysis above suggests that students can make use of analytic resources to resist or question the impulse to buttress a sovereign, unimplicated subjectivity that refuses coming into the kinds of uneasy relations when one learns from difficult knowledge (I extend my analyses and conclusions in two other publications: Taylor, 2011; in press).

My analysis raises important questions about the potential for pedagogies of ethical planetary citizenship to create as an antechamber within which learners might pause before seeking the consolation of hegemonic and habitual forms of knowledge, where they might experiment with imaginatively reorganizing "bits of experience into a temporarily connected sense of self" (Ellsworth

2005, 60) that might transform and be transformed within critically re-imagined ways of planetary cohabitation.

NOTES

1. This critique echoes one of the most radical and substantive critiques of contemporary globalization theorizing, made by the African historian Frederick Cooper (2001, 192–193), who argues that amongst the three predominant framings of globalization—the "Banker's Boast," the "Social Democrat's Lament" and the "Dance of Flows and the Fragments"—a common conceptual lacuna and gesture of renewed mastery is the "totalizing pretensions and their presentist periodization."
2. On 'planetarity' as a practice of responsibility and counterdiscourse to globalization, see Spivak, 2003, 101–102. I am indebted to Diana Brydon, whose paper "Difficult Forms of Knowing" (2009) sent me back to Spivak's 2003 work.
3. 11.7 percent of the students in the B.Ed. program are francophone, less than 3 percent are allophone (their first language being neither French nor English), 35.6 percent are from outside Quebec, and less than 10 percent are visible minority.
4. This exercise, using visual organizers to analyze the regimes of representation (or 'dominant gaze' as termed in the course) and discriminatory practices (systemic, institutional and interpersonal) explored in the documentary, is required of every group as part of their preparation to facilitate small-group discussion of their film/documentary. All three groups cited here prepared analyses of comparable quality.
5. Britzman makes this distinction out of concern that teacher education has tended to privilege instrumental knowledge (Horkheimer and Adorno 1982), knowledge whose usefulness lies in its capacity to be externalized and applied to others (Britzman 2000, 204). Questioning this rush to apply, she argues that '[w]orld making requires self knowledge . . . the work of knowing the self [which] entails acknowledging not just what one would like to know about the self but also what is difficult to know about the self, including features we tend to project onto others: aggression, self aggrandizement, destructive wishes, and helplessness' (Britzman 2000, 202).
6. As the documentary begins, the narrator reads a text adapted from Jamaica Kincaid's (2000 [1988]) "A Small Place": "If you come to Jamaica as a tourist, this is what you will see. . . ."
7. The concept of the gaze is introduced in earlier course readings and exercises (specifically, Hall 1997 and hooks 1992).
8. "Under the leadership of Emmanuel Ringelblum, a university trained historian, several dozen writers, teachers, rabbis, and historians compiled an archive documenting life in the Warsaw ghetto . . . On the eve of the final annihilation of the ghetto, Ringelblum buried all records and documents in metal containers and milk cans so they would be found after the war, after his death and the death of all other members of his historical society. So they would let the world know" (Wienberg and Elieli, cited in Ellsworth 2005, 110–111).

REFERENCES

Althusser, L. (1971) *Lenin and Philosophy and Other Essays*; trans. B. Brewster, London: New Left Books.

198   *Lisa Taylor*

Andreotti, V. (2008) 'Development vs Poverty: Notions of Cultural Supremacy in Development Education Policy', in Doug Bourn (ed.), *Development Education: Debates and Dialogues*, London: Institute of Education, University of London, 45–63.

Banks, J. (2004) *Diversity and Citizenship Education: Global Perspectives*, San Francisco: Jossey-Bass.

Black, S. (2001) *Life and Debt*, Tough Gong Pictures, http://www.lifeanddebt.org/ (accessed November 10, 2010).

Boler, M. (1999) 'The Risks of Empathy: Interrogating Multiculturalism's Gaze', in M. Boler, *Feeling Power: Emotions and Education*, New York: Routledge, 155–174.

Britzman, D. (1998) *Lost Subjects, Contested Objects: Toward a Psychoanalytic Inquiry of Learning*, Albany: State University of New York Press.

———. (2000) 'If the Story Cannot End: Deferred Action, Ambivalence and Difficult Knowledge', in R. I. Simon, S. Rosenberg and C. Eppert (eds.), *Between Hope and Despair: Pedagogy and the Remembrance of Historical Trauma*, Lanham, MD: Rowman & Littlefield, 27–56.

Brydon, D. (2009) *'Difficult Forms of Knowing': Enquiry, Injury and Translocated Relations of Postcolonial Responsibility*. Paper presented on July 17, Hamilton, ON: McMaster University.

Cooper, F. (2001) 'What Is the Concept of Globalization Good For? An African Historian's Perspective', *African Affairs*, 100: 189–213.

Ellsworth, E. (2005) *Places of learning: Media, architecture, pedagogy*, New York: Teachers College Press.

Felman, S. (1987) *Jacques Lacan and the Adventure of Insight: Psychoanalysis in Contemporary Culture*, Cambridge, MA, and London: Harvard University Press.

Hall, S. (ed.) (1997) *Representation: Cultural Representations and Signifying Practices*, London and Thousand Oaks, CA: Sage Publications, in association with The Open University.

Heron, B. (2007) *Desire for Development: Whiteness, Gender, and the Helping Imperative*, Waterloo, ON: Wilfrid Laurier University Press.

hooks, b. (1992) *Black Looks: Race and Representation*, Boston: South End Press.

Horkheimer, M. and Adorno, T. (1982) *Dialectic of Enlightenment*, J. Cumming (trans.), New York: The Continuum Publishing Corporation. (Original work published 1947)

Kincaid, J. (2000 [1988]) *A Small Place*, New York: Farrar, Straus, Giroux.

Levine-Rasky, C. (1998) 'Teacher Education and the Negotiation of Social Difference', *British Journal of Sociology of Education*, 19(1): 89–112.

———. (2002) *Working through Whiteness*, New York: SUNY Press.

McCarthy C. and Crichlow, W. (1993) *Race, Identity and Representation in Education*, New York: Routledge.

Morrison, T. (1992) *Playing in the Dark: Whiteness and the Literary Imagination*, Cambridge, MA: Harvard University Press.

———. (2000) *Local Histories/Global Designs: Coloniality, Subaltern Knowledges, and Border Thinking*, Princeton, NJ: Princeton University Press.

Mundy, K. and Manion, C. (2008) 'Global Education in Canadian Elementary Schools: An Exploratory Study', *Canadian Journal of Education*, 31(4): 941–974.

Pashby, K. (2009) 'The Stephen Lewis Foundation's Grandmothers-to-Grandmothers Campaign: A Model for Critical Global Citizenship Learning?', *Critical Literacy, Theories and Practices*, 3(1): 59–70.

Pitt, A. and Britzman, D. (2003) 'Speculations on Qualities of Difficult Knowledge in Teaching and Learning: An Experiment in Psychoanalytic Research', *International Journal of Qualitative Studies in Education*, 16(6): 755–776.

Radhakrishnan, R. (2003) *Theory in an Uneven World*, Oxford: Blackwell.

Said, E. W. (1978) *Orientalism*, New York: Vintage.

Schick, C. and St. Denis, V. (2005) 'Critical Autobiography in Integrative Anti-Racist Pedagogy', in L. Biggs and P. Downe (eds.), *Gendered Intersections: An Introduction to Women's and Gender Studies*, Halifax, NS: Fernwood, 387–392.

Schueller, M. J. (2009) 'Decolonizing Global Theories Today: Hardt and Negri, Agamben, Butler', *Interventions*, 11(2): 235–254.

Simon, R. I. (2008) Paper presented at Breaking the Silence: International Conference on The Indian Residential Schools Truth and Reconciliation Commission of Canada, Sept. 26–27, Montreal: University of Montreal. Forthcoming as Simon, R. I., 'Towards a Hopeful Practice of Worrying: The Problematics of Listening and the Educational Responsibilities of the IRSTRC', in P. Wakeham and J. Henderson (eds.), *Reconciling Canada*, Toronto: University of Toronto Press.

———. (2009) *A Shock to Thought: History and the Exhibition of Difficult Knowledge*, paper presented at Curating Difficult Knowledge Conference, April 16–18, Montreal: Concordia University. Forthcoming in E. Lehrer, C. Milton and M. E. Patterson (eds.), *Curating Difficult Knowledge: Violent Pasts in Public Places*, New York: Palgrave Macmillan.

Sleeter, C. (2001) 'Preparing Teachers for Culturally Diverse Schools Research and the Overwhelming Presence of Whiteness', *Journal of Teacher Education*, 52(2): 94–106.

Solomon, R. P. (2000) 'Exploring Cross-Race Dyad Partnerships in Learning to Teach', *Teachers College Record*, 102(6): 953–979.

Spivak, G. C. (2003) *Death of a Discipline*, New York: Columbia University Press.

Taylor, L. K. (in press) Feeling in Crisis: Vicissitudes of Response in Experiments with Global Justice Education, *Journal of the Canadian Association for Curriculum Studies*, 8(3).

———. (forthcoming) Teaching for a 'Sensate Democracy': The Implication of 'Frames of War' for Global Justice Education, in R. Naqvi and H. Smits (eds.), *Thinking about and Enacting Curriculum in 'Frames of War'*, Lanham, MD: Rowman & Littlefield.

Todd, S. (2009) Toward an Imperfect Education: The Task of Facing Human Pluralism, Invited Distinguished Lecture, American Educational Research Education, www.aera.net (accessed May 15, 2009).

Willinsky, J. (1998) *Learning to Divide the World: Education at Empire's End*, Minneapolis: University of Minnesota Press.

Winnicott, D. W. (1989) *Playing and Reality*, New York: Routledge.

11 Rerouting the Postcolonial University

Educating for Citizenship in Managed Times

Su-ming Khoo

"[T]his rupture is in fact a way of forgetting or repressing the past, that is to say repeating it and not surpassing it." (J. F. Lyotard 1992, 90)

"[T]he essence of colonialization lies less in political rule than in seizing and transforming 'others' by the very act of conceptualizing, inscribing and interacting with them in terms not of their own choosing, in making them into pliant objects and silenced subjects of our scripts and scenarios; in assuming the capacity to 'represent', the active verb itself conflating politics and poetics." (Comaroff and Comaroff 1991, 131)

This chapter explores some of the dilemmas and ambiguities of educating for global citizenship in a globalizing postcolonial university. It critically reflects upon two key moments in the experience of an Irish university through a postcolonial lens. The implications for global citizenship are discussed in terms of the 'colonial present,' a concept that highlights the continuities between the colonial past and the nominally 'post'-colonial present, where we are unsure of what the 'post' means (Gregory 2004). The colonial present echoes what Mamdani (1996) terms 'late colonialism' and 'the politics of the not-yet,' containing ambivalence, complicity, hybridity, mimicry (Bhabha 1994) and 'self-colonization' (Yoshioka 1995). These conditions are reorganized as new global educational governmentalities emerge. Readings rather expansively claims that the university has been ideologically "dereferentialized" and that it has become a 'posthistorical' phenomenon (1996, p. 166). Traditional conceptions of university education as constitutive of national culture and citizenship and as broadly educative are 'in ruins.' Globalization reorients universities towards different claims—of transnational mobility and bureaucratic excellence (op. cit.) and knowledge economy (Bastalich 2010). These shifts complicate the emancipatory projects and intents of postcolonial criticism, education and citizenship, making the task of pulling these three projects together difficult, yet necessary.

The 'post' in postcolonial signifies a number of different possibilities for the aftermath of colonialism—a liberatory rejection of colonialism, a continuation/reformulation of colonialism or something coming 'after' colonialism—signifying that colonialism is somehow 'finished.' Postcoloniality is often assumed to be an exceptional situation, pertaining only to a certain set of peoples, territories or dates corresponding to official empire, but its relevance is far wider. Legacies of colonization and decolonization, loss of empire and national liberation, challenge to cultural imperialism and cultural reassertion are ubiquitous whether the focus is the colonized periphery, a settler colony, the very center or the furthest edge of an imperial power. Postcoloniality is not solely a condition of victims and one of the major contributions of postcolonial theory is to show how colonizer and colonized have been mutually shaped by the colonial encounter and its aftermath. The colonized can be understood as agents, and not simply the victims of colonial modernity. They can also be understood as desiring subjects, practicing certain techniques of self (Gikandi 2001), their agency positioned somewhere between local histories and global designs (Mignolo 2000).

In the mid-1990s, Pieterse and Parekh (1995) suggested that the process of political decolonization was more or less complete, while critical, intellectual and cultural decolonization were underway. They optimistically heralded a new era for

> the imaginative creation of a new form of consciousness and way of life . . . an engagement with global times that is no longer premised either on Eurocentrism, modernization theory or other forms of Western ethnocentrism passing for universalism, or on Third Worldism, nativism and parochially anti-western views. (1995, 3–4)

Yet rapid globalization has led postcolonial theory to reevaluate itself in the decade since, and to reroute its concerns (Loomba et al., 2005; Wilson, Şandru and Welsh 2010). Schueller (2009) suggests that totalizing conceptions of the global work as colonizing forces must be ethically resisted. To challenge globalization, the postcolonial must reconfigure itself, "taking on cosmopolitanism, post-communism, revisionary pedagogies and critical practices" (Wilson, Şandru and Welsh 2010, 3).

Global citizenship may express dominant or resistant trends. It might represent an attempt at discursive closure for a form of neoliberal universalism that makes the world the "ungated playground of the elite," but it might equally reflect shifts towards equity, justice and inclusion (Shultz 2010, 7). The project of global citizenship contains its own colonial present in the form of a liberal imperialist heritage of world citizenship (Sluga 2010), yet it can also offer a platform for resisting marketized, homogenizing and dominating constructions of globality, education and citizenship. Progressive (Freire 1998) and capabilities-based (Saito 2003; Walker 2006; Flores-Crespo 2007) conceptions of education offer education as a space of unfinishedness and freedom that resists closure and totalization, where ethics are open for debate and engagement. Global citizenship education offers discursive and pedagogical spaces where troublesome and difficult knowledge can be confronted, and understandings of social justice and citizenship can be surfaced (Shultz 2010, 19). Postcolonial critique contributes a "decolonizing energy . . . [that] is effective precisely because it disrupts monolithic ideologies and creates 'cracks' in the global imaginary" (Wilson, Şandru and Welsh 2010, 7). The rerouting debate within postcolonial theory aims to retrieve and reassert the pedagogical and ethical import of the postcolonial, linking it to larger projects of public education and wider justice, education and equity movements at levels both below and beyond the nation-state (op. cit.; Brydon 2010).

This discussion reroutes and reroots debates on cultural and political decolonization (see Loomba et al. 2005; Wilson, Şandru and Welsh 2010 for the discussion of rerouting and rerooting) towards the question of education and global citizenship in 'managed times,' where new forms of *global governmentality* dominate—"hard times for higher education" (Walker 2006, 6). This brings forward the relevance of questions about decolonizing the mind (N'gũgĩ wa Thiong'o 1986) and the imagination (Pieterse and Parekh 1995). Recent postcolonial critiques of management scrutinize the complicity of Western systems of knowledge and representation with colonial control and domination (Prasad 2003) while problematizing the generic Enlightenment zeal to modernize and rationalize (Cooke 2003; 2008). At the same time, cultural critiques of global informational capitalism have drawn our attention to the growing power of deterritorialized 'e-Empires' (Raley 2004) based on the enclosure and uneven accumulation of information, mediated by electronic technologies. New forms of self-colonization and compensatory ideologies of self-effectiveness, consumerism and 'citizenism' (Lock and Martins 2009) have come to the fore in this context, to be challenged by utopian, cosmopolitan and humanist claims for education and citizenship.

FIRST RUPTURE: NOT QUITE 'TWO CHEERS' FOR POSTCOLONIAL RESISTANCE

Two 'ruptures' in an Irish university's history provide interesting points for reflecting on the colonial present. Spencer suggests that rerouting "entails the pulling up and examination of one's roots" (2010, 44). Hence the first rupture is an inaugural moment when three Queen's Colleges were founded in 1845 in Belfast, Cork, and Galway and united as the Queen's University of Ireland in 1850. In 1908, this became a new National University of Ireland, predating the postcolonial Irish Free State by some two decades (Manning 2010). The reference to the queen was removed as the Galway and Cork colleges were renamed University Colleges and merged into a federal structure with the Catholic University College Dublin. Mignolo (2000) describes the colonial encounter as 'local histories' confronting 'global designs.' Such was the nascent Irish national higher education system, which responded to two quite different global designs—one the nineteenth-century British strategy of union and pacification (O'Tuathaigh 1999), and the other a global expansion and local embedding of Catholicism (Casanova 1997). Between the 1801 Act of Union and Ireland becoming a Free State in 1922, Ireland was simultaneously constitutive of British imperial power, the site of nationalist resistance and a rising metropole for global Catholic expansionism. Higher education was essentially representative of imperial governance, governability and privilege, put in place to generate and reproduce imperial states of science and mind (see various contributions in Foley 1999), as well as the global spread of Catholicism (Hogan 1990).

One university existed well before the nineteenth century in Ireland—Trinity College Dublin, which was granted its charter by Queen Elizabeth I in 1592. However, Trinity remained autonomous with respect to the establishment of the three Queen's colleges under the patronage of Queen Victoria in 1845. This moment was the very height of the British Empire, but also the start of the appalling Irish famine (1845–52; see Kinealy 1994). The Queen's colleges were "dedicated to the fashioning of colonial masters and imperial subjects" (Foley 1999, xi) in the first half of its 150-year existence. Irish national consolidation took place in the 1920s, and for second half of their history, Irish universities had to address the formation of postimperial citizens in a new nation-state. "Throughout the entire nineteenth century, Ireland possessed most of the signs of being a colony [yet] . . . was constitutionally an intrinsic part of the British Empire" (ibid.). The aim of establishing the colleges was to render Ireland "safe, secure and loyal . . . taking the sting out of Irish nationalist political demands" (O'Tuathaigh 1999, 3). However, the nondenominational colleges garnered support from only a minority of the Irish, notably the nonsectarian Young Irelanders (ibid.). The so-called Godless Queen's colleges faced considerable opposition from the Catholic hierarchy, which aligned with the anticolonial Repeal movement to favor an explicitly Catholic national university. This became University College Dublin (UCD), brainchild of Cardinal John Henry Newman, famed for his paradigmatic lectures on the idea of the liberal university (Newman 1996/1854).

Benita Parry's essay *"Resistance theory/theorizing resistance or two cheers for nativism"* (1994) presents a partial defense of nativism as a countervailing stance during the liberation struggles of the late nineteenth century, up to the 1970s. While accepting that such 'reverse-discourses' of nativism were not based on fact, but on mythical 'false consciousness,' Parry defends the nativist 'structure of feeling' as a means for self-empowerment, to challenge, subvert and undermine the ruling ideologies and refuse subjugation (1994, 45, 40). Parry's materialist historical analysis considers nativism to be a historical necessity for cultural and imaginative freedom. Cultural or ethnic revivalism can act as reactionary forces—this has been lethally proven in her case of contemporary India (op. cit., 38; see also Sen

2006); however, she still gives it 'two cheers.' Her vindication of Fanon and Césaire traces the same route of progress that Edward Said envisaged, from nativist to nationalist, to liberation theory and a "mainstream pattern of cultural decolonization" (Pieterse and Parekh 1995, 6).

Ultimately, this emancipatory teleology returns to global citizenship's premise of universalistic, humanistic and cosmopolitan ideals. Fanon and Césaire ultimately envisioned a universalist, post-European transnational humanism as their ultimate goal, even if their nativism was more audible. Cultural-political resistance is deemed necessary to open the way for alternatives to colonial subjugation. Césaire's systematic defense of 'the non-European civilizations' is seen as a prelude to imagining alternatives to global capitalism and inequality: ". . . they were communal societies, never societies of the many for the few. They were societies that were not only ante-capitalist . . . but also anti-capitalist" (*"Discourse on Colonialism"* 1972, 20, 22–23, cited in Parry 1994, 46).

How well could this liberatory conception of nativism fit within the design for higher education established with the Queen's Colleges/National University system in Ireland? The controversial discipline of Irish provides some illustration. Queen's College Galway made provision for the teaching and study of Irish, under the disciplinary title of 'Celtic Languages' from 1850, but the historical record shows a lack of demand for the subject in the first few decades. Irish had been repressed under colonial rule from the sixteenth to early nineteenth centuries. It was not taught at primary or secondary schools, and the subject presented no employment prospects (O'Madagáin 1999, 349). The cultural mobilization of the Gaelic League turned the tide in favor of Irish in the 1890s. After the foundation of the Free State, Irish became the official language and its revival became an integral government policy. Irish language was made compulsory across the school system, leading to a steady increase in Irish-language competence (Walsh 2011, 16). In higher education, Irish was established as a compulsory subject for teacher training and law, and Irish language and Irish studies grew as academic disciplines within the humanities. Located in one of the more strongly Irish-speaking parts of the country, the renamed University College Galway assumed a statutory responsibility to use Irish as a working language in 1929. Yet promotion of the Irish language as a measure of cultural liberation yielded ambivalent results. Extensive measures to revive the Irish language have resulted in widespread competency in it as a second language within education, but it has nevertheless declined to the status of a threatened or minority language in everyday life, with only 1.8 percent of the population speaking it every day outside formal educational settings. Educated competence did not lead to widespread use (op. cit. 29, 37). Walsh argues that Irish historians have either ignored or marginalized the impact of 'language shift' from Irish to English. However, one influential commentator (Garvin 2004) characterized language revival as extremist and inimical to the development of a critical intellectual culture and socioeconomic development. Garvin blames the language movement, together with the Catholic Church, for 'smothering' rather than creatively energizing culture, 'preventing the future' and maintaining Ireland in poverty and underdevelopment for far longer than necessary. In response to Garvin's negative view, Walsh suggests that a new political economy of socioeconomic development might offer an alternative local design for Irish-language and economic development to mutually flourish, if language is accorded a central role in development policy. University academics could play an important role in developing this alternative, presenting new interpretive frameworks for development, thus pluralizing futures (2011, 412–413), as envisaged by Nandy (2000). Walsh notes that academics who could support an alternative vision have so far ignored the issues of economic development, and he calls for greater engagement to link language policy and practice with local community development.

Postcolonial theories and pedagogies can offer insights into how this pluralization of futures and connections between economic and language issues can be addressed. Tikly argues that a postcolonial reading of globalization and education problematizes the mainstream scripts and scenarios. A postcolonial reading seeks to "renarrativise the globalization story" (2001, 152), placing the peripheralized postcolonial countries at the center of the narrative, while drawing on critical political economy to highlight social inequalities and resistance to Western global hegemony. The aftermath of colonialism complicates the project of global citizenship with historical burdens of injustice, inequality and uneven development, demanding that these burdens be recognized and made good. These material demands raise complicated questions about culture, identity and power, complicity and autonomy, power as domination ('power over') versus power as expressive ('power to'). Hickling-Hudson advocates 'postcolonialising' as a strategy for developing identities that "leave constricting neo-colonial ideas and practices behind" (2003, 2). She suggests that education be restructured to promote intercultural cooperation. She advocates the pluralization of epistemologies, providing examples of 'culturally proactive' educational practices that are alternative to racist, ethnocentric and 'culturally problematic' schooling. Since 2009 in NUI Galway, the professional MA course in community development practice has introduced the "Through Other Eyes" approach to give learners tools to reflect on their own knowledge and engage with other knowledge systems (Andreotti and de Souza 2008). This approach comprises part of the learning program for a course entitled "Development in an International Context," which aims to connect local and global development concerns and 'renarrativise' development according to a global *and* grassroots imagination (Appadurai 2000).

Gandhi (1998, 167) suggests that postcolonialism is caught between the politics of structure and totality on the one hand and the politics of the fragment on the other. She indicates the need to mend the ideological wedge between histories of subjectivity and histories of subjection, engaging with internal histories of subordination and the continuing exclusions of post-colonial civil society (op. cit.). The case of Irish in Irish universities shows that attempts to pluralize epistemology and restore cultural identity yield ambivalent results since it is part of the West in a globalized world where questions about employability and economic relevance constantly impinge on projects of liberation and decolonization. The question of how to proceed past historic burdens is complicated ". . . [s]ince colonization was a highly complex process, decolonization lacks a clear focus" (Pieterse and Parekh 1995, 3). Colonizer and colonized are deeply intertwined and the embeddedness and power of English as local *and* global language makes it difficult to maintain the nativist position. The alternative is to re-embed economy and culture in a moment of transformation that is reducible to neither nativist resistance nor universalist transcendence, with the university playing a key role in developing culturally driven, alternative local economies. Lavia (2007, citing Appadurai 2000, 15) suggests that decolonizing pedagogy could include practices of 'deparochialization' and 'strong internationalization.' This might seem to be the very opposite of the localized community-development strategy proposed for the west of Ireland by Walsh (2011). However, local and global intersect through the issues and practice of community development, and through a tension and dialogue between deparochialized knowledge and community interests. Chambers advocates the perspective of 'critical professionalism' (Chambers 1995), which internalizes a strong critique of professional knowledge and its biases, emphasizing a development practice of empowerment and 'putting the last first.' Community development aims to bridge the very gap between structure and fragment, by facilitating local communities to analyze and articulate their own needs, while putting in place strategies that make community visions relevant, visible and powerful within larger power structures. Walker (1997) puts forward a praxis for 'subaltern professionals,' whose professionalism is rooted in reflexivity and oriented towards social justice:

> a form of professional development which involves continuous shifting between trying to alter a social situation in ways which bring us closer to living out our democratic values and revisiting what ought to be done, while simultaneously interrogating what we mean by social justice. (411)

SECOND RUPTURE—GLOBALIZATION AND THE NEW SPIRIT OF ACADEMIC CAPITALISM

The second rupture or point of departure here is the contemporary moment of managed reform and globalization. Higher education is claimed as the apotheosis of economic development under the sign of 'knowledge economy.'

While it is seen as a force for the growth and restructuring of the general economy, it is compelled to undergo management reforms to make it fit for this role. Bastalich (2010) suggests that 'knowledge economy' does not describe a new mode of economic production, but represents a discursive recasting of the relations between ideas and economy. She contends that the discourse of knowledge economy undermines universities' democratic and creative role. Policies to promote 'innovation' focus on resource exploitation and commodity fetishism, narrowing the distinctive and diverse knowledge innovations produced by universities' actual research practices (op. cit.).

This moment is marked by the rebranding of universities as posthistorical and postnational corporate entities. The national university system rearticulates itself as an engine of global governmentality, attempting to 'symmetrify the world' (Burawoy 2011) through the self-colonizing agency of educational policymakers, managers, workers and students. A seemingly banal example of transformative 'rebranding' illustrates the semantic and conceptual shifts taking place. In 2009, the official title of 'National University of Ireland, Galway' was replaced in public communications by a briefer, more corporate 'brand mark,' 'NUI Galway.' The 'brand mark' claims to embody unique "personality and positioning" (NUI Galway 2009, 4) rather than a specific content regarding identity or role. The displacement of the words *National, University* and *Ireland* from the signifier indicated a reimagination of a postnational, postuniversity enterprise informed by market researched 'brand values,' semiotically distanced from nationalist or liberal Enlightenment educational missions. The very conception of the university as a public institution and space is transformed as marketing and public communications become more dominant activities for the university.

A wider material context is provided by the global capitalist crisis of 2008, which resulted in particularly severe reversals for the 'Celtic Tiger' economy, which had boomed since the 1990s (Kirby 2010). The meltdown and implosion of proglobal developmentalism gave additional impetus to university corporatization and internationalization that was already underway. The resulting confusion is illustrated by the sudden unilateral announcement by the then minister of education, abolishing the national university entity (NUI) in 2010 as a cost-saving measure. The NUI defended itself on economic grounds too, arguing that abolition would lead to higher costs and administrative inefficiencies, while a recognizable 'national brand' is an economic necessity in a globalized marketplace (Manning 2010). In the face of these arguments, the announced abolition seems unlikely to be implemented. The recent Hunt Report on Higher Education Strategy states that the current funding model for Irish higher education is an urgent issue because it is unsustainable. While refraining from overt mentions of current and future cuts under planned austerity measures from 2008 to 2014, the report does note that public funding is unlikely to grow, while private investment has decreased (Strategy Group for Higher Education 2010, 32).

The unpopularity of proposals to reintroduce third-level fees (abolished in 1996) can only be mitigated by increasing international fees, turning to the private sector or hoping for philanthropic donations. A 'High-Level Group on International Education' was convened in 2010 to drive international-ization for higher education, with the aim of raising some €300 million (Department of Education and Skills 2010, 12) to plug domestic gaps.

'Internationalization' relies upon the matching of Orientalist and Occi-dentalist assumptions of buyers and sellers, as contending metropoles compete to be the chosen destination of the Other. The Other, primar-ily identified with fast-growing Asian economies, is targeted as a source of unequal exchange, but also as a source of research 'talent.' The frame is commodified and imperial, if not blatantly neocolonial. Irish universi-ties have turned to the global scramble for reputation only comparatively recently, but the drive for internationalization has heightened their reliance on global metrics and university rankings (Liu 2009; Hazelkorn 2009). In the colonial present, academics and students learn to insert themselves into a hierarchical global order as mobile individual producers and con-sumers, functioning simultaneously as resources and markets. Within the global design of internationalized higher education, Ireland plays down its peripheral postcolonial identity in favor of a metropolitan positioning as first world, English-speaking exemplar of bureaucratic excellence. Such a positioning is highly problematic for postcolonial and engaged pedagogy, which emphasizes ethical praxis, responsibility and care. Madge, Raghuram and Noxolo (2009) raise the problematic for UK higher education institu-tions which are active 'in creating the underdevelopment of individuals and families in poorer countries who are making horrendous financial sacrifices (for generations) to enable a family member to experience a (not-so) British education' (44).

Within the global design of commodified higher education, analyses of 'colonialism' take on a wider meaning. Habermas's idea (1984; 1987) of the *'colonization of the lifeworld'* and Yoshioka's *'self-colonization'* critically interrogate the spread and deepening of capitalist relations within the inter-nal territories of subjectivity and self. Habermas observes that runaway processes of modernization and capitalist-bureaucratic reform are coloniz-ing every lived space. Colonial spaces and frontiers have been recalibrated to bring in more extensive and intensive visions of globality, seeking to incorporate space, time and bodies into the logic of accumulation. These processes of conceptualizing, inscribing and interacting are termed 'bio-economisation' (Simons 2007). Zipin and Brennan (2003) observe that this transformation involves the quotidian suppression of ethical dispositions within higher education, while the monologic, colonizing and oppressive processes of transformation can arguably be described as the very antinomy of *ethical development*, defined as "a concept that involves improvements in the quality of human lives subject to the demands of social justice and freedom" (Qizilbash 1996, 1209). Postcolonial critiques of management highlight the continuities between colonial forms of administration such as indirect rule and twenty-first-century management techniques (Cooke 2003, 2008). There are certainly strong parallels between the central role played by enumeration in nineteenth-century colonial governmentality and governance reforms for 'accountability' in twenty-first-century managed times. Enumeration and hierarchical identities were essential to the colonial division of labor and regime of accumulation (Anderson 1991; Ludden 2003; Appadurai 1996). Colonial instrumentalism predominated in the nineteenth century through the epistemological privilege of European expertise, 'company experts' and legal texts (Ludden 2003, 251), while twenty-first-century instrumentalism relies on global informational media e-empires (controlling publications, citation and league tables), management expertise and intellectual-property regimes.

The new scripts and scenarios of academic capitalism (Slaughter and Leslie 1999) suggest a momentous rupture and transition from the postcolonial moment toward a posthistorical and deterritorialized biopolitics. While this line of thinking points to a grim reinscription of colonial continuities, Luke (2010) is less deterministic, suggesting that the current phase differs from colonial and Cold War forms. In his view, what has emerged is "a complex, chaotic and unpredictable *'edubusiness'* whose prioritization of a financial bottom line has supplanted clear normative educational and, indeed, overtly ideological intents" (44). This is "not a one way street of ideological indoctrination, marginalisation or exploitation—but rather an archetypal instance of the push/pull dialectics of cultural and economic globalisation" (loc. cit.; Rizvi 2000). Pieterse and Parekh (1995) largely glossed over the processes of economic development, but their volume on the decolonization of imagination notably includes Yoshioka's essay on Japanese self-colonization. Yoshioka suggested that Japan avoided Western political colonization by preemptively and rapidly colonizing itself, enabling its transformation into a modern, imperialist state. Postcolonial perspectives on organizational management highlight the hybrid epistemology of modern management as a discipline—especially with respect to the recent phenomenon of Japanization. Such perspectives reject simplistic views of cultural binarism and domination in favor of multiple voices and possibilities (Frenkel and Shenhav 2006).

Liesner is critical of the predominant governmentality as a capitalist, bureaucratic and managerial mode of social regulation. While reforms state that their aim is the "financial transformation of the university system" (2007, 72), she argues that the changes are really about the production of systemic compatibility between university and enterprise. Such systemic compatibility is produced by the commercial application of managerial principles, orienting universities and enterprise towards a shared economic calculus. This form of governmentality produces markets for educational commercialization and management as commodities in themselves, channeling universities to buy products as well as to produce and sell them.

Ball (2007) shows how the privatization of public-sector education has led to a proliferation of education businesses and products, and the increasing dominance of corporate logics of expansion, diversification, integration and profit. It is fascinating to note how little struggle is involved and how rapidly universities have taken to commodification and the business-managerial model. While the state may coerce the universities to comply with reforms using the carrot and stick of public funding, academics are by and large complying, while university managers seem genuinely compelled to complete the transformation as fast as possible, even if their reforms may justify threats and cuts to their core activities (Liesner 2007). The latest fiscal crisis merely deepens the existing trend for universities to go along with governments' planned retreat from higher education as a public good, even as they advocate for its expansion and its increased relevance. National, regional and global educational policymakers accept that governments cannot afford the higher education that societies want, hence the need for a radical realignment towards the market. The pressures and impossibilities of financing higher education are such that it is perhaps unsurprising that the turn to market solutions reflects a kind of magical thinking rather than rational calculus. Comaroff and Comaroff use the phrase *millennial capitalism* (2000, 292) to describe the social imaginary of the moment, appealing to magic and mimicry to bridge the gap between expansive desires for powerful new means of wealth creation and the improbability of their efficacy.

One theory that helps to explain the consent for reform is Boltanski and Chiapello's account of 'the new spirit of capitalism' (2005). They explain the social-psychological power of capitalism's 'new spirit' in terms of its ability to engage persons:

> [I]t is precisely because capitalism is hand in glove with freedom, does not have total sway over people, and presupposes the performance of a large number of tasks that cannot be carried out without workers' positive involvement, that it must furnish acceptable reasons for engaging. These reasons are contained in the 'spirit of capitalism'. (486)

Capitalism's growth-oriented insatiability comes up against the inherently satiable, critical and diversely oriented nature of human beings. Hence, capitalism requires a strategy that appeals to the human spirit, offering a moral vision of freedom that reformulates the critique of capitalism and harnesses its power. The human desire for accumulation is limited by the presence of alternative and competing desires, goals, norms and orders of status (op. cit., 488). This partly explains the drive to eliminate alternative human bases of educational values, and to standardize critique in the form of judgments against quantitative capitalist benchmarks. Critique itself ('*voice*') is crucial to the creation and transformation of the spirit of capitalism, through procedures of scrutiny and control which establish the capitalist order as morally just (op cit., 289–290). Privileged moments of judgment (*'supervised tests'*) identify individuals for remuneration or sanction. In providing an acceptable moral order, such mechanisms substitute self-control for external control. The resources of critique are rerouted through techniques of management which demand that individuals be evaluated more reliably and more often. Archer (2008) documents how younger academics have adopted neoliberal subjectivities, internalizing the evaluative order into their professional identities.

Following Boltanski and Chiapello's logic, the power of critique has become part of the problem, but it must also be part of any solution. While critique can be deployed to shore up and increase conditions of degradation and social inequality, generating a kind of political nihilism, the solution they propose is an optimistic *renewal of social critique* to "render the connexionist world less unjust" (2005, 518).

BACK TO THE FUTURE—SOCIAL CRITIQUE, CITIZENISM AND HUMAN RIGHTS

Scott (1999) allies the postcolonial present with the exercise of modern power, which he argues alters the terrain of struggle itself. He argues that critical postcolonialism must try to address the possibility of reshaping the postcolonial present in the future. Yet the idea of a ruptural transformation capable of producing a future that surpasses the present is hard to think of in globalized higher education. "The present invites us to take up the more difficult task of thinking fundamentally against the normalization of the epistemological and institutional forms of our political modernity"—a modernity of postcolonial misery (op. cit., 20). Morley (2003) writes of the consequences of managerial normalization—the presence of powerful discourses of crisis, loss, damage, contamination and decay—as the subjectivities and social spaces of higher education are reformed.

The two quotes used at the beginning of this essay point to a critical viewpoint that refuses the incorporation of social critique into the instrumentalities of the capitalist colonial present, but cannot in itself amount to a systemic ruptural break. It can only point to the idea that the 'knowledge economy' that looks like a transformative rupture is really a reconfiguration that effectively recruits critique, subjectivity and agency. Nandy (2000) suggests that universities can play a pivotal role in cultural resistance and the recovery of postcolonial societies through a democratization of knowledge (see also Delanty 2001). Their main responsibility "is to pluralize the future by pluralizing knowledge in the present," providing "a better, more honest range of options—material, ideational, and normative—for human beings and societies to choose from" (Nandy, 2000, 122). Arguing against critics who discount the modern university as irretrievably metropolitan and Eurocentric, Nandy suggests that they can play a positive mediating role by bringing marginalized indigenous knowledge to bear upon dominant Western knowledge formations. The postcolonial functions to 'crack' the imaginary, remaking the university as a site of "scepticism towards victorious forms of knowledge and as the means of recovering and transmitting knowledge that has been cornered, marginalized or even defeated" (2000, 117), while cautioning against "increasingly experimental, laboratory-based knowledge" sets up the postcolonial world as the object of enquiry and less than equal interlocutor (ibid.). For Nandy, the presence of marginalized knowledge creates a potential for dialogue between West and non-West, but this strategy requires the continued existence of a stable West/modern versus non-West/ nonmodern binary.

Nandy admonishes postcolonial universities not to mimic the engineered, industrial 'New Man' based on the template of nineteenth-century European utopias, as this did not work and served to "steal these cultures' concepts of their own futures during the war of categories that took place during colonial times" (Nandy 2000, 122). However, he also doubts that the search for a culturally authentic and uncontaminated culture can serve as a real source of confidence and creativity. The binary underpinning the awarding of "two cheers" to nativist affirmations of the cultural self loses its power amidst three cheers for managed globalization. For the posthistorical university, neither the uncolonized past nor the colonial present appear available. As an African academic recently remarked to me, 'We can't go back'; and meanwhile the lifeworld of the colonizer is itself colonized. The idea of syncretic or dialogic encounters between the modern, Western and nonmodern, non-Western worlds loses its purchase as the Manichean binary of modern-nonmodern dissolves.

What possible futures can emerge from such an enterprise of knowledge recovery? Theorizing in the critical postcolonial frame enables the West to address its own intellectual and epistemological exclusions, while allowing the non-West to present their cultural inheritance as knowledge. Gandhi's modest agenda for postcolonial theory is to "diversify its mode of address and learn to speak more adequately to the world it speaks for. In turn, it may acquire the capacity to facilitate a democratic colloquium between the antagonistic inheritors of the colonial aftermath" (1998, x). Nandy's pluralizing futures implicitly posit a choice between critical and cognitive recognition/liberation and functional capitalist transformation. However, postcolonial metropolitan universities have moved across this binary to recognize and even privilege the global Other. However, this remains part of a metropolitan strategy for unequal accumulation amidst a worldwide pattern of increasing inequality. Meanwhile, the privileged amongst the rising Others buy into this strategy in the hope that they will gain mobility across globalization's hierarchies, to become the 'winners' and not 'losers' of globalization.

Comaroff and Comaroff observe that neoliberal millennial capitalism is characterized by deep fissures between state, government and citizenship:

Everywhere there is evidence of an uneasy fusion of enfranchisement and exclusion; of xenophobia at the prospect of world citizenship without the old protections of nationhood; of the effort to realize modern utopias by decidedly postmodern means. Gone is any official-speak of egalitarian futures, work for all, of the paternal government envisioned by the various freedom movements. These ideals have given way to a spirit of deregulation, with its taunting mix of emancipation and limitation. Individual citizens, a lot of them marooned by a rudderless ship of state, try to clamber aboard the good ship Enterprise.' (2000, 299)

The postcolonial problem space concerns the transition from one 'politics of the not-yet' (Mamdani 1996) to another—from not-yet social citizens of only-just nations to not-yet consumer citizens hoping for futures of employment and potential consumption (see also Mullard 2004; Bauman 2008). The Comaroffs argue that the state's increasing hollowness pushes it to rely on "dramaturgy and improvisational content in order to secure the collusion of citizen-subjects" (2000, 328). The emptier nationhood becomes, the more urgent the need for collective reenchantment. Thus neoliberal reforms are accompanied by calls for engagement with the 'community' and 'civil society' through 'service' and volunteering. This plays an important role in 'performing fullness' for the nation. Civil society stands not in opposition but as a complementary discourse to millennial capitalism because it is "the battlecry that signifies that there is no battle." It reenchants by providing a moral imagination, and kindling a reformist spirit even as it reinforces the neoliberal status quo by voluntarily providing the services that the state has withdrawn from, and that the marginalized cannot access or afford (op. cit., 329).

Lock and Martins refer to a left critique of 'citizenism' and its impasse:

By 'citizenism' we mean an ideology of which the principal traits are 1) the belief in democracy as something capable of opposing capitalism, 2) the project of reinforcing the State (the States) so as to put this politics in place, [and] 3) the citizen as the active basis for this politics. The goal of citizenism is to humanize capitalism, to render it more just, in a certain way to give it a supplemental soul. Here the class struggle is replaced by the political participation of the citizenry, which not only elects representatives, but constantly acts to put pressure on them so that they apply themselves to what they were elected to do. (*"The Citizenist Impasse,"* 2001)

The roots of citizenism lie in the erosion of organized labor under globalization and the concomitant denationalization of the state: "States accompany this globalization by getting rid of the public sector inherited from the war economy (denationalizations), by becoming 'flexible' and by reducing the cost of work as much as possible" (ibid.). Citizenist movements present

themselves as interlocutors with the state, sometimes even staging spectacular 'radical actions'; however, they face an impasse since they simultaneously
offer support and opposition to the neoliberalizing state, but never attempt
to surpass it. There is no solution to the impasse, according to the collective
authors of this anonymous critique of citizenism, merely an exhortation to
practice critique and learn to wait. Lock and Martins (2009) contend that
the alternative to the impasse of citizenism is the promotion of properly
critical citizenship, entailing a properly critical system of higher education
and struggle against the 'consensus' model of citizenship. However, this
cannot be carried out in the abstract. Critical education for global citizenship must engage in pluralized, contested and 'dissenting futures' (cf. Nandy
2000). However, Nandy's modern Western/nonmodern peripheral binary
is exhausted within a globalized scenario where even resistant identities
and socioeconomic marginalization have become commodified by 'ethno-
preneurs,' a process described as 'Ethnicity Inc.' (Comaroff and Comaroff
2009). Identity and belonging comprises one of three components of citizenship, the other components being the collective benefits and rights that are
conferred by belonging and participation in political, economic and social
processes of the community (Bellamy 2008). The question of 'Whose vision
of entitlements and obligations?' must be balanced with 'What vision of
entitlements and obligations?' and 'How are priorities decided?'

For critical debate to proceed, substantive areas of discussion are
required. One key area where the meaning and content of global citizenship can be debated is that of human rights. Dower (2003), an influential
contributor to the debate, roots his conception of global citizenship in a
normative and ethical commitment to human rights. Hence, this chapter
concludes by suggesting that a critical approach to global citizenship education might address the globalization of human rights as a substantive
problem space. Debates about postcolonial cathexis, cultural contestation and epistemological claims can be rerouted to add important critical
dimensions to the substantive debates on human rights and 'claiming citizenship.' At both national and global levels, the real political problem is
how to make ethical commitments address a social world which maintains
inequality and reproduces privilege (Bourdieu 1993; 1999). The debates
on realizing human rights, contesting development and the role of citizen participation and knowledge transformation (Kothari 2005; Gready
and Ensor 2005; Kabeer 2005) reroute postcolonial critiques and reroot
critical concerns in debates about responsibility, social justice and humanity. A postcolonial reading implies a rerooting in nonperfectionist views
of human rights and education that remains open to otherness and difficulty. Todd (2009) calls for a more difficult form of cosmopolitanism that
subjects the founding tradition of liberal humanism to critical scrutiny.
After all, liberal humanism's particular forms are contestable and Western
liberal humanists cannot have a monopoly on what humanity means (cf.
Levinas 1997). Todd contends that a nonperfectionist approach does not

shy away from evil and wrong, conflict and tension, basing itself not an abstract principle of humanity but rooting itself in a world with others that demands us to face others (op. cit.).

Universities can only play their properly critical role with regard to human rights (Steiner 2002) and ethical development (Qizilbash 1996) by purposefully diversifying its educational spaces with these concerns in mind, for example, by at least including postcolonial, feminist and critical readings of the human-rights canon. Their democratizing role requires the engagement of a wider public in the production of knowledge about, and performative practice of, the public pedagogy of human rights (cf. Giroux 2003). This gives universities a role in keeping the possibility of other futures open, where the quality of human lives, social justice and human freedom can be democratically debated (see Delanty 2001). Burdick and Sandlin (2010) advocate the centrality of a concept of 'answerability' as an ethical and human obligation with respect to the Other. Human rights adopts such notions of answerability and constructive accountability (Freedman 2003) which provide a welcome critical and empowering alternative to the deadening bureaucratic conceptions of 'accountability' that have permeated public discourse, not least through the managed discourses of education and governance.

Aronowitz (1998) insists that the ethical and critical impulses of education must resist the attempts of administered judgment to incorporate them. Education invokes more kinds of rigor and innovation than that which is measured by positivistic and commercial management metrics. Likewise, Fielding (1999) defends the nuanced language of education in opposition to the 'harsh and metallic' language of the market. Espousal of freedom-based visions of education may seem wild, anachronistic and utopian in new managed times, but how else can education be justified as "that specifically human act of intervening in the world" (Aronowitz 1998, 4)? The managerial moment tries to immobilize history by redesigning the present to fit within a fully marketized global future, but this denies material, historical and human demands and maintains an unjust socioeconomic and cultural order. An alternative futurity depends on pedagogic spaces that keep providing alternative conceptions and valorizations of education. A radical approach does not have to demonstrate that a radically different future is likely, only that it is possible (op. cit.). The new strengths of managed neoliberalism—its appeal to subjectivity and incorporation of aesthetics (Klein 2000) as well as critical judgment (Boltanski and Chiapello 2005)—are precisely also its weakness, since critique, subjectivity and judgments retain the potential to be 'outside' the instrumentalities of capitalism. In progressive and capabilities-based ideas of education, educability is rooted in the learner's autonomy and freedom and their irreducibility to instrumental means. Progressive educators strive towards a critical educational philosophy that resists totalization and closure, and that can somehow become more adequate for thinking other-wisely in an economically and culturally interdependent world. Freire's pedagogy highlights the essentially dialogi-cal, creative and incomplete nature of the educational enterprise, which privileges human unfinishedness and learning as spaces of possibility. There is no closure as long as there is ontological openness in the imagi-nation and will of agents (Marginson 2008). As Pieterse and Parekh (1995) note, colonization was a highly complex process and the decolonization involves the imaginative creation of new forms of consciousness for both. The critical debate on global citizenship, and what that means in educa-tional terms, needs to be facilitated with pedagogical spaces. These must provide choices and opportunities for citizens to critically view the very dif-ferent positions from which claims of globalization, citizenship and postco-loniality are made, and to evaluate these claims in terms of what individual and shared futures might result.

REFERENCES

Anderson, B. (1991) *Imagined Communities: Reflections on the Origin and Spread of Nationalism*, London: Verso.

Andreotti, V. and de Souza, L. (2008) *Learning to Read the World through Other Eyes*. Derby, UK: Global Education.

Appadurai, A. (1996) *Modernity at Large: Cultural Dimensions of Globalization*, Minneapolis: University of Minnesota Press.

———. (2000) Grassroots Globalization and the Research Imagination, *Public Culture*, 12(1): 1–19.

Archer, L. (2008) 'The New Neoliberal Subjects? Young/er Academics' Construc-tions of Professional Identity', *Journal of Education Policy*, 23: 265–285.

Aronowitz, S. (1998) 'Introduction to Freire, P', *Pedagogy of Freedom: Ethics, Democracy and Civic Courage*, trans. by P. Clarke, Lanham, MD: Rowman & Littlefield, 1–20.

Ball, S. J. (2007) *Education Plc: Private Sector Participation in Public Sector Edu-cation*, London: Routledge.

Bastalich, Wendy (2010) 'Knowledge Economy and Research Innovation', *Studies in Higher Education*, 35: 845–857.

Bauman, Z. (2008) *Does Ethics Have a Chance in the World of Consumers?* Cam-bridge, MA: Harvard University Press.

Bellamy, R. (2008) *Citizenship: A Very Short Introduction*, Oxford: Oxford Uni-versity Press.

Bhabha, H. (1994) *The Location of Culture*, London: Routledge.

Boltanski, L. and Chiapello, E. (2005) *The New Spirit of Capitalism*, London: Verso.

Bourdieu, P (1993) *The Field of Cultural Production*, Cambridge: Polity Press.

Bourdieu, P. (1999) *The Weight of the World: Social Suffering in Contemporary Society*, Cambridge: Polity Press.

Brydon, D. (2010) 'Cracking Imaginaries: Studying the Global from Canadian Space', in J. Wilson, C. Şandru, and S. Welsh (eds.), *Rerouting the Postcolonial: New Directions for a New Millennium*, 105–117.

Burawoy, M. (2011) 'Universities in Crisis—a Public Sociology Perspective', address to the Royal Irish Academy, January 13, 2011.

Burdick, J. and Sandlin, J. A. (2010) Inquiry as Answerability: Toward a Meth-odology of Discomfort in Researching Public Pedagogies, *Qualitative Inquiry* 16(5): 349–360.

Casanova, J. (1997) Globalizing Catholicism and the Return to a "Universal" Church, in S. Hoeber Rudolph and J. Piscatori (eds.), *Transnational Religion and Fading States*. Boulder, CO: Westview Press, 121–143.

Chambers, R. (1995) Poverty and Livelihoods: Whose Reality Counts? *Environment and Urbanization*, 7(1): 173–204.

Comaroff, J. and Comaroff, J. (1991) *Of Revelation and Revolution: Christianity, Colonialism and Consciousness in South Africa*, Chicago: Chicago University Press.

———. (2000) 'Millennial Capitalism: First Thoughts on a Second Coming', *Public Culture*, 12: 291–343.

———. (2009) *Ethnicity Inc.*, Chicago: University of Chicago Press.

Cooke, B. (2003) 'Managing Organizational Culture and Imperialism', in A. Prasad (ed.), *Postcolonial Theory and Organizational Analysis: A Critical Engagement*, New York: Palgrave Macmillan, 75–94.

———. (2008) 'Participatory Management as Colonial Administration', in S. Dar and B. Cooke (eds.), *The New Development Management: Critiquing the Dual Modernization*, London: Zed Books, 111–128.

Delanty, G. (2001) *Challenging Knowledge: The University in a Knowledge Society*, Buckingham, UK: Open University Press.

Department of Education and Skills (2010) *Investing in Global Relationships: Ireland's International Education Strategy 2010–15*. Report of the High-Level Group on International Education to the Tánaiste and Minister for Education and Skills, Dublin: Department of Education and Skills.

Dower, N. (2003) *An Introduction to Global Citizenship*, Edinburgh: Edinburgh University Press.

Fielding, M. (1999) 'Target Setting, Policy Pathology and Student Perspectives: Learning to Labour in New Times', *Cambridge Journal of Education*, 29: 277–287.

Flores-Crespo, P. (2007) 'Situating Education in the Human Capabilities Approach', in M. Walker and E. Unterhalter (eds.), *Amartya Sen's Capability Approach and Social Justice in Education*, Houndmills, UK: Palgrave.

Foley, T. (ed.) (1999) *From Queen's Colleges to National University: Essays on the Academic History of QCG/ UCG/ NUI Galway*, Dublin: Four Courts Press.

Freedman, L. (2003) Averting International Death and Disability: Human Rights, Constructive Accountability and Maternal Mortality in the Dominican Republic, *International Journal of Gynaecology and Obstetrics*, 82, 111–114.

Freire, P. (1998) *Pedagogy of Freedom: Ethics, Democracy and Civic Courage*, trans. by P. Clarke, Lanham, MD: Rowman & Littlefield.

Frenkel, M. and Shenhav, Y. (2006) 'From Binarism Back to Hybridity: A Postcolonial Reading of Management and Organization Studies', *Organization Studies*, 27: 855–876.

Gandhi, L. (1998) *Postcolonial Theory—a Critical Introduction*, Edinburgh: Edinburgh University Press.

Garvin, T. (2004) *Preventing the Future: Why Was Ireland Poor for So Long?* Dublin: Gill and Macmillan.

Gikandi, S. (2001) 'Globalization and the Claims of Postcoloniality', *The South Atlantic Quarterly*, 100: 627–658.

Giroux, H. (2003) 'Public Pedagogy and the Politics of Resistance: Notes on a Critical Theory of Educational Struggle', *Educational Philosophy and Theory*, 35(1): 5–16.

Gready, P. and Ensor, J. (2005) *Reinventing Development: Translating Rights-Based Approaches from Theory into Practice*, London: Zed Books.

Gregory, D. (2004) *The Colonial Present*, Oxford: Blackwell.

Habermas, J. (1984; 1987) *The Theory of Communicative Action*, Vols. I and II, Boston: Beacon Press.

Hazelkorn, E. (2009) 'Rankings and the Battle for World-Class Excellence, Institutional Strategies and Policy Choices', *Higher Education Management and Policy*, 21: 1–22.

Hickling-Hudson, A. (2003) 'Multicultural Education and the Postcolonial Turn', *Policy Futures in Education*, 1: 381–401.

Hogan, E. (1990) *The Irish Missionary Movement: A Historical Survey 1830–1980*, Dublin: Gill and Macmillan.

Kabeer, N. (ed.) (2005) *Inclusive Citizenship: Meanings and Expressions*, London: Zed Books.

Kinealy, C. (1994) *This Great Calamity: The Irish famine 1845–52*, Dublin: Gill & Macmillan.

Kirby, P. (2010) *The Celtic Tiger in Collapse*, Houndmills, UK: Palgrave.

Klein, N. (2000) *No Logo*, London: Flamingo.

Kothari, U. (ed.) (2005) *A Radical History of Development Studies: Individuals, Institutions and Ideologies*, London: Zed Books.

Lavia, J. (2007). Repositioning Pedagogies and Postcolonialism: Theories, Contradictions and Possibilities, *International Journal of Inclusive Education*, 11(3): 283–300.

Levinas, E. (1997) *Difficult Freedom: Essays on Judaism*, trans. by S. Hand, Leiden: Brill.

Liesner, A. (2007) 'Education or Service? Remarks on Teaching and Learning in the Entrepreneurial University', in J. Masschelein, M. Simons, U. Bröckling and L. Pongratz (eds.), *The Learning Society from the Perspective of Governmentality*, London: Wiley-Blackwell.

Liu, Nian Cai (2009) 'The Story of Academic Rankings', *International Higher Education 54*, http://www.bc.edu/bc_org/avp/soe/cihe/newsletter/Number54/p2_Liu.htm (accessed March 7, 2010).

Lock, G. and Martins, H. (2009) 'The European Universities, Citizenship and Its Limits: What Won't Solve the Problems of Our Time', *European Educational Research Journal*, 8: 159–174.

Loomba, A. et al. (eds.) (2005) *Postcolonial Studies and Beyond*, Durham, NC, and London: Duke University Press.

Ludden, D. (2003) 'Orientalist Empiricism: Transformations in Colonial Knowledge', in C. A. Breckinridge and P. van der Veer (eds.), *Orientalism and the Postcolonial Predicament: Perspectives on South Asia*, Philadelphia: University of Pennsylvania Press.

Luke, Allan (2010) 'Educating the Other: Standpoint and the "Internationalisation" of Higher Education', in V. Carpentier and E. Unterhalter (eds.), *Global Inequalities in Higher Education: Whose Interests Are We Serving?*, London: Palgrave/Macmillan, 43–65.

Lyotard, J. F. (1991) *The Postmodern Explained to Children: Correspondence 1982–1985*, J. Pefanis and M. Thomas eds. and trans., Sydney: Power Publications.

Madge, C., Raghuram, P. and Noxolo, P. (2009) Engaged Pedagogy and Responsibility: A Postcolonial Analysis of International Students, *Geoforum*, 40: 34–45.

Mamdani, M. (1996) *Citizen and Subject: Contemporary Africa and the Legacy of Late Colonialism*, Princeton, NJ: Princeton University Press.

Manning, M. (2010) 'The National University of Ireland's Abolition?', *Public Affairs Ireland* (February): 16.

Marginson, S. (2008) 'Global Field and Global Imagining: Bourdieu and Worldwide Higher Education', *British Journal of the Sociology of Education*, 29: 303–315.

Mignolo, W. (2000) *Local Histories/Global Designs: Coloniality, Subaltern Knowledges and Border Thinking*, Princeton, NJ: Princeton University Press.

Morley, L. (2003) *Quality and Power in Higher Education*, Buckingham, UK: Open University Press.

Mullard, M. (2004) *The Politics of Globalization and Polarization*, London: Edward Elgar.

Nandy, Ashis (2000) 'Recovery of Indigenous Knowledge and Dissenting Futures of the University', in S. Inayatullah and J. Gidley (eds.), *The University in Transformation: Global Perspectives on the Futures of the University*, Westport, CT: Bergin & Garvey.

Newman, J. H. (1996) The Idea of a University, F. M. Turner (ed.), New Haven, CT: Yale University Press. (Original work published 1854)

N'gũgĩ wa Thiong'o (1986) *Decolonizing the Mind: The Politics of Language in African Literature*, London: Heinemann.

NUI Galway (2009) *Brand Book*, Galway, Ireland: NUI Galway.

O'Madagáin, B. (1999) 'Irish: A Difficult Birth', in T. Foley (ed.), *From Queen's Colleges to National University: Essays on the Academic History of QCG/ UCG/ NUI Galway*. Dublin: Four Courts Press, 344–359.

O'Tuathaigh, G. (1999) 'The Establishment of the Queen's Colleges: Ideological and Political Background', in T. Foley (ed.), *From Queen's Colleges to National University: Essays on the Academic History of QCG/UCG/ NUI Galway*, Dublin: Four Courts Press, 1–16.

Parry, B (1994) *Resistance Theory/Theorizing Resistance or Two Cheers for Nativism*, reprinted in B. Parry (2004), *Postcolonial Studies: A Materialist Critique*, London: Routledge.

Pieterse, J. and Parekh, B. (1995) 'Shifting Imaginaries: Decolonization, Internal Decolonization, Postcoloniality', in J. N. Pieterse (ed.), *Decolonization of the Imagination*, London: Zed Books.

Prasad, A. (2003) 'The Gaze of the Other: Postcolonial Theory and Organizational Analysis', in A. Prasad (ed.), *Postcolonial Theory and Organizational Analysis: A Critical Engagement*, New York: Palgrave Macmillan.

Qizilbash, M. (1996) 'Ethical Development', *World Development*, 24: 1209–1221.

Raley, Rita (2004) 'eEmpires', *Cultural Critique*, 57 (Spring): 111–150.

Readings, B. (1996) *The University in Ruins*, Cambridge, MA: Harvard University Press.

Rizvi, F. (2000) 'International Education and the Production of Global Imagination', in N. Burbules and C. Torres (eds.), *Globalisation and Education*, New York: Routledge, 205–226.

Saito, M. (2003) 'Amartya Sen's Capability Approach to Education: A Critical Exploration', *Journal of Philosophy of Education*, 37: 17–33.

Schueller, M. J. (2009) 'Decolonizing Global Theories Today', *Interventions*, 11: 235–254.

Scott, D. (1999) *Refashioning Futures: Criticism after Postcoloniality*, Princeton, NJ: Princeton University Press.

Sen, A. (2006) *Identity and Violence: The Illusion of Destiny*, New York/London: W.W. Norton & Company.

Shultz, L. (2010) 'What Do We Ask of Global Citizenship Education?', *International Journal of Development Education and Global Learning*, 3: 5–22.

Simons, M. (2007) 'Learning as Investment: Notes on Governmentality and Biopolitics', in J. Masschelein, M. Simons, U. Bröckling and L. Pongratz (eds.), *The Learning Society from the Perspective of Governmentality*, London: Wiley-Blackwell.

Slaughter, S. and Leslie, L. (1999) *Academic Capitalism: Politics, Policies, and the Entrepreneurial University*, Baltimore: Johns Hopkins University Press.

Sluga, G. (2010) 'UNESCO and the (One) World of Julian Huxley', *Journal of World History*, 21: 393–418.

220   *Su-ming Khoo*

Spencer, R. (2010) 'Cosmopolitan Criticism', in J. Wilson, C. Şandru, and S. Welsh (eds.), *Rerouting the Postcolonial: New Directions for a New Millennium*, New York: Routledge, 105–117.

Spivak, G. (1988) 'Can the Subaltern Speak?', in C. Nelson and L. Grossberg (eds.), *Marxism and the Interpretation of Culture*, London: Macmillan.

Steiner, H. J. (2005) 'The University's Critical Role in the Human Rights Movement', *Harvard Human Rights Journal*, 15: 317–328.

Strategy Group for Higher Education (2010) *National Strategy for Higher Education: Draft Report of the Strategy Group (The Hunt Report)*, Dublin: Strategy Group for Higher Education.

The Citizenist Impasse: A Contribution to a Critique of Citizenism (2001, English translation by Pygmalion Books, 2007), http://www.notbored.org/citizenism.html (accessed February 20, 2011).

Tikly, L. (2001) 'Globalisation and Education in the Postcolonial World: Towards a Conceptual Framework', *Comparative Education*, 37: 151–171.

Todd, S. (2009) "Toward an Imperfect Education: The Task of Facing Human Pluralism", Invited Distinguished Lecture, Philosophical Studies in Education SIG AERA, San Diego, April 15, 2009.

Walker, M. (1997). Subaltern Professionals: Acting in Pursuit of Social Justice, *Educational Action Research*, 4(3): 407–425.

———. (2006). *Higher Education Pedagogies*, Maidenhead, UK: Open University Press.

Walsh, J. (2011). *Contests and Contexts: The Irish Language and Ireland's Socio-Economic Development*, Oxford and Bern: Peter Lang.

Wilson, J, Şandru, C. and Welsh, S. (2010) *Rerouting the Postcolonial: New Directions for a New Millennium*, London: Routledge.

Yoshioka, Hiroshi (1995) 'Samurai and Self-Colonization in Japan', in J. N. Pieterse and B. Parekh (eds.), *De-colonization of Imagination: Culture, Knowledge and Power*, London: Zed.

Zipin, L. and Brennan, S. (2003) 'The Suppression of Ethical Dispositions through Managerial Governmentality: A Habitus Crisis in Australian Higher Education', *International Journal of Leadership in Education*, 6: 351–370.

12 Equivocal Knowing and Elusive Realities

Imagining Global Citizenship Otherwise

Vanessa de Oliveira Andreotti,
Cash Ahenakew and Garrick Cooper

We start this chapter with a powerful story told in New Zealand contexts about Māori ways of knowing. In this story, a Māori grandmother is asked whether there were many gods or just one God. She replied with reference to the Bible: 'There is only one God: our father who lives in heaven.' The grandmother is then asked: 'What about the other Māori Gods?' She responded: 'And there are those as well!' This chapter suggests that, for many aboriginal cosmologies, there is absolutely no contradiction in this grandmother's response. We propose that such cosmologies are inherently multiepistemic—or pluri-versal (Mignolo 2007): They can hold competing and contradictory systems of meaning in tension without having to come to a dialectical synthesis or resolution. We suggest that the basis of this epistemic possibility could be a conceptualization of language, knowledge, reality and metaphysics that differs significantly from dominant conceptualizations in Western humanist thought. These different conceptualizations emphasize a metaphorical and equivocal relationship between language and an elusive metaphysical reality that is perceived to be beyond the limits of language or of full cognitive comprehension. We suggest that these conceptualizations open new possibilities for a postcolonial project of global citizenship 'otherwise.'

In this chapter, we weave different insights from Aboriginal and postcolonial scholars on the political economy of knowledge production; we focus particularly on the relationships between language, knowing, metaphysics and reality. We begin with a brief overview of the epistemic privilege of modernity and Christianity in creating root metaphors that are still prevalent and perceived to be natural and universally true. We then explore issues related to language, knowing and reality in the works of Māori and First Nations scholars. We suggest that a different conceptualization of the relationship between language and reality offers different possibilities for interpreting 'myths.' Next, we use postcolonial scholarship to examine the implications of bringing forward open metaphysical questions in the production of knowledge. In the last section of this chapter we offer four examples of the use of the medicine wheel in Aboriginal literature to illustrate ideas related to global citizenship education and the possibility of knowledge construction that takes account of spirituality and relationality through contingency, situatedness, fluidity and partiality. In our conclusion, we consider the ethical responsibilities involved in the process of knowledge construction and the implications for a project of global citizenship education that has the potential to create "a non-coercive relationship or dialogue with the excluded Other of Western humanism" (Gandhi 1999, 39).

We have made a conscious decision to make explicit the cultural/genealogical positionings and disciplinary affiliations of the theorists used in this chapter in order to highlight the geo- and body-politics of knowledge production (Mignolo and Tlostanova 2006) in this field of study. By bringing forth these hybrid positionings, we aspire to move beyond essentialist categorizations and to emphasize the multiple and intersubjective nature of each locus of enunciation.

THE EPISTEMIC PRIVILEGE OF MODERNITY AND CHRISTIANITY

Some Aboriginal scholars have questioned the use of the word *myth* to refer to their stories and metaphors for creation. They argue that the word *myth* often evokes a distinction between myth and fact or myth and history that serves to discredit and infantilize oral traditions that construct knowledge based on different ideas of reality (Allen 1986). Along with postcolonial scholars, they also question the lack of awareness and scholarly engagement with Christian myths/stories that are seen to be foundational for the construction of modernity and of secularism itself. Cree playwright and novelist Tomsom Highway, for example, highlights the power of the Christian narrative of creation in shaping social relations in the Americas and elsewhere:

> When Christopher Columbus arrived in North America in October of the year 1492—a date arguably among the most important in our history as a people—probably the most significant item of baggage he had on his ship was the extraordinary story of a woman who talked to a snake in a garden and, in doing so, precipitated the eviction of human kind from that garden. This seminal narrative has created severe trauma in the lives of many, many people and ultimately, one might argue, the life of our entire planet. I don't think that it is any coincidence that the mythology/theology this story comes from, Christianity, has at its centre the existence of a solo god who is male and male entirely. (Highway 2005, 163)

Nakota historian Vine Deloria Jr. (2003) also emphasizes that many characteristics of this Christian mythology of a single male god, including its notion of time, history, self and manifest destiny, are foundational to our secular modern world. Similarly, Argentinean semiotician Walter Mignolo (2002) asserts that the idea of epistemology in 'modern space' was "first Christian and then White" (935). He argues that Christianity and modernity occupy a double space of 'epistemic privilege' where they can define (or enunciate) what is universally good, true and real in dichotomous terms and at the same time make it sound as if these definitions are natural and objective:

> Christianity and its aftermath, secular epistemology, had the privilege of being at the same time part of the totality enunciated and the universal place of enunciation while being able to make believe that the place of enunciation was a nonplace. Consequently, the order of the enunciated was the natural order of the world and the world, alas, was organized in dichotomous hierarchies. (Mignolo 2002, 935)

Blackfoot social scientist Betty Bastien (2005) argues that the idea of the universal nature of humanity is also grounded in such dichotomous hierarchies. She states that the notion of a universal humanity provided the license for Europeans, through colonialism, to alter the natural order and processes of indigenous cultures and people. Reiterating Said's insights into orientalism, she quotes Ani (1994) to map the perceptions and relationships between five interconnected European ideologies and their implications in relation to Europe's cultural others. She asserts that Christianity projected a self-image of Europeans as religious and moral, while non-Europeans were perceived to be nonreligious, immoral and in need of salvation. Other ideologies followed the same pattern: while Europeans perceived themselves as modern, progressive, civilized, literate, scientific, pure and human, others were perceived as traditional, backward, primitive, illiterate, dirty, non-human, objects of study who needed to be developed, advanced, educated, civilized, helped, studied, known, controlled, avoided, pitied, enslaved or destroyed (Bastien 2004).

As Highway suggests, in this historical context, a certain myth/story had the power to (violently) shape collective consciousness and institutions around the globe in ways that were not available to different myths/stories. Portuguese sociologist Boaventura de Souza Santos (2007) refers to the key legacy of this epistemic universalization as 'abyssal thinking.' He defines abyssal thinking as a system consisting of visible and invisible distinctions established through a logic that defines social reality as either on 'this side of the abyssal line' or on 'the other side of the abyssal line.' He explains:

> The division is such that 'the other side of the line' vanishes as reality becomes nonexistent, and is indeed produced as nonexistent. Nonexistent means not existing in any relevant or comprehensible way of being. Whatever is produced as nonexistent is radically excluded because it lies beyond the realm of what the accepted conception of inclusion considers to be its other. What most fundamentally

characterizes abyssal thinking is thus the impossibility of the co-presence of the two sides of the line. To the extent that it prevails, this side of the line only prevails by exhausting the field of relevant reality. Beyond it, there is only nonexistence, invisibility, non–dialectical absence. (Souza Santos 2007, 2)

The denial of co-presence is translated into a hegemonic contact that "converts simultaneity with non-contemporaneity [making up] pasts to make room for a single homogeneous future" (3). The project of a homogeneous future justifies the violence and appropriation carried out in its name. Thus, one part of humanity (considered subhuman), on the other side of the abyssal line, is sacrificed in order to affirm the universality of the part of humanity on this side of the line (Souza Santos 2007).

Therefore, Souza Santos (2007) argues that the struggle for global social justice is inseparable from the struggle for global cognitive justice and that both struggles require 'post-abyssal thinking' (5). This implies that political resistance must be "premised upon epistemological resistance" (10), which calls not for 'more alternatives' but for an "alternative thinking about alternatives [which requires] the symbolic amplification of signs, clues, and latent tendencies that, however inchoate and fragmented point to new constellations of meaning as regards both to the understanding and the transformation of the world" (10). Souza Santos suggests that, from this side of the abyssal line, recognition of cultural diversity does not necessarily translate into recognition of epistemological diversity. Therefore, he proposes that the recognition of epistemological diversity entails a provisional renouncing of any general epistemology:

Throughout the world, not only are there very diverse forms of knowledge of matter, society, life and spirit, but also many and very diverse concepts of what counts as knowledge and the criteria that may be used to validate it. In the transitional period we are entering, in which abyssal versions of totality and unity of knowledge still resist, we probably need a residual general epistemological requirement to move along: a general epistemology of the impossibility of a general epistemology. (Souza Santos 2007, 12)

Souza Santos argues that the limits and value of knowledges should be attributed according to the notion of 'knowledge-as-intervention-in-reality' and not 'knowledge-as-a-representation-of-reality' (Souza Santos 2007, 13). He proposes that "the credibility of cognitive construction [be] measured by the type of intervention in the world that it affords or prevents" (ibid.). He suggests a break with the notion of linear time that constructs the denial of co-presence in order to open the possibility of radical co-presence through egalitarian simultaneity. This drive towards egalitarian simultaneity is based on an idea of incompleteness: "Since no single type of knowledge can account for all possible interventions in the world, all of them are incomplete in different ways [hence] each knowledge is both insufficient and inter-dependent on other knowledges" (Souza Santos 2007, 17).

In the second section of this chapter, we suggest that 'egalitarian simultaneity' leading to the recognition of the existence of multiple epistemologies could already be an inherent feature of some Aboriginal cosmologies. We propose that focusing on the relationship between knowledge construction, language and reality can offer productive insights into this area.

LANGUAGE, KNOWLEDGE AND REALITY

Cherokee sociologist Eva Garroute (1999) suggests that some Aboriginal conceptualizations of language present a relationship between word and world (or language and reality) that is very different from Western humanism. Rather than an indexed relationship, where language describes reality in unequivocal ways, in such Aboriginal ontologies language is perceived as a symbolic code for a reality that is constantly on the move and that allows for multiple symbolic and situated interpretations. Each of these interpretations produces a different effect in reality itself—they "bring a different reality into being" (953). Garroute states that "different readings [of the same, single text] are created for different ceremonies, and they produce different effects" (ibid.). She explains that

> [d]iscursive performances not only shape the world, but the same text can do so in different ways, depending upon which reading is selected from the various possibilities available within it. Here, different accounts clearly matter, and they matter very much. New accounts are never simply a matter of an infinite regress of equally defensible readings: each distinct account is powerful. Speakers or writers assuming such a philosophy of language would have reason to take great care over the texts that they produce—because they would understand that, in doing so, they also produce the world—the Real world—in a very literal sense. (954)

This philosophy of language can also be associated with Ngāti Porou (Māori) international human-rights lawyer and scholar Moana Jackson's (2010) interpretations of how stories take a special form in the Māori notion of 'whakapapa' (genealogy). Jackson talks about whakapapa as a series of stories with never-ending beginnings that maintain the nurturing of interconnectedness in the process of construction of meaning. He also extends this conceptualization to the notion of time and knowledge in Māori cosmologies. Time of never-ending beginnings would be very different from linear time and produce stories that may never end. This in turn reflects the never-ending scope of knowledge itself (27). In the same way, Ngāti Raukawa (Māori) philosopher Charles Royal (2009) describes knowledge production in Māori cosmologies as a process of weaving where knowledge is presented as "an energy rather than a finite product, . . . as equivalent to the world, rather than as representation of it" (14).

According to Cree anthropologist Yvonne Dion-Buffalo (1990), this languaging-as-equivalence is enacted in the creation of imageries or metaphors that provide the interface between perception, emotion, spirit and the physical body, working as "seeds of thought or arrows of change" (129). She states that good storytellers use metaphors to communicate spiritual knowledge and "to create moods, to form patterns, and to evoke various physical and mental changes" (120). Thus, metaphors are used as a "means to relay information about the unconscious and spiritual realms" (121). Hence, Dion-Buffalo conceptualizes myths as "rituals or language constructs that contain the power to transform something or someone from one state to another" (122). Like Jackson, she emphasizes the flexible nature of myths as stories that have many variants and that are told differently according to the context. She quotes Allen (1986) to assert that

> Myths are stories that allow a holistic image to pervade and shape consciousness thus providing a coherent and empowering matrix for action and relationship . . . this creative ordering capacity of myth frightens and attracts the rationalistic, other centered, mind (Allen 1986, 105, in Dion-Buffalo 1990, 122)

Like Dion-Buffalo, Pueblo philosopher Gregory Cajete (2000) makes a distinction between a rationalistic mind and a 'metaphoric' mind that engages with the kind of metaphysical knowledge that stories and metaphors convey. He asserts that the metaphoric mind, unlike the rational mind, is used to "describe, imagine, and create from the animate world with which we constantly participate, [and bring] forth the descriptive and creative 'storying' of the world by humans" (50). For Cajete, the metaphoric mind creates these stories from collective subconscious or semiconscious images. Cherokee psychiatrist and scholar Mehl-Madrona (2007) argues that Aboriginal elders speak of these images as masks held by spirits, ancestors or entities that aim to communicate beyond the rationally trained, skeptical, doubtful and scripted mind. Cajete (2000) proposes that engaging these images/masks/metaphors requires a conceptualization of language as a "symbolic code for representing the world that is perceived by our senses" (50) and a conceptualization of truth not as a fixed point, but as "an ever-evolving point of balance, perceptually created and perceptually new" (48).

Cree ethicist Willie Ermine (1995) explains the relationship between a metaphoric and a rational mind in terms of different quests of knowledge production and their effects: "One was bound for an uncharted destination in outer space, the physical, and the other was on a delicate path into inner space, the metaphysical" (101). According to Ermine, while the extreme of one trajectory leads to an obsession with order and control of the physical world, the other leads to immanence through the insight that all existence is connected by a force beyond complete human understanding. This immanence is based on the understanding that the 'languaging' or creation of meaning about this life force will always be provisional, partial, contextual and subjective (hence the notion that the life force is a mystery). On the other hand, it is the life force itself that propels the creation of meaning and the possibility of knowledge construction. He affirms that the recognition and affirmation of this mystery is crucial for a quest of knowledge at the conjunction between physical and metaphysical realities. Ermine emphasizes the importance of having this quest for knowledge grounded in an inner space consciousness—or "in the spirit" (108). He quotes Lewis Thomas to argue that for the quest for knowledge to be humble and relational, it needs to be centered around the idea of the 'unknown':

> Teach on the outset, before any of the fundamentals, the still imponderable puzzles of cosmology. Let it be known, as clearly as possible, by the young minds, that there are some things going on in the universe that lie beyond comprehension, and make it plain how little is known ... Teach ecology later on. Let it be understood that the earth's life is a system of interlinking, interdependent creatures, and that we do not understand at all how it works ... teach that. (Thomas 1983, 213, as cited in Ermine 1995, 107)

For Ermine, the journeys into the unknown are mediated by stories—or myths that speak of "unfinished explorations in the inner space" (105). In Native American traditions, the trickster-transformer is the character that enacts that function. In Māori cosmologies, the interplay between the known and the unknown is enacted in the stories of the characters Māui and Tawhaki (Cooper 2008).

We turn now to Indian political theorist Ashis Nandy (2002) and Trinidadian social theorist Jacqui Alexander (2005) to explore the implications of engaging with epistemologies that privilege the sacred unknown-innerspace that Ermine refers to and that language the world through metaphors. We argue that the idea of the unknown—or an elusive reality, used as a root metaphor for being/knowing—generates 'plural traditions' where metaphysical questions remain consciously open (i.e., reality is elusive), where knowing is perceived as 'storied,' situated and partial (i.e., knowledge is equivocal) and where different (equivocal) stories of (an elusive) reality can coexist (albeit in tension).

KNOWING THAT EMANATES FROM BEING: EQUIVOCAL KNOWLEDGES AND ELUSIVE REALITIES

Nandy's (2002) differentiation between religion as a plural tradition (religion-as-faith) and religion as monolithic political tool (religion as ideology) is useful to explain why a relationship to an unknown or elusive reality produces very different effects from organized religion or secularism. Nandy states that

> One way of explaining the difference between [religion-as-faith and religion-as-ideology] is to conceive of ideology as something that, for individuals and people who believe in it, needs to be constantly protected, and faith as something that the faithful usually expect to protect them. (63)

His differentiation associates faith with "a way of life, a tradition that is definitionally non-monolithic and operationally plural" (62), while religion-as-ideology is defined as

> a sub-national, national or cross-national identifier of populations contesting for or protecting non-religious, usually political or socioeconomic, interests. Such religion-as-ideologies usually get identified with one or more texts, which, rather than the ways of life of believers, then become the final identifiers of the pure forms of religions. The texts help anchor the ideologies in something seemingly concrete and delimited and, in effect, provide a set of manageable operational definitions. (62)

Resonating Deloria's (2003) argument that secularism is inherently linked to Christianity-as-ideology and its obsession with chronological descriptions of reality (i.e., history) that culminates with divine unfoldings (of the nation-state in this case), Nandy conceptualizes secularism as an import of Europe into South Asia that has an ambivalent relationship with other religions-as-ideology. On the one hand, he asserts that secularists in south India conceptualize religion-as-ideology as something to be contained because it sits "in opposition to the ideology of modern statecraft" (64). On the other hand, secularists foreclose the religious (i.e., Christian) roots of the modern statecraft ideology itself. Nandy argues that secularists are also wary of religion-as-faith as it has the potential to deny "the state and the middle-class ideologues of the state the right to be the ultimate reservoir of sanity and the ultimate arbiter among different religions and communities" (65).

In this sense, he suggests that modern states find religion-as-faith too inchoate and unmanageable and therefore prefer to deal with religion-as-ideology. He further contextualizes both categories with historical examples from India.

> It is religion-as-faith which prompted 200,000 Indians to declare themselves Mohanmedan Hindus in the census of 1911; and it was catholicity of faith which prompted Mole-Salam Girasia Rajputs to traditionally have two names for every member of the community, one

Hindu and one Muslim. It is religion-as-ideology, on the other hand, which prompted a significant proportion of Punjabi-speaking Hindus to declare Hindi their mother tongue, thus underlying the differences between Sikhism and Hinduism and sowing the seeds for the creation of a new minority. Likewise, it is religion-as-ideology which has provided a potent tool to the Jamaat e Islami to disown traditional, plural forms of Islam in the Indian subcontinent and, by separating official religion from everyday life, producing a pre-packaged Islam for Muslims uprooted and decultured by processes of engineered social change in the region. (63)

Our interpretation is that religion-as-faith, for Nandy, corresponds to an equivocal epistemology while religion-as-ideology corresponds to an unequivocal and universalizing epistemology. This implies that religion-as-faith is always already plural, as it is open to the undecidable, the unthinkable, to what is beyond language, rationality or human authority. In other words, religion-as-faith is a spiritual-political practice. Conversely, religion-as-ideology forecloses its choices of what exists, and what should be done, which, according to Nandy, has many parallels with secularism.

In her work with nonanthropocentric African spiritual practices, Jacqui Alexander (2005) emphasizes the inseparability of the spiritual and the political, but, just like Nandy conceptualizes faith, she conceptualizes the spiritual as a social practice/epistemology that is equivocal and pluralist by nature. Like Santos, she highlights the difficulty of engaging with or seeing through the eyes of social practices that transform modern/Christian/secular conceptualizations of nature and society and builds relationships around sentience, reciprocity and solidarity, rather than order, discipline and control. For her, one of the greatest challenges for the imagination of one who has been oversocialized in a 'thinking-as-knowledge' paradigm is to wrestle with the sacred and its permanent impermanence and undecidability, which frame ways of being that "are intimately and tangibly paired to the world of the invisible" (327). The first difficulty of rationalizing the sacred would lie not only in reducing it to a 'thought' or a 'name' (e.g., 'metaphysics') but in grappling with a system where knowing emanates from being and not from language.

The second difficulty would be to wrestle with the dynamic and constant reinterpretation of dominant 'grounding' categories, such as embodiment, language, interpretation, progress, history and time—and with paradoxes such as the notion that change and changelessness are both constant. Alexander's description of a conceptualization of time and memory illustrates this process. She explains that how sentient beings are remembered

is continually being transformed through a web of interpretive systems that ground meaning and imagination in principles that are ancient with an apparent placement in a different time. Yet, both the boundaries of those principles as well as what lies within are constantly being transformed in the process of work in the present; collapsing, ultimately, the rigid demarcation of the prescriptive past, present and future of linear time. (392)

She calls for a move beyond understanding spiritual practices as merely cultural retention and survival towards an understanding of the spiritual as epistemology—an epistemology of the sacred, or an 'epistemology of ceremony':

The constructs that constitute the praxis of the Sacred would thus have to be taken as real and the belief structures of its practitioners as having effects that are real. The constituents within its ambit, such as Truth, cannot be superficially positioned as multiple choice, contested situational claims or lapses in communication, but as *metaphysical* principle. The knowledge derived from faith is not uninformed epiphenomena, lapses outside the bounds of rationality that need to be properly corrected with rationality, but rather knowledge about Sacred accompaniment, knowledge that is applied and lived in as a consistent and as committed way as possible so as to feel and observe the meaning of mystery, not as secret, but as elusive—hence the constancy of work. (327)

Similar metaphysical principles are also represented in Australian Aboriginal dreamtime:

The dreaming ... [is] ... the other of Australian awareness, for it embodies the hidden dimensions or the shadow, that which is unconscious, strange and unknown to the model of being which is Australian and White. (Cain 1991, cited in Grieves 2009, 27)

According to Worimi historian Vicky Grieves (2009), Aboriginal elders affirm that Tjukurpa—often translated as dreamtime—is not appropriately represented by any single word in English as it evokes a force of past, present, future, oneness, ancestral beings, relationships, natural laws, ceremonies and the creation of knowledge itself. Grieves states that

The reasons for the debasement of Aboriginal philosophy—its relegation to the category of quaint myths and legends, suitable only for reproduction as children's stories—lie deep within settler colonial constructions of Aboriginal society as primitive, stone age and inherently backward, with nothing to offer the modern, progressive ideals of the colonial project. These ficto-narratives, including terra nullius, the myth of an empty land, are the necessary rationale for the take up of Aboriginal lands and the salving of White consciousness from the violence of the colonial project. The subsequent base poverty of Aboriginal Australians only adds to the constructions of their worthlessness as a people

and the subsequent ignorance of the source of wisdom about ways of
managing the natural resource base, and of human populations, held
within Aboriginal spirituality. (Grieves 2009, 27)

Thus, the difficulty in engaging with such sacred knowledges is directly
related to the epistemic blindness that arises from Santos's (2007) abyssal thinking. Engaging with this blindness has been an explicit project of
postcolonial theory. The focus on knowledge/power and constructions of
reality is also evident in postcolonial projects informed by poststructuralist
ideas. However, such projects have often focused on Western knowledge
construction and not on how such relationships may be different in the construction of knowledge in other contexts. We argue that a renewed focus on
this relationship in (some) Aboriginal processes of knowledge production
can enable the emergence of different possibilities for a project of global
citizenship education 'otherwise.' In order to illustrate such possibilities
and the potential contributions of indigenous knowledges to debates about
global citizenship education, we will turn to representations of the medicine wheel in Aboriginal literature in North America.

THE MEDICINE WHEEL AS AN EXAMPLE

The representations of the medicine wheel provided in this section exemplify the construction of situated, partial and equivocal knowledges that
are bound to context and time. They can also be interpreted as global
citizenship pedagogies from the perspective of First Nation philosophies
in North America. The medicine wheel is usually associated with learning
processes and represented as a circle consisting of six directions: north,
south, east and west, above and below. As a metaphor, its meaning is constructed in context, and, therefore, different people will attribute different meaning to its different dimensions according to their own contexts.
Thus, it is impossible to pin the medicine wheel down in a fixed way, and
many of the representations may involve both indigenous and nonindigenous ideas.
    Our first example comes from Sharylin Calliou (1995), a member of the
Michel band of Alberta in Canada. She represents the medicine wheel as a
model for a peacekeeping pedagogy.[1] She associates the movement of the
wheel (represented by seasonal cycles) with the continuity of learning as the
condition of all beings. In her construction of the wheel, the north is associated with the winter and with a cognitive realm that is best expressed in the
quality of wisdom and pedagogically enacted in an antiracist stance. The
east is associated with spring, the realm of spirituality and enlightenment,
enacted in a pedagogical practice of peacekeeping. The south is associated
with the summer, the realm of emotions and the practice of unconditional
love as a response to discrimination. The west is associated with fall, the

physical realm and the groundedness of a shared Earth as the basis of a multiculturalist pedagogy—of reaching out to others in our condition of interdependence in only one planet, one mother.

Our second example comes from Gregory Cajete (2000), a Pueblo sociologist from New Mexico. He represents the four directions of the medicine wheel as a way of engaging with different perspectives:

> The four or more directions generally serve as allegories for sacred orientations to places in Indigenous traditions. Each has associated plants, animals and natural phenomena. And each of the plants and animals represent a perspective, a way of looking at something in the centre that humans are trying to know. The idea of moving around to look from a different perspective, from the north, the south, the east and the west, and from above, below or within, is contained in the creative process. . . . Indigenous logic moves between relationships, revisiting, moving to where it is necessary to learn or to bring understandings together. This might be called the sacred dimension of Indigenous science. Western science has struggled mightily to remove the role of spirit from understanding the world. Indigenous science works from the other side, continually infusing relationships with spirit through its discovery and rediscovery. (Cajete 2000, 210–211)

Cajete emphasizes the importance of the use of metaphor in education so that learners can establish affective relations with what is being taught and engage their intuition in the learning process, exploring the realm of the unknown. He also uses the medicine wheel to propose a curriculum for indigenous learners based on creativity where students would explore both indigenous and nonindigenous scientific and nonscientific narratives and mythologies.[2]

Chickasaw scholar Eber Hampton (1995) uses the medicine wheel as an organizing principle for learning and movement. He says that there is a risk in representing it as a model emerging from thought and contained by words rather than something that guides thought and that is much more complex and dynamic than the imperfect picture that can be represented in text or visuals. He identifies six dimensions of the medicine wheel as principles for standards of Indian education.[3] The 'above' dimension is associated with the realm of metaphysics, spiritual identities and respect for spiritual connections between all things. The idea of a spiritual identity is related to freedom based on the acknowledgment of the necessity of diversity and of everyone's right to be who they are meant to be at the service of the collective cycle of life. The east of the medicine wheel is associated with spring, cultural identity and responsibilities, and the acknowledgment of diversity between indigenous cultural groups. The south is associated with summer and growth and the commemoration of indigenous traditions as living and evolving ways of living: summer is the time for the powwows where different tribes reunite to exchange and celebrate together based on the principle of respect. West is associated with fall and the death of the grass that hides its seed under the snow so that it can live again in the next cycle. Therefore the focus of the west is on education related to indigenous histories and the affirmation of the power of survival. Hampton asks: how does the acorn unfold into an oak? He argues that the answer is within the acorn itself and this direction brings the message that relentless courage is at the heart of the indigenous struggle for life in often hostile institutional environments (such as schools). The north is associated with winter and night, endurance and wisdom. Hampton sees the north as where Indian people need the vitality to face and challenge the worst effects of racism, especially in Western schooling, which he sees as being affected by a pathology consisted of unconscious processes which he identifies as:

> 1) a perverse ignorance of the facts of racism and oppression; 2) delusions of superiority, motivated by fear of inadequacy; 3) a vicious spiral of self-justifying action, as the blame is shifted to the victims who must be helped, that is, controlled for their own good; and 4) denial that the oppressor profits from the oppression materially, as well as by casting themselves as superior, powerful and altruistic persons. (Hampton 1995, 36)

The sixth direction is below—the Earth as a shared place. Here is where there is potential for healing as a partnership between indigenous and non-indigenous peoples to bring about personal, social and structural changes. However, he emphasizes that this partnership needs to acknowledge the violence of the past in order to make room for indigenous expression and revitalization—something that indigenous peoples themselves need to be able to do.

Working in the field of social work, Herb Nabigon (Anishinabe) and Anne-Marie Mawhiney (Cree) (1996) draw on Cree teachings to propose a model for balance and well-being based on the medicine wheel. Their model emphasizes key Aboriginal principles that

> all humans need healing [which] is a life long journey . . . Spiritual life is not separate from everyday life. Every aspect of existence is spiritual. Emphasis is on being rather than doing. [A]ll things are related. There is no sense of object and subject: all is one. Mind, body, emotions and spirit are not separate, and humans are not separate from the earth and everything on and in it. (21)

Their representation of the medicine wheel is unusual because it consists of the four directions in three nested circles.[4] The inner circle represents the inner self in its relationship with the metaphysical aspects of existence (the inner fire at the core of one's being), and the outer circles the external selves in their relationship with the outside world framed by culture, history and time. The external outer circle is associated with negative (disabling) sides of the external self; the middle circle is associated with positive and enabling sides of the external self. The internal circle also has negative and positive sides to it (represented by connectivity and relationality versus refusal to listen or learn). The circles are divided into four directions. The purpose of the movement of (and between) the circles is learning and healing towards balance of the three circles and six dimensions of the wheel. Feelings of inferiority/superiority and shame are represented in the outer circle in the east. The corresponding enabling/positive aspect of the external self represented in the middle circle is the acknowledgment, expression and sharing of feeling with a view to create the possibility of unconditional acceptance of one's learning journey and where one is at. The outer circle south represents envy and greed, while the corresponding middle circle represents a connection with one's inner voice and a sense of inner value. The outer circle in the west represents resentment and attachments to past emotions enacted in a single view of a situation. The corresponding middle circle represents respect—for self and others—through acknowledgment and honoring of different perspectives. The outer circle in the north represents apathy and disregard for the self, which means that one cannot contribute to the healing and learning of others as one cannot do it for the self. The corresponding middle circle represents caring first for the (balance and healing of) the self, which then translates into caring for everything else one is interconnected with. Nabigon and Mawhiney's medicine wheel emphasizes the need for looking at and healing the self first before one tries to change one's environment (or 'the world') because a person's imbalance can be projected in his/her relationships with everything else, creating more imbalances as a consequence.

We have chosen to show different examples of the use of the medicine wheel to illustrate how the relationship between language, knowledge and reality can be interpreted as different from traditional Western conceptualizations. Rather than fixing one meaning for the medicine wheel that should be placed in an encyclopedia or dictionary, some Aboriginal ways of knowing are open to and welcoming of multiple perspectives as long as such perspectives are accountable to their contexts of production, and their communities/relations in terms of their consequences in practice. In this sense, such Aboriginal knowledges demonstrate that all knowledge is connected to a context (it comes from somewhere), no knowledge is individual knowledge, and every knowledge is also an ignorance of other knowledges produced in different contexts, as Souza Santos defends.

On the other hand, ethical epistemological pluralism calls for different kinds of ontological responsibilities (Bastien 2004). Speaking from a Māori context, Jackson (2010) draws attention to the notion that stories and knowledge have power and need to "be treated with the same respect as a naked flame" (27). However, when a story is told, it is up to the listener to find the threads in it and create their own connections and symbolic interpretations based on root metaphors that are collectively shared. Hence, different from stories told from mainstream Western traditions, there is no single fixed meaning or moral to a Māori story. The process of interpretation is one of provisional co-construction of symbolic meaning related to the immediate context and an elusive shared reality that is constantly shaped, reshaped, made and invented in the process of knowledge construction in language. Therefore, echoing Royal and Garroute, Jackson argues that knowledge production should always be an ethical process at the service of the collective: "[o]ur intellectual tradition gives us the freedom to ask whatever questions we want to ask but in asking whatever we are free to ask there is also an obligation to ask, 'why do we need to know?' " (29). If language and knowing challenge and reconstruct realities, and if the quest for knowledge is one of seeking different realities, one should be always attentive to the collective risks that this entails (Jackson 2010). Similarly, Ghanaian educator George Sefa Dei (2011) highlights this connection of ethics and epistemology and affirms that "resistance as a part of the creation of new future/visions of education and society is a long, physical, material, metaphysical and emotional struggle" (10).

CONCLUSION

If we take Dei and Jackson's insights seriously in a project of ethical global citizenship education, certain questions need to be asked, such as: Whose myths, stories or metaphors inform our thinking? What do they say about our locus of enunciation? What other metaphors or myths could provide new possibilities for new constructions or transformation of selves and communities? Why and how is this going to be different from (or disrupt) previous constructions, inventions and inequitable power relations? Who should decide on the content and form of these new constructions? How can more people take part in these conversations? Who will benefit from these new constructions? What risks and ethical responsibilities are involved in this process?

We believe that the epistemological pluralism proposed by Santos and made possible in the conceptual frameworks proposed by Aboriginal and postcolonial scholars in this chapter is paramount for a project of global citizenship education that has the potential to break epistemological insularities (Dei 2011) and open the imagination to other ways of being, especially those that have been repressed by colonialism. Such epistemological pluralism should emphasize the gifts and limitations of every knowledge system and support both indigenous and nonindigenous people to expand their frames of references and open new possibilities for thinking, seeing, knowing, relating and being. However, there is a need to recognize both the historical absence and invisibility of certain knowledges in important debates in education and in society, and the resulting ethnocentric blindness and arrogance in mainstream knowledge systems in the belief that only one knowledge system can 'get it right.' If every knowledge system is insufficient (as it is situated) and represents an ignorance of other knowledge systems developed in other contexts, what we propose is not the elimination of ignorance (as a Cartesian universalist project would demand) but the removal of blinders to one's own ignorance in order to create the conditions for critical genealogy, humility, mutuality, reciprocity and solidarity necessary for an ethical project of global citizenship education. In the words of Mignolo (2002), what we propose is not "a mere reversal of epistemic privilege" (941) but the "making of non-modernity a legitimate locus of enunciation" (942) through pedagogies that emphasize the epistemic potential of border thinking and crossing (rather than border fixing). As an initial step in that direction, we invite educators to think about the implications of considering indigenous knowledges and ways of knowing seriously in equipping indigenous *and nonindigenous* people for living together as part of a shared planet and a global and very diverse community consisting of human and nonhuman beings.

NOTES

1. Summary of associations (I): North—Winter, cognitive realm, wisdom, logic, praxis, anti-racism; East—Spring, beginnings, spiritual realm, transformation, praxis, peacekeeping; South—Summer, emotional realm, racism, awareness, denial; West-Autumn, physical realm, multiculturalism, insight, groundedness.
2. Summary of associations (II): North—encounters with perceptions, metaphors, cultural content, experience; East—comparison and contrast between indigenous and Western perspectives; South—explorations, art, role play, experiments; West—reflections and symbolic orientations, evaluating what one has learnt.
3. Summary of associations (III): Above—Spirit, spirituality, service, identity, freedom, affiliation; East—Spring, identity, culture, diversity; South—Summer, affirmation, freedom, tradition, respect; West—Fall, education, service, history, relentlessness; North—Winter, education, culture, vitality, struggle; Below—Earth, affiliation, transformation.
4. Summary of associations (IV): East outer circle—inferiority/superiority; middle circle—feeling; south outer circle—envy; middle circle—inner voice and value; west outer circle—resentment; middle circle—respect; north outer circle—apathy and disregard; middle—care.

REFERENCES

Alexander, J. (2005) *Pedagogies of Crossing: Meditations on Feminism, Sexual Politics, Memory and the Sacred*, Durham, NC, and London: Duke University Press.
Allen, P. (1986) *The Sacred Hoop*, Boston: Beacon Press.
Ani, M. (1994). *Yurugu: an African-Centred Critique of European Cultural Thought and Behavior*, Trenton: Africa World Press.
Bastien, B. (2004) *Blackfoot Ways of Knowing: The Worldview of the Siksinaitsitapi*, Calgary: University of Calgary Press.

Cajete, G. (2000) *Native Science: Natural Laws of Interdependence*, Santa Fe: Clear Light Publishers.

Calliou, S. (1995) 'Peacekeeping Actions at Home: A Medicine Wheel Model for a Peacekeeping Pedagogy', in M. Battiste and J. Barman (eds.), *First Nation Education in Canada: The Circle Unfolds*, Vancouver, BC: UBC Press, 47–72.

Cooper, G. (2008) . Tawhaki and Māui: critical literacy in indigenous epistemologies. *Critical Literacy: Theories and Practices*, 2(1): 37–42

Dei, G. S. (2011) 'Introduction', in G. D. Dei (ed.), Indigenous Philosophies and Critical Education: A Reader. New York: Peter Lang, 1–14.

Deloria, V. (2003) *God Is Red: A Native View of Religion*, New York: Fulcrum Publishing.

Dion-Buffalo, Y. (1990) 'Seeds of Thought, Arrows of Change: Native Storytelling as Metaphor', in T. Laidlaw and C. Malmo (eds.), *Healing Voices: Feminist Approaches to Therapy with Women*, San Francisco: Jossey-Bass, 118–142.

Ermine, W. (1995) 'Aboriginal Epistemology', in M. Battiste and J. Barman (eds.), *First Nation Education in Canada: The Circle Unfolds*, Vancouver, BC: UBC Press, 101–112.

Garroute, E. (1999) 'Getting Serious about Interrogating Representation: An Indigenous Turn', *Social Studies of Science*, 29(6): 945–956.

Gandhi, L. (1998). *Postcolonial theory: A critical introduction*, New York: Columbia University Press.

Grieves, V. (2009) 'Aboriginal spirituality: Aboriginal philosophy, the basis of Aboriginal social and emotional wellbeing', Casuarina: Cooperative Centre for Aboriginal Health.

Hampton, E. (1995) 'Towards a Definition of Indian Education', in M. Battiste and J. Barman (eds.), *First Nations Education in Canada: The Circle Unfolds*, Vancouver, BC: UBC Press, 5–46.

Highway, T. (2005) 'Why Cree Is the Funniest of All Languages', in D. Taylor (ed.), *Me. Funny*, Vancouver, BC: Douglas, 159–168.

Jackson, M. (2010) 'Restoring the Nation: Removing the Constancy of Terror', in J. S. Te Rito and S. M. Healy (eds.), *Proceedings of Traditional Knowledge Conference 2008: "Te tatau pounamu: The Greenstone Door"*, The University of Auckland, Auckland, New Zealand, 27–33.

Mehl-Madrona, L. (2007) *Narrative Medicine: The Use of History and Story in the Healing Process*. Rochester, Vermont: Bear & Company.

Mignolo, W. (2002) 'The Enduring Enchantment (Or the Epistemic Privilege of Modernity and Where to Go from Here)', *The South Atlantic Quarterly*, 101(4): 927–954.

———. (2007) 'DELINKING', *Cultural Studies*, 21(2): 449–514.

Mignolo, W. and Tlostanova, M. (2006). Theorizing from the Borders: Shifting to Geo- and Body-Politics of Knowledge, *European Journal of Social Theory* 9: 205–221.

Nabigon, H. and Mawhine, A. (1996) 'Aboriginal Theory: A Cree Medicine Wheel Guide for Healing First Nations', in F. Turner (ed.), *Social Work Treatment: Interlocking Theoretical Approaches*, Toronto: The Free Press, 18–38.

Nandy, A. (2002) *Time Warps: Silent and Evasive Pasts in Indian Politics and Religion*, London: Hurst & Company.

Royal, C. (2009) '*Te Kaimānga: Towards a New Vision for Mātauranga Māori*', lecture of the Macmillan Brown Series, Macmillan Brown Centre for Pacific Studies, University of Canterbury, Christchurch, New Zealand, September 16, 2009.

Souza Santos, B. (2007) 'Beyond Abyssal Thinking: From Global Lines to Ecologies of Knowledges', *Revista Critica de Ciencias Sociais*, 80, http://www.eurozine.com/articles/2007-06-29-santos-en.html (accessed February 26, 2010).

Contributors

Ali A. Abdi is professor of education and codirector, Centre for Global Citizenship Education and Research (CGCER), University of Alberta. His areas of research include comparative and international education; globalization, citizenship and human rights education; social foundations of education; cultural studies in education; and colonial and post-colonial studies in education.

Cash Ahenakew lectures in the International Indigenous Studies program at the University of Calgary (Canada) on Aboriginal health & well-being; indigenous and Western methodology; and indigenous theory and practice. He is involved in research that focuses on Aboriginal population health, Aboriginal education and Aboriginal governance. Cash's doctoral dissertation, "The Effects of Residential Schooling, Social Capital and Geography on Health Conditions in Canada's Aboriginal Communities," interprets quantitative data through indigenous theories. Cash is Plains Cree and his family comes from Ahtahkakoop.

Vanessa de Oliveira Andreotti holds a professorial chair in global education at the University of Oulu, Finland, and is also associated with the University of Canterbury, in Aotearoa/New Zealand. Her research background is interdisciplinary and informed by postcolonial, (post)critical and poststructural theories. Her research focus is on building bridges between contemporary theories and debates around globalization and diversity and pedagogical practices; she is also interested in indigenous/Aboriginal studies and education. Vanessa is the current program chair (2011) and chair elect (2012) of the postcolonial studies in education special interest group of the American Educational Research Association (AERA).

Nancy Cook is an Associate Professor of Sociology at Brock University and a faculty member of the graduate programs in critical sociology and social justice and equity studies. She is the author of *Gender, Identity and Imperialism: Western Women Development Workers in Pakistan* (2007), an ethnographic study of transcultural interactions among development volunteers and local populations in northern Pakistan and their political effects. In her current research project, Dr. Cook is studying the impacts of a newly opened road to Shimshal, northern Pakistan, on women's lives and gender relations in the village.

Garrick Cooper is a lecturer and program coordinator at the School of Māori and Indigenous Studies at the University of Canterbury in New Zealand. Garrick is from Ngāti Ranginui of Tauranga Moana and Ngāti Whanaunga of Hauraki. His research on the interface between indigenous and nonindigenous epistemologies highlights critical ontological dimensions of indigenous knowledge systems. Before his current position he was a researcher at the New Zealand Council for Educational Research.

David Jefferess is an Associate Professor of English and Cultural Studies at UBC Okanagan in Kelowna, British Columbia, Canada. His current research examines how benevolence, as a structure of attitude and reference, informs North Atlantic discourses of global citizenship, humanitarianism and development.

Karen Pashby is a PhD candidate in the Philosophy of Education Program in the Department of Theory and Policy Studies at OISE/University of Toronto. Her dissertation investigates the real and assumed theoretical and pedagogical relationships between global citizenship education and multiculturalism in Canada. She is an experienced secondary-school teacher, having taught in downtown Toronto, northern Quebec and suburban Brazil. She currently works in the Initial Teacher Education program at OISE/UT. Karen coedited *Citizenship Education in the Era of Globalization: Canadian Perspectives* with Michael O'Sullivan.

Lynette Shultz is an associate professor and codirector of the Centre for Global Citizenship Education and Research (CGCER), University of Alberta. While the common focus of her teaching and research is education and social justice, particular areas of work include international educational policy; children's rights; citizenship education; participatory governance; and deliberative policy processes.

Lynn Mario T. M. de Souza is Professor of English at the Modern Languages Department of the University of São Paulo. He works and has published widely in the areas of language education, postcolonial theory, literacies and teacher education. With Vanessa Andreotti, Lynn Mario coordinated the UK-based international initiative 'Learning to Read the World Through Other Eyes' (www.throughothereyes.org.uk).

Nick Stevenson is a reader in cultural sociology at the University of Nottingham. His most recent publication is *Cultural Citizenship and Education,* published in 2011 by Sage. He is currently working on a short volume called *Freedom*, to be published by Routledge in 2012.

Paul Tarc is Assistant Professor in the Faculty of Education at the University of Western Ontario. His research interests/initiatives in progressive and critical modes of education are articulated through 'post'-informed theories of representation, subjectivity and pedagogy. He has taught in K–12 schools in South America, Southeast Asia and Ontario. His recent book, *Global Dreams, Enduring Tensions: International Baccalaureate (IB) in a Changing World*, uses IB as the focal point to historicize the 'international' of international education under globalization.

Lisa Taylor is an associate professor at Bishop's University. Taylor's research and teaching are in the areas of critical literacy, anticolonial and social justice teacher education, critical global education, postcolonial perspectives in TESOL, and transnational feminist literature. She publishes in *TESOL Quarterly, TOPIA: Canadian Journal of Cultural Studies*, and *Critical Inquiry in Language Studies*. She coedited "CONTESTED IMAGINARIES/Reading Muslim Women and Muslim Women Reading Back: Transnational Feminist Reading Practices, Pedagogy and Ethical Concerns"—as a special issue of *Intercultural Education* (2007) and *Muslim Women, Transnational Feminism and the Ethics of Pedagogy: Contested Imaginaries in Post-9/11 Cultural Practice* (forthcoming, Palgrave).

Su-ming Khoo is a lecturer in the School of Political Science and Sociology at the National University of Ireland, Galway, Ireland. Her teaching and research focus on decolonization, democratization, ecology, human development and rights-based approaches to development. Recent publications include articles and book chapters on rights, development, Millennium Development Goals, sustainability, consumer activism, citizenship and development education.

Colin Wright is Director of MA Programmes in the Department of Culture, Film and Media, and Codirector of the Centre for Critical Theory at the University of Nottingham. His general areas of research interest include French critical theory, Lacanian psychoanalysis and political and postcolonial theory. Specific interests currently include Alain Badiou's philosophy and the history of Jamaican conflict and culture from a postcolonial perspective. He is currently completing a book entitled *Alain Badiou in Jamaica: The Politics of Conflict*.

Talya Zemach-Bersin is a PhD candidate in the American Studies Program at Yale University. She received her BA with honors in American studies at Wesleyan University in 2007. She has published several articles on the politics of international education, including "Selling the World: Study

Abroad Marketing and the Privatization of Global Citizenship" and "American Students Abroad Can't Be 'Global Citizens.' " Her additional research interests include postcolonial studies, ethnography, cultural tourism, knowledge production and diplomatic history. Zemach-Bersin's doctoral dissertation will be on the cultural politics of twentieth-century U.S.-initiated study abroad and international education.

Index